Ribbons Among the Rajahs

Ribbons Among the Rajahs

A History of British Women
in India Before the Raj

Patrick Wheeler

PEN & SWORD
HISTORY

First published in Great Britain in 2017 by
PEN AND SWORD HISTORY
an imprint of
Pen and Sword Books Ltd
47 Church Street
Barnsley
South Yorkshire S70 2AS

ISBN 978 1 47389 327 6

Printed and bound in Malta
by Gutenberg Press Ltd.

Typeset in Times New Roman by
CHIC GRAPHICS

Pen & Sword Books Ltd incorporates the imprints of Pen & Sword
Archaeology, Atlas, Aviation, Battleground, Discovery,
Family History, History, Maritime, Military, Naval, Politics, Railways,
Select, Social History, Transport, True Crime, Claymore Press,
Frontline Books, Leo Cooper, Praetorian Press, Remember When,
Seaforth Publishing and Wharncliffe.

For a complete list of Pen and Sword titles please contact
Pen and Sword Books Limited
47 Church Street, Barnsley, South Yorkshire, S70 2AS, England
E-mail: enquiries@pen-and-sword.co.uk
Website: www.pen-and-sword.co.uk

Contents

Foreword 6

Introduction 8

Chapter 1   The Voyage 12

Chapter 2   Arrival and Establishment 38

Chapter 3   The Pioneer Women 55

Chapter 4   Housewife and Household 79

Chapter 5   Society and Propriety 103

Chapter 6   Dine and Wine 133

Chapter 7   Leisure, Pleasure and Endeavour ...155

Chapter 8   Indian Impressions 190

Chapter 9   Health and Death 206

Notes 225

Bibliography...238

Index..242

Foreword

Few of us can have given much thought to the presence of European women in India 200 years ago but, unquestionably, they should be remembered. For all the varied and complex reasons that took them there so many years ago, under such daunting circumstances, and largely under the social pressures of those days, and not least because so many of them lie there still. They were mostly ordinary, everyday individuals, in surprisingly large numbers, who had shared the experiences of the men of that time, but who could not themselves have any great impact on the interaction of the British with India because of their repressed social status.

The seeds of this book were sown while I was dabbling with some family history research a few years ago. Part of the reason for this was to assemble something of interest for the next generation, completely overlooking the possibility that they might prefer to do it for themselves or, more likely, that they might not be remotely interested. In the course of such probing, I spent some time looking at the life and career of a respectable and quite successful family forbear, who was a senior judge in Madras in the early 1800s. My interest was inevitably enhanced by my fascination in that country, its people and especially its history. I found that all sorts of historical data and correspondence existed for our judge, and much was known about his life and work, but, to my astonishment, absolutely nothing was known about his wife; not her date of birth, nor of her death, nor even whether she had accompanied her husband to India and nearby territories. Somehow she was just a blank; airbrushed out of history. From this point on it was a simple step towards recognising that this was true of legions of women who went to India in the eighteenth and early nineteenth centuries. They are a forgotten community. Not being contributors to the great events of the day, they have been swept into a corner, and long since lost to history. In the main, these women went out of duty, following husbands or brothers, or because they were shipped out to the care of family or friends, being difficult to marry off in Georgian England. Occasionally they were despatched to that country because they were the illegitimate offspring of the wealthy. In this, they were akin to the luckless second sons of the great and the good who did not inherit, and were perhaps not fitted for a life wedded to the Church, or the army, and

6

who were therefore packed off to India to make their fortune; or so it was hoped. Other women went out of desperation. Perhaps their fathers had died, too indigent to leave enough to support several daughters, as well as a widow, and yet a prospective husband could not be found. India was a clear option, where there were numerous lovelorn bachelors all set to make a fortune, or so these girls had been told, and therefore anticipated. Furthermore there was, from their point of view, a convenient shortage of potential brides and thus of competition; Caucasian at least. Lastly, some women clearly went from a sense of adventure and excitement. As like as not they had a family member already there, and this was a ready excuse to explore and fulfil some romantic fantasies. In Indian British society it was possible to do what would have been unthinkable in Britain, and that was to cross social boundaries, so deeply engraved on the backbone of life back home, and hopefully to elevate one's status in society. Nevertheless, thinking of going to India was one thing, getting there was quite another. The considerable expense of the journey had to be paid in advance, and the journey itself was lengthy, hazardous, tedious and unhealthy. There had to be, they thought, something secure and worthwhile at the end, after taking such an arduous gamble.

I have used frequent quotations from the available texts because the original language gives a stronger flavour of the period; an immediacy and authenticity, which, in a small way, brings those times to life. I have also strayed from convention by referring to them as Indian British. This is slightly more in line with their own custom, which was to refer to themselves as Indians, hardly appropriate today. Many current texts use the terminology Anglo-Indian which is confusing, in that this is a term very commonly used for those of mixed Indian and British blood, especially in contemporary India. It also rather overlooks the well known fact that a very high percentage of the Indian British were in fact Scottish. I have also inserted occasional words in brackets in the quoted texts to better convey the meaning of the writer, where this may be unclear. Otherwise I have not interfered with the often imperfect punctuation, and have retained the original wording. If there is any deviation, it is more than likely due to the difficulty of reading some of these faded handwritten letters.

Finally, I should like to acknowledge the assistance and guidance of various individuals and groups, including Rosie Llewellyn-Jones; Penny Brooks; the staff of the Asia, Pacific and Africa Collections at the British Library; Barbara Roe; Richard Virr, and the staff at Pen and Sword Books Ltd.

Introduction

This book is chiefly a social history. Any study of the lives of women during the Georgian and Regency period, and before the Victorian era with its Imperial power, could never have any flavour of politics or economics. They were simply barred from any consideration of that sort, unless they had unusual influence over their husbands. Therefore it can only be an account of everyday living; of the duties, responsibilities and amusements of women 200 years ago. This is not as long ago as it sounds. For older individuals, who possibly remember their grandmothers quite well, one is referring only to their own grandmothers, albeit in their childhood. As time passes, the first historical reality to become forgotten is an individual's everyday manner of living and coping. Politics and great national or military events live on, and rightly so, because it is they which dictate the subsequent course of a nation's life. Nevertheless, the day to day minutiae of the lives of these women had relevance, partly because of the effect they may have had on how the decision-makers (the men) conducted their lives, but also being of historical interest in their own right.

The period chosen begins with the arrival of British women in the East in the second half of the eighteenth century, and ends with the beginning of the Raj in the early Victorian period. The Raj, or Imperial India, dates approximately from the First War of Independence (Indian Mutiny) in 1857, and the dissolution of the East India Company shortly afterwards, right up to full independence in 1947, ninety years later. This later period was accompanied by a major social change. By then, the British regarded themselves less as visitors and traders in India, who had derived enjoyment, interest, and profit from the Indian people's way of life, and had, in many cases, become closely associated with it. They behaved instead as overlords, acting with an austere aloofness from Indian people and culture, simply taking it all for granted. Although there may have been a detached curiosity about Indian social practices and religions and, among some, an admiration of the richness of Indian art and history, it was generally superficial, the real interest lying in matters political, military and sporting, and an evening session in the club, deep in an armchair, armed with whisky and soda. By then, India was just an oriental extension of the British Empire, exercising absolute control over most aspects of the Indian way of life, apart from its religions – although even that too became a source of suspicion among the Indian people.

An emphasis on Britishness at every level, within work or daily life, was a necessary part of maintaining this control over the jewel in the crown that was 'our Indian Empire'. Any significant degree of fraternisation was out of the question, whereas in Georgian and Regency times, there was a tendency towards a merging of the two cultures. There was a honeymoon period of British fascination with India and its culture, an admiration that sometimes operated both ways. Local Indians found a means of employment when they might otherwise have struggled to make ends meet, and regional princes found military support to defend themselves against their neighbours.

There were notable names from that period, such as Sir William Jones and Warren Hastings. Jones was a judge, linguist, great orientalist, Sanskrit scholar and founder of the Asiatic Society; Hastings, although politically undermined by Edmund Burke, was, despite his faults, a sensitive supporter of intellectual learning about India, encouraging officials to learn the languages and study Indian texts. Hastings was also a founding supporter of the Asiatic Society, was a patron of Indian music and could even sing Hindoostani songs and, unlike most of his contemporaries, energetically encouraged an interest in all Indian culture, which he regarded as a prerequisite for sound administration. There were others, of course, who were less seduced, especially Richard Wellesley, Governor-General from 1797, who found little to attract him about Indian life. There were still others, middle-ranking officials and traders, who were there just to feather their Georgian nests. Very many in those earlier years, however, relished the oriental world: the colour, mystery and romanticism of language and custom, so much so that several took on Indian ways and learnt the languages. Many women of the time were equally fascinated, and wrote lengthy descriptions in their correspondence home about their enchantment with this new and strange world. Inevitably, not all felt this way. There were some, as always, who were just out to have a good time, and to score a good husband.

This was the time of the Honourable East India Company (HEIC), that remarkable business empire having its origin in the Charter given by Elizabeth the First. The HEIC, and its court of Directors, saw itself primarily as a trading entity with initial resistance to territorial acquisition, due as much to the cost implications as anything. Larger amounts of territory did not necessarily increase profit, but to have its own army was essential for defending its trading outposts from the predations of local Indian princes, and also the French. Maintaining this quite often put a large hole in the company's finances. Unfortunately, tempting offers of cash, or the gift of useful villages or coastline, in exchange for the use of the company's regiments for the defence of a local potentate against his acquisitive neighbour, led inexorably to the company's tentacles spreading from the coastal towns into the interior. Often they would find themselves facing their opposition, likewise backed by a foreign national force acting in mercenary fashion: the French. Apart from Clive's individual territorial ambitions after the Battle of Plassey in 1757, the India Bill of 1784 brought a parliamentary Court of Directors into political control of the company. Once the politicians were involved, territory and Empire became a gradually expanding concept, overcoming the East India Company's prior ambition to profit from trade only, much like a modern multinational with its shareholders in mind.

At that stage, India was not much involved in the tea trade, which then came by Company ships from China. The tea was purchased with specie, or silver, but this was a drain on financial resources, and so the idea was born to grow opium in India, and use this to trade for the tea. There was already a market for opium in China; the British hadn't especially introduced it, and there were large numbers of immigrant Chinese elsewhere in the East Indies growing opium for shipping back to China; something Sir Stamford Raffles attempted to control during his time in Java, and later. Nevertheless, the use of opium as a trading entity by the British has to be questionable, certainly to modern minds. The main Indian trade in the earlier years, before tea, was the export of cotton, textiles, saltpetre and indigo. The British tried to export wool in exchange, which not surprisingly didn't have a ready market. The threat posed to the cotton mills of the Midlands by this textile trade led to the bizarre situation whereby cotton was imported to England, transformed into textiles for subsequent export back to India, in an attempt to replace the textiles that the Indians could perfectly well make for themselves.

This book is based on the diaries and letters of the women that were there at that time, several of which can be found in various libraries and elsewhere, although the number is pitifully few compared to the number of women who actually travelled there in that pre-Victorian era. Not surprisingly, nearly all of these writings are the work of middle-class women and above, despite the fact that there were soldiers' wives, servants and trades people, who also found their way out there. These latter women were mostly either illiterate, or disinclined to put pen to paper or, if they did, the results have long since been lost. One impression gained from reading documents of that era is how the intellectual power of the period was no less extraordinary than it is today.

INTRODUCTION

It just followed a different line. Among some, linguistic ability, application of logic, political judgment, rationalisation, and the ability to absorb vast amounts of information about a people's culture and history was immense. This was, after all, the later stages of the Age of Enlightenment, containing such luminaries as Adam Smith, John Locke, Newton, Gainsborough, Samuel Johnson, Rousseau, Mozart, Handel, Wordsworth, Shelley and, among women, Mary Wollstonecraft. Even this list carries only a handful of the high achievers of that age. Unlike philosophy, politics, music and economics, technological or scientific topics were still in their infancy, especially medicine, which was still archaic. What had also not yet arrived in the West, let alone anywhere else, was a maturity of social conscience; a recognition of a need for redistribution of wealth, and of human rights for the sick, poor and elderly; education for all, and a development of what today we would call infrastructure. Such maturity of thinking was gradually coming, but did not really take off until the 1830s onwards.

Interestingly, there is a hint, among their personal correspondence that some women were beginning to sense a lack of social provision of this kind, particularly when witnessing the extreme poverty, and potential for famine, among ordinary Indian people. A number of British women in India became closely involved in the running of schools for the children of less well-off Europeans, and of institutions for the growing number of orphans, but even this diminished a good deal during the era of Imperial loftiness, by which time the numbers of European poor and orphaned were lessening in any case.

Described here are the complex social circumstances in which European women of that era lived in India; the personal pressures, tensions and discomforts; the complexities of household management; the endless dinners and balls; the food and beverages that were available, and the overall domestic responsibilities. Also described are their skills, leisure pursuits and occupations and, finally, their role in circumstances of ever-present illness. This they experienced in large numbers themselves, but they also nursed members of their own families, their staff and, above all, their children. They painfully watched many of these succumb; the inevitable fate of many such women themselves.

Chapter 1

The Voyage

It isn't difficult to imagine the feelings of those women headed for India a few decades either side of 1800, facing the prospect of four or five months in a ship smaller than the Isle of Wight ferry, and at the mercy of endless sea and all extremes of weather. They had to be apprehensive to say the least, and perhaps fearful for their lives, depending on the gossip they had listened to. Every now and then a ship was lost or, if at war, captured by the French, and most of these women's experience of travelling on water was at best an afternoon's rowing on a lake or river near home.

Having made the decision to take such a voyage, or for the most part had that decision made for them, there was plenty of time to consider all the extraordinary and worrying possibilities that lay ahead. But they were resilient people in Georgian times, and life in general was risky, from sudden disease, bankruptcy, fire, theft, violence and all those experiences from which we are so protected today. Apprehension is likely to have been coloured by a hint of excitement. What, after all, might lie ahead in the way of social prospects, wealth and the overall amazement of experiencing the mysteries of an oriental land?

East Indiaman ships were the universal mode of transport, and were, at most, 180ft long – or the length of three rowing eights in line ahead, although happily somewhat wider. This is little more than half the length of the ferry running from Portsmouth to Ryde, on the Isle of Wight. Despite this, they were considered large by merchantmen standards of that era. They were absolute workhorses; built mainly for trade, but also able to ferry passengers to and from the East Indies. The great majority were built in the Thames, in areas such as Blackwall, Deptford and Rotherhithe, in yards able to handle up to a dozen at once, such as Perry's or Pitcher's. In the years 1793 to 1813, ninety-eight Indiamen first baptised their hulls in the pewter stream of the tidal Thames, averaging around five a year at that time. Each had a displacement of 500 to 1200 tons, the commonest being about 800 tons. This latter was calculated by an archaic method that encouraged a relatively narrow beam, and a deep hold; good for cargo capacity, but which made it corkscrew lurchingly in a heavy sea.

The captain was already appointed by the launch, and invariably present for it, and the whole affair was a major social event with much junketing for a few hundred people.[1] These East Indiamen were actually fine ships, and in some respects better than the men-of-war of the time, because of less reluctance to consider innovation in design, as well as the incorporation of ideas from India, where the art of shipbuilding was in many ways more advanced than anywhere in Europe. They were armed with thirty-eight guns, mostly 18 pounders, and crewed by up to 130 men. They were sometimes confused by enemy shipping for Royal Navy frigates, which had its obvious advantages, although, under the East India Company charter, the guns were for defence rather than for aggressive purposes. Cargo was carried on the lower deck where it stood a reasonable chance of remaining dry from rain, or shipped seas; crucial if it was to retain its value. The officers were invariably British, although not invariably of high calibre but, thankfully for the passengers, most were good or adequate. The crew was a motley selection of Europeans, Chinese and Lascars (Moslem natives of India), among others, and could be of less good quality on the return trip if the better calibre of men had been impressed by Royal Navy ships, or squadrons. This often happened in the anchorages off the Indian coast, and was a distinct disadvantage in that the return trip was made more vulnerable to predatory attack, at a time when a valuable cargo was being imported to England.

The journey by sea to India, which at that time had to be round the Cape of Good Hope, measured approximately 12,000 sea miles. East Indiamen sailed between 75 and 150 miles per day, and thus at four to five knots, and so the length of the journey took about four to five months depending on any ports of call, and the vagaries of the weather; not a pleasing prospect for any woman with no experience of the sea. At the extreme, the voyage could be as little as three and a half months, or as long as seven. Ships would tend to sail singly in times of peace, or in convoy during war, usually with a naval escort. The introduction of copper-sheathed hulls increased the speed, and also the life, of these ships to about six round trips, over about twelve years, rather than the pre-existing four. In later years ships were kept going for longer still, but needed a very thorough structural check after three return journeys.

The cost of a passage to India was astronomical by today's standards. There was no question of one's employer paying for this, although the price was officially graded according to civil or military rank from about £250 for a general to £110 for a company writer, or a subaltern. In a sense these were subsidised prices, as independent ladies and gentlemen paid about £400–500, which was negotiated with the captain.[2,3] Later arrivals even had to barter for a junior officer's accommodation, if they were lucky enough to get agreement to this. When one remembers that £1 sterling in 1810 is worth around £34 in modern times (2005 – National Archive Office), the price of such a journey, one way, is equivalent to £17,000 in today's world; an unimaginable expense when one knew that it might end in death, either at sea or, more commonly, in the East. One really had to be quite strongly motivated – although premature death did at least save the cost of a return journey.

Having found the payment for a passage, it was then a matter of deciding where in the ship to install oneself. This partly depended on the amount paid, but for a single woman this would nearly always be in the roundhouse. This curiously named entity was by no means round, but formed part of that larger accommodation space on the rear part of the upper deck, covered over by the poop deck, which formed its ceiling. The Captain's stateroom and the cuddy (dining area) were in its forward part, opening onto the upper deck, and the roundhouse was the stern-most part. It could be subdivided into six or more smaller cabins, perhaps 9ft square, for individual ladies, or couples, by lightweight wooden, or even canvas, screens. The degree of visual privacy might have been reasonable, but the audible must have been non-existent. It requires little imagination to speculate on the array of sounds from neighbours, particularly in heavy weather. These sub-cabins were light and airy, having port holes which rarely had to be shut, they were secluded from the riff-raff in steerage and, in the case of a lady, they were close to the captain for his supposed protection. A berth here was the recommendation of Emma Roberts in the East India Voyage 1845, but with reservations:

It may seem fastidious to object to meeting sailors employed in getting up different stores from the hold, or to pass and repass other cabins, or the neighbourhood of the stewards pantry; nevertheless, if ladies have the opportunity of avoiding these things, they will do well to embrace it; for, however trivial they may be in a well-regulated ship, very offensive circumstances may arise from them. Neither during the night nor the day can the inmates of the poop-cabins (roundhouse) expect peace: persons on duty are always stationed above their heads, and it is a favourite walk with the passengers; added to this, the hencoops are usually placed upon the poop.... In bad weather, or during the working

*of the vessel, the noises made by trampling overhead, ropes dragging,
blocks falling etc. etc. are very sensibly augmented by the cackling,
chuckling, and screaming of the poultry, while throughout the day,
whether fair or foul, they are scarcely ever silent.*[4]

Below the roundhouse was the great cabin, also in the extreme aft of the ship,
and with its floor flush with the middle, or main deck (gun deck). This was
again divided by partitions into eight or twelve smaller cabins, which were
usually the domain of the unmarried civilian men, and army officers. The
wealthy could afford to purchase a third or a half of the great cabin for
themselves and their wives, if present; any children might be in a smaller
cabin elsewhere, in the charge of a nurse. Even this supposed luxury was
relative only, as William Hickey described on planning his berth for his return
to England in the *Castle Eden*, in 1807, for which he paid the huge sum of
£1,000.

*But on the gun deck, if you avoid the noises above specified, they are
more than counter-balanced by a variety of inconveniences, the grand
one that of being completely debarred of all daylight in tempestuous
weather by what is very expressively termed the dead lights being then
fixed in all the windows in order to prevent the sea breaking in, which
nevertheless it does not effectually do, for I was often set afloat in my
cabin by heavy seas breaking against those dead lights, and entering
at the seams, especially so at the quarter gallery door and window,
where it poured in in torrents, beating even over my bed. You have
also at times the horrid screeches and crying of children going home
for education, or what is full as bad, their vociferous mirth when
playing their gambols in the steerage, added to which grievances is
frequently being half poisoned by a variety of stinks, and that
notwithstanding the Company's ships are considered, and certainly
with truth, as being remarkable for their cleanliness, being regularly
purified twice a week by a complete washing of the deck from the
forecastle to the aftermost part, and last but not least of the evils, the
perpetual creaking of bulkheads, accompanied by the music of the
rudder working, all of which unpleasant circumstances are avoided
by being in the upper cabin or round house.*[5]

It seems as if there were problems in every place, and it was therefore a matter
of what bothered one the least.

Attached to the sides of the great cabin and roundhouse were quarter galleries projecting from the ship's side. These contained a flight of steps connecting the two levels, so avoiding the mayhem of the main part of the ship. They also contained a lavatory; an advantage over using one's own cabin, and doubtless any commodes in these were emptied by one's servant, or even a hapless sailor. Seen from the outside, these quarter galleries were rather beautifully carved and painted structures, somehow belying their purpose, but the fact that they projected made them vulnerable to heavy seas, and they were quite often smashed and washed away. It is said that this once occurred just after some lucky fellow had vacated it.[6] This must have made a good story over the port and cigars, although perhaps not in front of the ladies.

In front of the great cabin, between the upper deck and the middle, or main, deck were the numerous small cabins for the use of the junior officers of the ship, and the military, as well as the surgeon and purser: the more humble a person, the closer to the mess decks and the soldiers' accommodation. Occasionally late-arriving, or impecunious, passengers used these spots and the experience was not always pleasant, as recounted by the loquacious Mrs Sherwood in 1805:

> When Mr Sherwood hurried to the ship to make what preparations he could, every cabin was already taken with the exception of the carpenter's, and had he not been able to secure this I must have stayed behind.
>
> No woman who has not made such a voyage in such a cabin as this can possibly know what real inconveniences are. The cabin was in the centre of the ship, which is so far good, as there is less motion there than at either end. In our cabin was a porthole, but it was hardly ever open; a great gun ran through it, the mouth of which faced the porthole. Our hammock was slung over this gun, and was so near the top of the cabin that one could hardly sit up in bed. When the pumps were at work, the bilge water ran through this miserable place, this worse than dog-kennel, and, to finish the horrors of it, it was only separated by a canvas partition from the place in which the soldiers sat and, I believe, slept and dressed, so that it was absolutely necessary for me, in all weathers, to go down to this shocking place before any of the men were turned down for the night..............Our cabin was just the width of one gun, with room beside for a small table and single chair. Our cot, slung cross-ways over the gun, as I have said, could not swing, there not being height sufficient. In entering the

cabin (which, by the way, was formed only of canvas) we were forced to stoop under the cot, there not being one foot from the head or the foot of the cot to the partition. The ship was so light on the water that she heeled over with the wind so much we could not open our port, and we had no scuttle. We were therefore also in constant darkness. The water from the pump ran through this delectable cabin, and I as a young sailor, and otherwise not in the very best situation for encountering all these disagreeables, was violently sick for days and days, the nights only bringing an increase of suffering. The cabin could not be borne during the daytime.[7]

Having secured a cabin, a passenger was then faced with wooden walls, deck, and deck head, or ceiling, and absolutely nothing else. All the internal fittings, furnishings and decoration were his or her responsibility. In addition, there was an allowance of 1½ to 2 tons of baggage in the hold. Although this sounds generous, passengers returning from India might have a good deal to bring home, and these ships were additionally laden with cargo for sale. One passenger allegedly succeeded in bringing back 63 tonnes to the consternation of the East India Company.[8] There was published advice for what a passenger should take with him on board ship to India and what follows is a list of Necessaries for a Lady Proceeding to India.[9]

Cot, neatly trimmed	Coloured evening dress	Turbans
Hair mattress and bolster	White ditto	Caps
Down or feather pillow	White bedgowns	yards of fine French cambric
Fine upper blankets	Corsets	Ditto fashionable Lenos
Common under ditto	Pairs of white silk stockings	Ditto fine Irish linen
White counterpanes	Ditto black silk ditto	Ditto Velvet
Coloured chintz quilts	Ditto white cotton ditto	Ditto fine Welsh flannel
Pair of calico sheets	Ditto silk gloves or mitts	Pieces of white satin ribbon
Pillow cases	Ditto leather ditto	Assortment of millinery
Set of cot curtains	Ditto fashionable kid shoes	Ditto of stationary
Matting and screws	White cambric pocket handkerchiefs	Towels
	Neck handkerchiefs	Sofa, with drawers under, fitted up with curtains to serve as a bed
Shifts, made to pattern		
	Black silk dress complete	Mahogany table with drawers
Night ditto	Spencers	Pairs of scissors
Flannel petticoats	Nightcap	Penknives
Middle ditto	Straw hats	Pocket-book
Upper ditto	Ditto, drawing box, complete	Quarter chest of oranges
Coloured morning dresses		

White ditto	Toothbrushes	Boxes of Le Manns biscuits
Wash hand stand etc. complete	Nail ditto	Pints of Raspberry vinegar
Chairs	Hair ditto	Ditto capillaire
Yards of printed calico for lining cabin	Comb ditto	Pound pots of raspberry jam
Yards of carpeting for floor	Tortoiseshell dress combs	Ditto currant jelly
Ditto green baize for ditto	Small tooth ditto	Ditto strawberry jam
Ditto oilcloth for ditto	Pounds of Windsor soap	Pounds of gingerbread nuts
Cabin lamp	Bottles of lavender water	Ditto portable soup
Line for fastening furniture	Ditto of Arquebusade	Ditto chocolate
Brass hooks	Small looking glass with slider	Dozens of Bristol water
Piano-forte	Pounds of wax candles	Black leather trunks
Solid mahogany writing desk	Flat candlestick, snuffers, etc	Boxes of tooth powder

The East India Register and Directory for 1821

Having accumulated all this, at no mean price over and above the passage fare, the prudent person then ensured that the furniture stayed where it was put when the ship started rolling, by tying everything down to rings or cleats on the deck, especially those ladies who had brought a harp or piano. The cot was slung from an overhead beam, hopefully with enough space to allow one to sit up, and the walls and deck would often have been lined and carpeted, as implied by these recommendations. Elizabeth Grant gives a description in her memoirs from 1827:[10]

> *With Fatima's help our cabin was soon set in order. It was well filled; a sofa bed, a dressing table that closed over a washing apparatus, a writing table, a pianoforte, a bookcase, and a large trunk with trays in it, each tray containing a week's supply of linen. In the locker was a good supply of extra stores, water well bottled, in particular. A swing tray and a swing lamp hung from the roof, and two small chairs filled corners; there was a pretty mat upon the floor, and no little room could look more comfortable. The whole locker end was one large window, closed till we left the colder latitudes, open ever after, and shaded by Venetians during the heat of the day. A small closet called a galley, in which Ayah kept her peculiar treasures, had a shower bath in it, readily filled by the sailors, and a most delightful and strengthening refreshment to us.*[10]

She proved to be one of those passengers who, unlike many, learnt to be contented with shipboard life, and she goes on:

We soon learned to employ our days regularly, taught by the regularity round us. The life we led was monotonous, but far from being disagreeable, indeed after the first week it was pleasant; the quiet, the repose, the freedom from care, the delicious air, and a large party all in spirits, aided the bright sun in diffusing universal cheerfulness. Few were ill after the first weeks, the soreness of parting was over, a prosperous career was before the young, a return to friends, to business, and to pay awaited the elder; and we had left misery behind us and were entering on a new life free from trials that had been hard to bear.

Before the start of the voyage there would be a turmoil of visitors on deck, with boxes and baggage still being loaded, or scattered chaotically about waiting to be stored, like jetsam on a beach. It was at this stage that sad separations occurred. Sherwood commented:

Unhappy as I was I could not but feel that there were others more wretched than myself. Each company [of the army] *was allowed to take 10 women, and I had the privilege of choosing one who was to be my servant on the voyage. I, of course, could do no other than choose Luke Parker's wife, Betty, Mrs Andrew's old servant, although she had behaved most indiscreetly; I could not, however, be cruel, and Betty was assured of her passage as my servant; but when the rest of the women came to be mustered in the Devonshire there was one too many, and lots were drawn on deck to determine who was to be sent back. I saw this process, I saw the agony of the poor woman whose lot it was to be carried back to shore; I saw her wring her hands, and heard her cries; and I saw her put in a boat and sent back to Portsmouth; and I felt that whatever my hardships might be, my trials were nothing to hers.*

There are other such examples. Mary Doherty, and her husband Major Doherty, both sailed to India in early 1819. She was not the least keen to go, having had a presentiment of disaster, but her husband had overruled this, as he also did with her wish not to take their children.[11] 'We had two children, Henry was one year and nine months old, Charles was only eight months. I wished much not to take them with us but to leave them with my sister but their father would not consent to it.' She had earlier witnessed the embarkation of the Regiment and, like Mrs Sherwood, had seen the painful partings: 'The scene was heartbreaking. Wives who were not allowed to go taking leave of their husbands, and others of their children.'

One can only wonder at the thoughts of these women travellers, leaning on the taffrail of the poop deck, watching the coast of England diminish across the grey intervening sea; serenaded by clucking chickens and clinging on to their bonnets in the stiffening breeze. The first pangs of a permanent home sickness may have been catching at them; wondering if they would ever see family and friends again; and perhaps also the first pangs of a different sickness, as the swell grew greater, and the slowly mounting smell from below decks made its presence felt; the smell from men in crowded conditions; from sheep stowed in the ship's boats; and from cattle and goats in pens that were hardly roomy. This is assuming that they had got away at all, and were not stuck in an anchorage waiting for a fair wind. When Sir Stamford Raffles sailed to the East for the second time, in 1817, he was trapped in Falmouth for two weeks by adverse winds and severe weather, and when Mary Doherty arrived at Table Bay at the Cape of Good Hope, on her trip home to England in 1821, her ship spent a week beating about at the mouth of the Bay before they could work it inshore.[12] This must have been pretty frustrating after a long voyage, much of the time looking forward to the chance of a bit of comfort on land.

Seasickness was immensely common, and anyone who has experienced it can readily feel for those women, suffering the energy sapping, shivering ghastliness of it. It was very much the norm until after the Bay of Biscay, perhaps two or three weeks away, and many women and men made no public appearance throughout this time, lying prostrate on their cots or sofa beds, being ministered to, if they were lucky, by a companion or spouse between bouts of breath-stopping retching into a canvas or a leather bucket. With neighbours only feet away, on the other side of a matchwood or canvas screen, the noises offstage must have been indescribable, and fairly nausea-inducing in themselves. How crawlingly embarrassing this must have been for the gently refined and elegant Georgian lady. Most on board recovered in due course, and gained their sea legs, although there was the odd person who continued sick most of the way. The majority were eventually able to think again about food which, on the whole, was of a very adequate standard on an East Indiaman, certainly compared to a man-of-war.

Meals began with breakfast at 8 am.[13,14,15,16] This consisted of tea, which barely disguised the disgusting water, accompanied by biscuits and butter of variable quality, but adequate quantity. Milk was available from goats or cow, and sometimes bread was made, but it was usually fairly bad.[17] Dinner, the main meal of the day, was at two or three o'clock and this was sometimes held in two sittings as the cuddy only accommodated twenty people and there could be twice this number of passengers all told. Ladies and gentlemen dined together, the officers with them, and all were summoned by a drum beating *The Roast Beef of Old England*. The food was often rather good, and C.N. Parkinson quotes from primary sources that passengers relished joints of beef and mutton, fresh to start with and then slightly salted; poultry, pork, tongue, pickles, pastry, potatoes, rice, hams, puddings etc., all diminishing in quality with time.[18] This was washed down by an ample sufficiency of punch, beer, wine and even occasional champagne. The women indulged along with the men, but later left them in order that they could pass the bottle round, and unfetter their conversation into realms outside presumed feminine sensibilities. Sometimes the wealthy brought quantities of their own provisions, and William Hickey took three dozen bottles of Madeira on his last homeward trip, along with claret, beer and brandy, and thirty dozen bottles of water; the latter being a scarce and well worthwhile commodity aboard ship, and gave him about three bottles a day.[19] Dinner was quite a formal affair for which people dressed, some better than others in Martha Sherwood's experience:

> *Those of our ladies who had had as many months perhaps to prepare for the voyage as I had had days, came out every day very elegantly and richly adorned, to walk the deck or sit down to the captain's table. Dinner was presided over by the Captain, who made a point of asserting his authority, and it ended when he left the table.[20]*

Bad weather reduced the number of diners, for obvious reasons, and often meant that the food was cold because the cooking fires had gone out. In anticipation of the deteriorating weather:

> *The chairs round the table and the table itself were lashed down to iron staples driven into the deck. The dishes were kept in their places by means of long cushions of green baize stuffed with sawdust stretched across the table, and of smaller ones of a semicircular form placed under each dish, thus both raising its leeward edge and preventing it from slipping....[21]*

Dinner was followed by tea at 6 pm, of the same unappetising quality as at breakfast, and accompanied by poor bread, and usually molten butter. Supper occurred at 9 pm, with cheese and biscuits, cold beef, soup and the usual range of liquors. After this it was lights out and to bed. The use of candles was restricted by the captain for safety reasons.

Life for passengers aboard an Indiaman verged on the tedious, and some form of occupation was necessary. Almost everyone could read, but the ladies could also sew or embroider. The redoubtable Mrs Sherwood also took on the responsibility of teaching a soldier's son to read. The opportunity for study was considerable. Stamford Raffles learnt Malay on his first voyage out and Lady Lucretia West was taught geography and astronomy by her husband – a logical occupation when sailing halfway across the world, and the skies radiant with stars.[22] Walking up and down the deck for exercise and conversation were inevitable and pleasurable activities, and passengers must often have been diverted by some of the shipboard sights. There would be occasional excitements such as meeting another ship, hopefully friendly, and conversing through a speaking trumpet if possible. Letters could be written on the off chance of meeting an Indiaman returning home, to whom they could be transferred. Those with the talent exercised their drawing or painting skills or, for the men especially, beating their opponents at backgammon, whist or piquet.[23] There was also the ceremony of 'crossing the line' (equator) with the usual ducking and shaving; indignities from which the ladies were spared. Doubtless they enjoyed the opportunity of watching the men suffer what could be slightly rough treatment at times. Occasionally this reached the point of inducing a violent reaction at gunpoint.[24,25] Other events might be the King's birthday, or Christmas, both being excuses for a bit of a party, the highlight being a bowl of punch.

Music was a regular pleasure, and quite often a lady would have brought her pianoforte, or a harp, the latter being portable enough to take on deck, although at other times it was often necessary to tie down one's chair to achieve a single note of music.[26,27] She might have been accompanied by some of the young men singing, or even by her husband, if she had one. As Lucretia West wrote during her voyage to India: 'Edward begins to sing very nicely, both in concert and solo.'[28]

The music might be accompanied by the dancing of a quadrille on the quarterdeck, to a piano, violins, or the ship's band of fifes and drums, and sometimes with the quarter gallery lighted with lamps.[29] On special occasions, such as New Year, there might be fancy dress, decorative flags and even fireworks, and at other times amateur theatricals. Any of these entertainments could be inhibited by the rolling of the ship, a constant problem in a narrow-beamed Indiaman. Lucretia West refers to this with some feeling:

THE VOYAGE

We have passed such a wretched night rolling about, besides our sofa bed breaking down with us... we roll so amazingly it is impossible to sit on the sofa; one runs from one end to the other. One nearly swings up to the top of the cabin [in the cot at night]. [30,31]

Her nights were disturbed by other interests as well: 'A third calm night but the cockroaches so active we had a hunt instead of sleeping.'

Poor weather, and a big sea, can only have been a trial for the women; slipping about on wet decks in thin-soled leather shoes, and clinging for stability to coarse ropes and heavy bulkheads with their dresses clinging wetly to their ankles, let alone the tedium of confining oneself to a none-too-spacious cabin.

One of the greatest preoccupations and interests of shipboard life, as in any confined environment, would have been the behaviour, habits and personalities of one's fellow passengers. These could be disconcertingly variable, although often there was a reasonably harmonious mix of army officers, civilian staff of all ranks from within the East India Company, merchants, and the odd chaplain, surgeon or adventurer. Some of these were accompanied by wives, sisters or daughters, but a few women travelled alone at the invitation of a family member in India, or close family friend, and nearly always with a companion. There were more single women on the return journey, often with children, having left India as a consequence of the death of a husband. In addition to all these there were, of course, the ships officers who mixed socially with the passengers as well.

Some of the women did not cope well with the male passengers, especially if sobriety and language plummeted. Stanford quotes a Mrs Tottingham as sentencing herself to solitary confinement in her cabin for thirteen weeks in order to avoid the liquor-induced vulgarity of the menfolk. Similarly, Mary Doherty makes the following comment:

A ship certainly was not exactly the place for ladies. Into the cabals and quarrels I entered not and heard little of them except the extraordinary language and conduct of Mrs Knowles who hardly ever was sober. It was the joke of the house to fill her glass and laughing with her and at her, many forgot the respect due to ladies in general. Another source of discomfort was the conduct of Captain Gregorie, which at last obliged Major Doherty to put him under arrest, but this business was hushed up. [32]

Disappointingly, quite what Captain Gregorie had done is not related. Other women obviously enjoyed the variety of people present, and commented on them with an amusingly unstilted degree of perception and wit in their journals:

> Our passengers are Mr and Mrs Wilde (he is going to St Helena as Chief Justice: they go with us to the Cape, and there wait for a homeward bound ship to take them to St Helena);-the O'Briens;-Miss Shields, good-humoured and lively, going out as a missionary;-Miss Knight, sick and solemn;-several Irish girls apparently on their promotion;-Captain Faulkner, very good-humoured and civil, and rather original and clever, but the most incessant talker I ever did meet with in all my life: he can talk down the whole ship's company, and be quite fresh to begin his rounds again: he is the universal adviser to the whole company on every subject: I suspect he teaches the captain to sail;-Mr Harvey, who plays chess, and takes care of his flowers; he has them in an hermetically sealed glass case, which he is taking to the Cape;-a number of hitherto unnamed gentlemen, who sit down to eat and drink, and rise up to play;-one or two pretty boys, who saunter about with Lord Byron in hand;-and Mr Stevens, the missionary, who is good and gentle, but so sick that we have not yet made much acquaintance.[33]

Flirtation, or more, with the opposite sex was probably hampered by the complete lack of privacy, and cramped quarters, although some managed to form a relationship, if only limited while on board. Warren Hastings, on his way out to India, was greatly attracted to a lady, the wife of a German count, also on board. After a divorce had gone through, she later became his second wife. Lady Elizabeth Barlow, wife of an Acting Governor-General, Sir George Barlow, returned home to prepare for her husband's imminent departure from India, but was escorted on the journey by a young man distantly related to her husband. So, in 1807, began a lengthy affair, which caused a mounting scandal over the next two or three years, led to at least one pregnancy, and eventually ended in a messy and very public divorce in 1816.[34]

In the main, shipboard social life was rather more mundane, and is well illustrated in the journal kept by Mary Doherty on the return journey to England with her two young children. It too has its humour, but also pathos, and it bears relating in full:

THE VOYAGE

Never were a stranger set of people collected together, ill and out of spirits as I was, they afforded me a fund of amusement.

Captain Clark was a vulgar but a good-tempered man, and by no means ignorant.

Mr Hippison was a great dandy; very silly and very ignorant.

Mr Cole it was the fashion to abuse and dislike, but I found him in his medical capacity very clever, and his conduct to me was always extremely respectful.

Adjutant Wiggins no one would believe had been 19 years in India. He was going home to see his friends. He was a fat, jolly, good-tempered man, not unlike the landlord of a public house, so fine in his scarlet regimentals, fringed with yellow, and his rosy fat face.

Lieutenant Butler was a gentlemanly handsome young man, extremely reserved, and suffering from the liver complaint. Mr Featherstone was a missionary going to the Cape for the recovery of his health. He was extremely clever, well-informed, and pleasing in his manners. Mrs Featherstone was also a missionary; she was also going to the Cape for her Health. She never spoke.

Captain Everest. The greatest oddity ever seen; he was a radical in principles and always took the opposite side on an argument, besides he was so extremely greedy. He had had a fever which generally leaves people craving for food, but this charming gentleman not only wanted more than his share, but he also wanted the best of every thing. He was called Ginger Tea because his black servant was walking about the first thing in the morning with a little teapot of ginger tea for his master.

Mrs Simpson was the widow of a merchant (in plain English, a shopkeeper) at Madras. Her husband had died of the cholera on the road to Bangalore, where he had been sent against his will to give evidence on some trial, in consequence of which the company's government allowed her a pension. She was a little, ugly, smart-looking woman. She had two children with her, Caroline, about three years old, whom she was whipping from morning till night, and Anne, a baby, certainly not more than eight months old, whom she tried to pass off for year and a half old. Even by her own account of the matter, this child was born eleven months after her husband's death and it was so strikingly like Mr Cole, and its apparent age agreed so well with the date of his last voyage that strange tales were told, and her conduct during the voyage did anything but contradict reports. She had also the care of an unfortunate half-caste girl of nine years old, called Helen, whom she neglected dreadfully. Her servant was called Mrs Hickey, a dirty ragged old woman.

Mrs Davidson was the widow of an assistant surgeon of the Bengal establishment. She had been several years in India up the country in Bengal. She was a young good-looking Scotch woman and had three children, two of whom she had sent in another ship because she did not like the trouble of them. The youngest, Sophie, a baby of a year old, she had with her. Her sole aim was to get another husband as soon as she came on board. She left off her weeds and dressed herself in blue and pink gowns, which she had taken to India with her 10 years before. They were rather antique but they had the desired effect on Ginger Tea, or more likely he was amusing himself. She first tried the missionary but by her own account he had been first a Roman Catholic, then a Presbyterian, and he would have nothing to say to her. Ginger Tea lasted till we left him at the Cape. She then attacked the unfortunate Adjutant Wiggins, who got so entangled with her that I don't know how he got out of the scrape, for I left them together at Exeter (?). All this perhaps did not so much signify, but her conduct as a mother was shameful. She left her poor babe, who was just old enough to lift up her little hands, and with tears in her eyes beg her to take it to the care of an infamous woman, one of the very lowest description, who ill treated, beat and starved it. She used to make it lay the whole day on her lap and, if it darest move, she used to run her needle into its face!! This wretched woman's name was Kenny and her conduct too bad to be recorded, suffice to say drunkenness was her least fault. There were also on board two poor children, Amelia and William Gregg, under Mr Coles care, without any servant to attend them. The girl was seven years old, the boy four: where any of the gentlemen had nothing to amuse them, to tease Billy Gregg was their constant employment. He a fine high-spirited boy and, in a short time, he did them out. The young lady, however, was not the better for the voyage. She was a delicate, elegant, girl when first she came on board, but before she reached England she was the colour of mahogany, more from diet than sunburnt, and as rude and ill bred as possible. Never did I look at these poor children without thanking the Almighty that my life was spared to protect my treasures from such ill usage.

Captain Turner was not particularly polished in his manners and his temper had suffered from my severe illness, but he had a warm heart and conducted himself in a very honourable, gentlemanly manner. His kindness and attention to me was a real comfort.

Mrs Turner, who was extremely pretty and young, was very well disposed, amiable and an excellent mother. Her sweet baby was but three months old. She did everything for it herself, her only servant Maria Fortune, was a young girl of 15, daughter to the poor woman who died on board the Windsor. She lost her father also and was going home to her friends.

In the evening the other passengers came on board and, from the confusion they were in, I had good reason to be thankful my cabin was arranged. Mrs Davison very foolishly took her baby from its wet nurse without it ever having fed; consequently it was extremely fretful and suffered much. Mr Cole came on board the next morning and we sailed with a fair wind. It certainly was more comfortable in every respect than on board the Windsor coming out, the table was very good whereas in the Windsor we were starved. Nobody interfered with the children. They were allowed to play in the cuddy and on the deck at their pleasure. The ship certainly was not so clean, but the worst part of the diet, [was] the table linen, which a hint from me to Captain Clark remedied. The weather was beautifully fine and, while the passengers continued in a good humour, it was pleasant enough. The missionary and Captain Everest were clever men, and their conversation entertaining. Rational conversation, however, did not suit Mrs Simpson or Mrs Davidson and they actually interrupted an argument respecting the comparative merits of mathematical instruments by different makers with, Prey, gentlemen, don't talk politics. They could not endure me because Mrs Doherty was so proud, and the gentlemen paid her so much attention, mistaking reserve for pride, and the civilities which correctness of manners commanded, for attention they coveted. I sat at dinner between Captain Clark and Ginger Tea and I am sure I could not say much in praise of the politeness of either, for the one turned his back to talk to Mrs Simpson, and the other to Mrs Davidson, and I was nearly starved between them, so much so that I begged leave to go to the other side of the table. Mrs Turner they hated still more, for she had youth and beauty which neither of them possessed. Next we were disturbed by a quarrel between Captain Clark and Mr Cole. Mrs Simpson, in the early part of the voyage, allowed Mr Cole to be in her cabin at rather unusual hours. She got tired of him and Captain Clark became the favourite. Her conduct was shameful even in public. Captain Clark and Mr Cole were both married men.

Mrs Davidson's flirtations were more innocent, and even diverting, but she never could get Ginger Tea to give her any of the plums and sweetmeats till he had plentifully helped himself. It was the diversion of the gentlemen to send my little Charles, the only child who dared do it, to steal Captain Everest's plums. If they had been pagodas [an Indian currency] *he could not have made more fuss about them. One day in particular, just as the dessert was placed on the table, the ship required some alteration in its sails and the crew was very small, and every gentleman rose from table to assist them, except Ginger Tea. Who, drawing the fruits towards him without asking any of the ladies if they would have some, helped himself to half. I could not forbear looking at Mrs Simpson, who immediately burst into a loud laugh, when Captain Everest saying Oh Mrs Davidson will want some, sent the other half downstairs.*

The servants and maids could not endure me because I always attended at the children's dinner at one o'clock and prevented them from eating Billy and Emily's pudding. Nanny took good care my boys had enough, but if I was not there Mrs Kenny and Mrs Hickey starved the other poor children. Though I repeatedly told Mrs Simpson and Mrs Davidson of it, nothing could induce them to look after their children. Little Sophie, Mr Cole actually kept alive with medicine, and both she and Mrs Simpson's children were all over sores from diet, to the great terror of Mrs Turner who was fearful her baby would catch it.

Nothing of any consequence occurred, nor had we one day's bad weather, till we got off Table Bay at the Cape of Good Hope. The wind was contrary and we were beating about at the mouth of the Bay for a week. This was in November. At last we worked our way in and cast anchor, when all at once the sailors gave a great shout and a cry for all the women to go below. I was on the deck and enquired what was the matter, to which Mr Butler answered 'Don't talk to Mrs Davidson, or we shall have a scene, but we are receiving foul of another ship.' I went into my cabin and saw we were going backwards against the Clandine; the crack was dreadful; tore away the bowsprit of the other ship but did no serious damage, though both ships were injured before they could be disentangled. Mrs Davidson made a practice of fainting

but, unfortunately for the full effect, I poured a glass of pure brandy
which was on the table rather quickly down her throat, which made
her open her eyes instantaneously to the no small amusement of the
bystanders.

Captain Everest, or 'Ginger Tea', was in fact none other, in later years, than
the great Surveyor-General of India who completed the south-north
triangulation of the subcontinent, and enabled the first accurate triangulation
of the Himalayan peaks. The highest of these was eventually named after
him.

Life on an Indiaman was not always a source of entertainment. There
were very real threats such as storms, shipwreck, fire, shortage of food and
water, and the dangers of enemy warships. During a five-month passage it
was inevitable that there would be a few babies born and, more so, that some
of the crew or passengers would die. In the main, this would be the result of
disease, rife everywhere at that time, or shipboard accidents, such as falling
overboard or out of the rigging; a not uncommon occupational hazard. Mary
Wimberley, wife of the Rev Wimberley, seems to have taken a true church
wife's interest in such matters, and records every event in her five-and-a-half
month outward journey in 1825.[35] There were five babies born on board, but
three other children died. Eleven adults died, which seems to be quite a high
number, mostly of unspecified disease. These were of course all committed
to the deep with due ceremonious gravity. Such events were part of daily life,
as were accidents. Mary Docherty described a Dragoon falling overboard,
but who was thankfully saved by enormous effort on the part of the crew. On
the same voyage there was a storm with thunder and lightning and:

The electric fluid struck the mainmast, killed farrier Maclennan, and
wounded several sailors and soldiers, set fire to a bag of oakum [tarred
fibre for caulking] *in the gun deck and occasioned universal alarm.*
The farrier had his wife and three children on board. He was killed
instantaneously. The fire with some difficulty was got under control.

Shortage of water was a constant menace and the usual ration was six pints
per day; no doubt this was why William Hickey took his own water on his
final return home, as well as to counteract the ship's foul-tasting supply.[36]
This latter inconvenience was an inducement for many to make their
predominant fluid intake wine or beer. The allowance of water was not
adequate for washing oneself, or one's clothes, although neither was a popular

pastime in those days. This notion tended to impinge on the minds of some as a reasonable idea when the weather grew hotter. Lucretia West, wife of Sir Edward West, was sailing to Bombay in 1822 for him to take up the office of Judge, and in her diary she comments that:

> *It has poured torrents all day so much so that 12 vats of water have been caught which are very valuable. Today the scene cannot be believed, the sailors almost all nearly in buff on their knees beating, stamping on and washing shirt cloaths on the deck in the water which ran in torrents.*[37]

And later, in December, she notes that 'We now get up at 6 o'clock as Edward bathes in a tub'. At another time, however, she and the others had had their water allowance for washing reduced to one pint a day – hardly enough to bathe in. Mary Wimberley, in turn, noted on her journey that, 'We use the shower bath constantly now, which is very refreshing.'[38,39]

Severe weather at sea was an inevitable risk, and most passages were complicated by a blown out mainsail or topsail and, occasionally, a sprung topmast, all of which the ship's crew were used to handling. Elizabeth Grant, clearly a bold young lady, describes having herself lashed to the companionway in order to view the mountainous seas. The waves rose to the masthead, apparently: 'we were up on top of them one minute, down in such a hollow the next, the spray falling heavy on the deck.'[40]

A really full-blown storm was not inevitable, but happened quite often, to the great terror of all the passengers, and the crew. There was a regular loss of ships from this, and other maritime causes, but this never reached the exceptional loss rate of the two years 1808 and 1809 when no less than fourteen Indiamen went down.[41] If a ship was short-handed, the ability to control it in heavy weather was greatly diminished, as for instance when some of the better quality of the crew had been pressed into a Royal Navy vessel. The loss of ships has to be set against the number overall in service. In the first ten years of the 1800s this averaged 100 ships a year, sailing mainly to the three Presidencies in India: Calcutta, Madras and Bombay, as well as to the East Indies islands and of course China. There are a few detailed accounts of a storm at sea in an East Indiaman but one of the fullest, and best known, is that in William Hickey's memoirs during his second voyage to India in 1782, in company with his common law wife, Charlotte Barry. He offers a whole chapter on the hurricane they experienced, and what follows are extracts from this:

THE VOYAGE

At daylight on Sunday, 17th November, (a memorable day to me) finding as I lay in bed the motion of the ship particularly uneasy, I got up to look out; and never, to the last day of my existence, shall forget the shock I experienced at what I beheld. The horizon all round of a blackish purple, above which rolled great masses of cloud of a deep copper colour moving in every direction with uncommon rapidity; vivid lightning in every quarter, thunder awfully roaring at a distance, though evidently approaching us; a short irregular sea, breaking with a tremendous surf, as if blowing furiously hard though then but moderate; the wind, however, whistling shrill as a boatswain's pipe through the blocks and rigging. The scene altogether was such as to appal the bravest men on board.... The sea suddenly increased to an inconceivable height, the wind roaring to such a degree that the officers upon deck could not make themselves heard by the crew with the largest speaking-trumpets. Between nine and ten, it blew an absolute hurricane, far surpassing what I had any idea of. As it veered all round the compass, so did the sea increase infinitely beyond imagination, one wave encountering another from every direction and, by their mutual force in thus meeting, ran up apparently to a sharp point, there breaking at a height that is actually incredible but to those who unhappily saw it. The entire ocean was in a foam white as soap-suds.

At a quarter to eleven, the foretop mast, yard, rigging and all went over the side, the noise of it being imperceptible amidst the roaring of wind and sea. In a few minutes, it was followed by the mizzen mast, which snapped like a walking stick about eight feet above the quarter-deck; part of the wreck of it unfortunately got foul of the rudder chains, and every moment struck the ships bottom with excessive violence. At half-past eleven, the foremast went, being shivered into splinters quite down to the gundeck.... Thus, in the short space of four hours, was this noble vessel reduced to such a state of distress as few have ever been in. Our situation seemed hopeless; not a creature on board but thought every minute would be the last of their lives. When the masts were gone, she immediately began to roll with unparalleled velocity from side to side, each gunwale, with half the quarterdeck, being [sub]merged in water each roll, so that we every moment expected she would be bottom uppermost, or roll her sides out.

Mr Bateman, at the commencement of the gale, had gone upon deck, from whence he dared not again venture to stir, but was obliged to lay himself down under the wheel and there remain. Mr Kemp and Mr Brown had lashed themselves to the gun-rings of the aftermost port in the great cabin to prevent their being dashed from side to side. Whilst thus situated, three out of the five stern windows, frames and all, suddenly burst inward from the mere force of the wind.

The ship was apparently full of water, and seemed to be so completely overwhelmed that we all thought she was fast settling downward. Nevertheless, the velocity and depth of her rolling abated nothing, tearing away every article that could be moved. Not a bureau, chest, or trunk but broke loose and were soon demolished, the contents, from the quickness and constant splashing from one side to the other of the ship, becoming a perfect paste, adhering to the deck between the beams, many inches in thickness, so as, near the sides, actually to fill up the space to the deck. During the severity of the hurricane, about twenty noble fellows, such as would not have disgraced the British Navy, at the head of whom stood the boatswain, acted with the same determined spirit they had shown on 9th September, doing all that could be performed by men, while the rest of the crew gave themselves up to despair, clinging round their priest, and screeching out prayers for pardon and mercy in such dismal and frantic yells as was horrible to hear. By two in the afternoon, every bulkhead between decks, except that of my cabin, had fallen from the violent labouring of the ship.

The sea, indeed, had already done much towards it for us by carrying off the whole of the masts, yards, rigging, and everything that was upon the upper deck. An attempt was therefore made to throw the guns overboard; but only five were so, and those at the imminent risk of the lives of the men from the excessive motion. An attempt was likewise made to start [i.e. move] the madeira wine. The two first men that went into the hold for that purpose were immediately jammed in between two pipes [barrels containing 418 litres each] and killed; after which, no other would try. After exerting himself in a wonderful manner, by one of the violent jerks from a tremendous sea breaking on board, the captain was thrown down with such force as to break his right arm and receive a severe contusion on his head, which rendered him insensible.

Thus hour after hour passed with us in utter despair; but still to our amazement we remained afloat, which seemed to us little short of a miracle for a ship in such a state as ours was, so tossed about at the

32

mercy of such a sea as never was seen, so involved in ruin and desolation on every side, making too, as she did before the hurricane commenced, thirty inches of water every hour, and not a single stroke of pump after half-past eleven in the morning; nor could anybody account for her not going to the bottom but by supposing she actually rolled the water out of her as fast as it came in!

At eight at night, the gale had evidently subsided or, to use a seaman's language, it had broken up. This encouraged the few men who had throughout behaved themselves like heroes to further exertions. At the imminent risk of their lives, some of them went over the stern and ultimately succeeded in cutting away considerable quantities of the rigging, sails, and yards that got so entangled with the rudder and rudder-chains as totally to prevent the ships steering; by which our danger of foundering from the overwhelming sea was greatly increased. They also afterwards accomplished the throwing overboard of fourteen more of her guns, besides much lumber from between decks, by which the ship was importantly benefited, the rolling being less rapid and not so deep.

I joined in searching amongst the heap of rubbish in the great cabin for anything worth preserving. We soon collected from thence a parcel of six-and-thirty-shilling pieces, or half-Joes as they are called in Portugal, two watches and various bits of gold and silver ornaments and trinkets. After ransacking in a mass of dirt, so blended together it was difficult to separate for a long time, I got hold of a small tin case, much bruised but unbroken. Thirteen of the crew lost their lives, the greater part of them, as was conjectured, being washed overboard. Besides the two persons killed by the pipes of wine, three other bodies were found in different places, two of them under the beams upon which the boats had been stowed, the third between the coppers and ships side, a space of only a few inches wide. It was a shocking spectacle; being so jammed in by the working of the ship, the intestines were squeezed out and the head forced completely round, the face being towards the back. These miserable corpses were committed to the deep in the afternoon.

By any stretch of the imagination this was a desperate storm, and a terrifying experience, but also a remarkable delivery; which left the ship with no masts and no provisions, but a good many people feeling profoundly relieved. Charlotte Barry appears to have coped with true fortitude, although she had resigned herself that they would both drown. Her behaviour seems to have been something of an example to the crew, who loved her 'for the peculiar gentleness and suavity of her manners'. A Dutch vessel came to their assistance, having heard the regular gunfire alert, and provided spars for a jury mast, sufficient to enable the ship to limp into Trincomalee on the island of Ceylon. The relief of arrival was rather dashed by finding it had fallen into French hands, and was now occupied by the celebrated Admiral Suffren. Thus the ship and its passengers survived the hurricane, only to become French prisoners of war.

Another hugely feared disaster at sea was fire. Not surprisingly, wooden ships were rather susceptible to this and, despite the paradox of being surrounded by water, they can be entirely destroyed by fire unless it is extinguished rapidly. One of the most terrible and tragic examples of such an experience was that of Stamford Raffles, and his wife Sophia, returning home from Bencoolen in Sumatra, at the end of his time there as Lieutenant Governor. In addition to being a high-achieving civil servant and administrator with the East India Company, he was a consummate historian, naturalist and linguist, with a profound knowledge of the people and places where he lived and worked. Consequently he was carrying home hundreds of cases containing his unsurpassable collection, as well as multitudes of manuscripts, and even live caged animals. The fire started in the evening; was caused by carelessness, and progressed rampantly. Everyone just about escaped – Sophia still in her nightgown, and the crew rowed them the fifty miles to shore through the night, no mean feat, and obviously to the grateful relief of all. This relief was offset, however, by the awful awareness by Raffles and Sophia that they had lost everything. They had had to leave their four dead children in Bencoolen, and now all Raffles' official papers and valuables were gone, even the precious ring given to him by Princess Charlotte. Gone too were his notes for a history of Sumatra and Borneo; his account of the founding of Singapore; his natural history specimens, along with 2,000 drawings; dictionaries, grammars, a detailed map of Sumatra, and a very large collection of animals and plants heading for England, including a living tapir, a new species of tiger, birds etc.[42] A loss such as this was incalculable but, with true fortitude, he set about redrawing the maps, and rewriting many of his articles while waiting for another ship; a real measure of the almost obsessive conscientiousness of the man. In reality, what else could he do?

If one was fortunate enough to escape these horrors, there was still the possibility of being attacked by the enemy, if at war. Britain was much of the

THE VOYAGE

time at war with France during those years. Such was the near experience of Martha Sherwood during her outward voyage in 1807 after sighting three ships bearing down on them:

Passing close to our rear, [they] hoisted French colours almost before we had time to form our conjectures of what they were. The colours were no sooner up than they began to fire, and at the same crisis all hands were engaged on board our ship to clear for action. Every cabin which had been erected between the last gun and the forepart of the ship was torn down, ours of course amongst the rest, and everything we possessed thrown in heaps into the hold or trampled underfoot. All the women without respect of person were tumbled after the furniture of the cabins into the same dismal hole at the very bottom of the ship, and the guns prepared in the shortest possible time to return the compliment which the enemy had already paid us. One of the enemies ships was a seventy-four, or eighty gun, the other a frigate...after some broadsides the French showed a disposition to withdraw... . It was quite dark when the contest ceased and we poor women were set at liberty. The hold was a dismal place and there was no light but what came from above. There were six ladies and eight or ten soldiers wives in it... . We were then considerably under [the] water-mark, in darkness, and quite certain that if anything happened to the ship nothing could save us, for they had taken away the ladders, probably to keep us in our places. Our husbands and all our late companions were above, and we heard the roar of the guns, but had no means of learning what was going on. There was, however, no fainting, screaming or folly amongst us; it is not on occasions of real trial that women in general behave weakly.[43]

Before reaching India many ships stopped, either to drop off passengers or, more commonly, to take on water and revictual, as well as to have a short period of respite from shipboard life. One of the first ports of call was Funchal in Madeira, but this was with a very definite purpose in mind, that of taking on board Madeira wine for shipping to India to sell, or for personal use. The opportunity was taken to collect water and fresh vegetables, and even to have a wander around the island. The next and most common port was the Cape, where the intrinsic Protestantism made the British feel at home, unlike Madeira. It was easier to call at the Cape if England was at peace with Holland or if, at the time, they were in possession of Dutch colonies such as

Java, but the stay was generally pleasant and offered good food (at a price), accommodation and the opportunity of exploring the vineyards at Constantia, or climbing Table Mountain. After 1796, the Cape became British, following the recent Napoleonic annexation of the Netherlands, which gave the British some excuse to take control of Dutch settlements, and therefore stops became more frequent. Lucretia West mentions pretty streets with a canal in the centre of each settlement, and clean white houses, only too reminiscent of Holland:

> [We] *walked past the Governors house to see the wild beasts and the secretary birds... . We are at Morrison's boarding house which looks clean and comfortable tho we have some bugs, but no mosquitoes. Most of the inhabitants are Dutch; everything appears abominably clean.*

This last observation could be of a Dutch town today.

After the Cape, passengers often became restless and tired of one another, according to Julia Maitland, and squabbled a little for amusement.[44] Some men even challenged others to duels, to be consummated upon arrival on land; all being a consequence of cramped living conditions, and faces that had become all too familiar. Further on lay Mauritius, a considerable threat from the French during times of war, but a possible watering hole otherwise, and eventually Point de Galle, at the southernmost tip of Ceylon. This was the first Indian landfall, and land vegetation could be scented from near twenty miles away.[45] At this point, those going to Bombay turned left, but the majority headed East towards Madras (the Coast) or Calcutta (the Bay). The time of year at which one arrived was obviously dictated, approximately, by the time of departure from home. This, in turn, had to be fixed according to the likely prevailing wind in the Indian Ocean when one got there. Fortunately this was more or less predictable, being either the South-West monsoon running from April to October, or the North-East monsoon from October to May. Both were of immense importance to sailing ships in all those waters, because they largely dictated where and when one could go, and certainly with any safety. If heading for Bombay or the Malabar coast one tried to time one's arrival for the S-W monsoon; at best July or August. This was also the best monsoon for travelling to the East coast. On the other hand, voyages to the westward, either homewards from Madras or the Bay of Bengal, or towards the Malabar Coast, had to be done during the N-E monsoon, which was the complete converse, and the best months were January and February. Any attempt to do the opposite was likely to fail. This is very much an oversimplification, but it explains the timings of voyages, and also why those on shore might not see any ships (nor receive any letters) for weeks, or even months, on end.

Having coped with all potential, or actual, tribulations of the journey, most women must have been exceedingly glad to see the buildings, and other landmarks, of their destination, and temporarily forgotten any homesickness in an eager desire to get ashore. That is except the prim Lucretia West who, on the point of disembarkation, remarked: 'It is odd but I am not at all anxious to arrive. I have been so comfortable [astonishing!] and must expect a good deal of bustle and annoyance...'

The next interesting problem, however, was how to effect a landing, especially at Madras which had no harbour whatsoever before the late nineteenth century.

Chapter 2

Arrival and Establishment

Having first sighted land, and so imagining herself to be on the home straight, a few nasty surprises lay in wait for any timorous Georgian woman. The commonest landfall, if heading for India, was Point de Galle at the southern end of Ceylon. Here ships steered left to head for Bombay, Surat and the Malabar Coast, or right to head for Madras on the Coromandel Coast, and Calcutta in the Bay of Bengal. The latter was the commonest destination, Calcutta being the senior Presidency (and later the seat of the Governor-General), and West Bengal being of such economic significance in the earlier years of the East India Company. Ships en route to the Bay often stopped for a while in Madras, before heading on to Calcutta, while some sailed eastwards to Penang, the Malacca Straits or beyond.

Ships heading for Calcutta arrived at the mouth of the Hooghly River, which was effectively the lowermost navigable part of the Ganges as it flowed through Calcutta, and lay at a point some fifty miles downriver from the city. At this point ships became beset by shifting sandbanks, and rapid tidal streams, and usually anchored at this point in Sangar Roads, in what later became known as Diamond Harbour. It was certainly possible to take full-sized ships further upstream but this was not regularly done because of these hazards. Therefore passengers usually disembarked here into smaller boats, such as a brig, to sail, or even be rowed, up to Calcutta itself. Luggage often went separately. If the pilotage had been poor, or there was nasty weather, these smaller craft could capsize, causing a drenching, or even drowning, for unlucky individuals who had survived months at sea. Occasionally, full-sized Indiamen went aground, or broke their moorings, or were even harried by French privateers. The journey up to Calcutta was a good opportunity for ladies to tidy themselves after the wet and windblown sea journey, and to review the state of their possessions but, above all, to gaze in amazement at the unfamiliar Eastern view around them. The dense, verdant exuberance of the jungle-like water's edge, lined with billowing strange trees and shrubs, giving way after some miles to a gradually increasing magnificence of lavish riverside estates, with numerous colonnaded houses lining Garden Reach stretching up to the outskirts of Calcutta. This city's stately splendour in the early 1800s would have stirred a feeling of comfortable reassurance in the hearts of passengers who would be wondering what on earth they faced, after all those miles of desolate sea, and so far from England.

Arriving at Madras was quite another matter, and rather more hair-raising. There was no harbour, nor any river inlet, and ships moored a mile or two offshore, away from the rolling surf that pounded the beach. At peak times of the year, such as the first arrival of the season of a fleet of Indiamen from England, and perhaps in the company of Royal Navy vessels, there could be as many as 100 ships lying at anchor. An exchange of fluttering flag signals and the boom of gun-salutes passed between the ships and Fort St George, which lay almost on the beach, well before anchor chains had rattled through hawses. Before, too, the catamarans had come from shore to greet them, and exchange mail to and from the city. These catamarans were essentially three lightweight pointed tree trunks, tied together in a bundle, and carrying two men perched on top, manoeuvring the craft with paddle power. They carried the all-important letters in their close-fitting conical caps to keep them dry. Pictures of these craft appear in engravings of the early nineteenth century, and they are completely unchanged 200 years later, except that they are now powered by an outboard motor of sorts; usually pirated from a road vehicle. Mary Doherty, wife of Major Doherty of the 13th Light Dragoons, comments on arriving at Madras in 1821:

> *The scene on board was very entertaining; the catamarans bringing us provisions, the natives begging to be engaged as servants, and soldiers preparing to disembark which they did with the greatest regularity early on Monday morning, and in the best spirits, little thinking the country before them is destined to be the grave of the greater part.*

By means of the catamarans, letters of introduction could be sent ashore to friends or relatives who might be able to help with accommodation, and to other introductions so useful during that period of time soon after the first nervous leap ashore, for in the 1700s and early 1800s there were no adequate hotels or boarding houses, and the invariable practice was to throw oneself upon the hospitality offered as a consequence of these letters. As Mary Doherty records: 'We immediately sent our letters onshore and impatiently waited for an invitation from some kind friends to their house, Mr Holland having furnished us with letters of introduction to several of the first [i.e. most important] inhabitants of Madras.' From time to time such visitors were a little less welcome than might be implied by the hospitality of their hosts, but in the main the system worked well.[1]

Invitations subsequently arrived from all those who had received letters and, having accepted an offer, it was then a matter of getting ashore through the surf. Stories of this were told in England, and old hands from India would alarm the ladies with paralysing accounts of what was involved. The Indian boatmen were practised and skilled however, and the *Masulah* boats they used were designed for the purpose. Their flexible *Anjali* planks and timbers were not held together by nails, but tied with coconut fibre and caulked with the same, allowing these high sided, flat bottomed, craft to flex with the great force of the beaching surf.[2] Passengers were shielded from sun and spray by an awning, with chairs to sit on while the twelve oarsmen would chant rhythmically in time with the oar stroke, and at an increasing rate to poise the boat on the crest of a roller before charging down the other side, eventually arriving on the sand.[3,4,5] An overview of the experience of landing at Madras was well expressed by Lady Maria Callcott in 1810:

I do not know anything more striking than the first approach to Madras. The low flat sandy shore extending for miles to the north and south, for the few hills there are appear far inland, seems to promise nothing but barren nakedness, when, on arriving in the roads, the town and fort are like a vision of enchantment. The beach is crowded with people of all colours, whose busy motions, at that distance, make the earth itself seem alive. The public offices and store-houses which line the beach, are fine buildings, with colonnades to the upper stories supported by rustic bases arched, all of the fine Madras chunam, smooth, hard, and polished as marble. At a short distance Fort-George, with its lines and bastions, the government house and gardens, backed by St Thomas's Mount, form an interesting part of the picture, while here and there in the distance, minarets and pagodas are seen rising from among the gardens. A friend who, from the beach, had seen our ship coming in, obligingly sent the accommodation-boat [Masulah] for us, and I soon discovered its use. While I was observing its structure and its rowers, they suddenly set up a song, as they called it, but I do not know that I ever heard so wild and plaintive a cry. We were getting into the surf; the coxswain now stood up, and with his voice and his foot kept time vehemently, while the men worked their oars backwards, till a violent surf came, struck the boat, and carried it along with a frightful violence; then every oar was plied to prevent the wave from taking us back as it receded, and this was repeated five or six times, the song of the boatmen rising and falling with the waves, till we were dashed high and dry upon the beach. The boats used for crossing the surf are large and light, made of very thin planks sewed together, with straw in the seams, for caulking would make them too stiff; and the great object is, that they should be flexible, and give to the water like leather, otherwise they would be dashed to pieces. Across the very edge of the boat are the bars on which the rowers sit; and two or more men are employed in the bottom of the boat to bale out the water (they are naked all but a turban, and half a handkerchief fastened to the waist by a pack-thread). They are wild-looking, and their appearance is not improved by the crust of salt left upon their bodies by the sea-water, and which generally whitens half their skin. At one end of the boat is a bench with cushions and a curtain, for passengers, so that they are kept dry while the surf is breaking round the boat.

Upon coming ashore passengers were met by dozens of individuals pressing for employment and willing to carry luggage and people onto the beach, for a fee. Sometimes there was competition from the young men out of Fort St George, looking for an opportunity to meet any eligible young ladies waiting to come on land and, better still, to carry them.[6] An engraving by J.B. Hunt, published in 1856, wryly shows the details of the event: a large, smiling lady is carried in a chair by two bare-torsoed natives, while a young man disconsolately wades through the surf in his highly polished best boots. Once ashore they would be carried off to their hosts by any one of a variety of local transports. The commonest was the palanquin, or palkee, which was effectively a rectangular box with sliding doors and small Venetian, or curtained, windows and a mattress to lounge on. It was about high enough to sit up inside, and just long enough to lie full-length. There would be two bearers (or *hamauls*) at front, and the same at the back, and the single central pole projecting forwards and backwards ensured that, in one plane at least, the whole thing stayed horizontal over rough ground. A *tonjon* was not dissimilar, being more like an open sedan chair, with again a single pole fore and aft, and a movable hood. On the road outside the Fort, and above the beach, might be some carriages. These could be two-wheeled, two-person gigs, or four-person landaus, or one of a variety of closed carriages such as broughams. A popular choice was the one-person, one-horse chair called a bandy. Bullock-drawn carriages – or *hackeries* – were extensively used in India, but less so in cities, unless going into the countryside and carrying heavy luggage. The variety of carriages in India at that time was overwhelming, or would be to the modern observer:

> *This avenue forms the evening drive, and at sunset it is thronged with carriages of every description, and equestrians mounted upon all sorts of horses. Chariots, barouches, brichtskas, and double phaetons, fresh from the best builders of London or Calcutta, appear amid old coaches, old sociables, rickety landaus, buggies, stanhopes, tilburies, and palanquin-carriages – the latter not infrequently drawn by bullocks, and all in various stages of dilapidation, for no one in India cares about being seen in a shabby vehicle.*[7]

And so the uncertain traveller, after four to five months at sea, began his or her sentence in the sultry and thrilling East. No doubt they wondered what lay in store, but must have been reassured to see all the signs and trappings of Englishness, and so to know that many individuals had gone before and, hopefully, were there to lend a helping hand.

After stepping ashore, the overriding priority was to find somewhere to live. As already outlined, this would initially be at the house of someone introduced from home, and young men, be they civil or military, often stayed with a family of note for weeks, or months, before moving up country with their Regiment, or to another Presidency, to fulfil their job commitments. Single males arriving in India would invariably join family, or very close friends by prior arrangement. Wives would often accompany their husbands, but sometimes arrived at a later date, having travelled from Britain alone, apart from the company of a maid or acquaintance. The main reasons for this delay might have been preoccupation with the education and care of her children, or perhaps that the great expense of travel obliged a staggered start after some financial consolidation.

The home was the responsibility, and perhaps the life sentence, of ladies in the Georgian, and even the Victorian eras and its situation, design and facilities would have been an important preoccupation. As at home in Europe, the running of the household was down to the lady of the house. She would have some cash for simple expenses, and would usually keep the household accounts, but her husband held the purse strings; how tightly depended on his character and generosity. In India it was more common to rent than buy houses, and the grandeur of the house reflected the importance, or self-importance, of the owner. It was perhaps a secondary matter as to whether he could afford it. Richard Wellesley, Lord Mornington, was Governor-General of India from 1797 and built, with hubristic grandiosity and somebody else's money, the enormous and stunning Government House in Calcutta. He incurred considerable displeasure from the Court of Directors of the East India Company, who paid for this bit of megalomania and were, as usual, strapped for cash. Sadly, one can hardly see it today, as it is ringed by trees and men in uniform, being now the seat of the Governor of Bengal. Beyond this, lesser mortals would rent, buy or build what they could, but mostly they rented. The owners of rented properties might possess a handful of them around the city, and these early property developers became wealthy from the income and capital gain that accrued. Not such an unfamiliar story today.

Sir Henry Gwillim, a judge at the Supreme Court of Madras, his wife Elizabeth and her unmarried younger sister Mary, lived for a while in a house in Madras owned by an Armenian, while their house close to the coast, and pleasantly cooled by the sea breeze, was being renovated. This temporary home was at St Thomas's Mount which, being on higher ground, was also cooler than those on the plains. Some lived in the Fort, both in Madras and the other presidencies, but this was mainly the domain of single men, soldiers and others, a hangover from the earlier years of the 1700s. Elizabeth Gwillim likened St Thomas's Mount and the surrounding area to:

> *One of the villages about London; perhaps Clapham Common is most like it. There are 40 or 50 villas in the Italian style, enclosed in gardens of most luxuriant foliage. ... The road from the Fort to this place is said to be the most beautiful and interesting in India... about 3 miles before you come to this place it is a sort of forest scenery with roads wandering under the groups of trees in various directions, all constantly filled with travellers and droves of cattle of various descriptions.*[8]

Today the trees have been replaced by a forest of housing, and the droves are of cars, auto-rickshaws, motorbikes, bicycles and people in a constant whirligig of noise and haze. It is unlikely that any but the most ardent Madras inhabitant would now call it beautiful but, as ever in India, it has its fascination.

Many of the buildings of the eighteenth and early nineteenth century in India were fine, elegant and stylish. William Hickey, in Calcutta in the late eighteenth century, describes a friend as: 'Purchasing an excellent country house, beautifully situated at the head of Garden Reach, commanding an extensive and rich view both up and down the river, taking in Fort William [and] the range of houses, fairly enough termed palaces, along the Esplanade.'[9]

Here, and in Madras, those with any means chose to live in more rural areas giving the opportunity for tranquillity, rural beauty, and slightly cooler weather than to be found in the Fort or town centre, and they would commute to work by horse, palanquin, or bandy. In Madras these were the garden houses; picturesque Palladian-style buildings erected during the more genteel and refined Georgian period, and now almost extinct. They were built to live in, and their design reflected the taste of the period with elegant colonnades of pillars, paired or single, fronting a deep shady veranda in which the occupants could stroll or dine, with some respite from the heat of the sun. They were often flat-roofed, but sometimes with a well-proportioned pediment above a graceful staircase and portico, or the latter might extend outwards from the entrance to form a shelter from sun or rain for carriages bringing visitors.

To a large extent the buildings resembled the eighteenth century structures of London or Paris, but in miniature, or even the great villas of that time in the southern United States. The columns, and the building itself, were made of brick, and rendered with a hard, shining lime plaster, mostly peculiar to Madras called *chunam*. This was made from seashells, and other arcane ingredients such as egg white and coarse sugar (*jaggery*); the recipe is now largely lost to history. *Chunam* could be polished to a smooth, marble-like appearance, with a similar consistency, and was often painted to mimic this to perfection. It would have been quite similar to the scagiola well-known to Italian art historians. The exact roundness achieved in these columns is remarkable, giving the complete appearance of a Greek Doric column. This could only be achieved by first building the column with specially constructed bricks, one face of each forming part of a circle, so that an assembly of many forms the column, before applying the *chunam*.

The houses were set in extensive gardens in which amateur botanists could delight in collecting the more beautiful regional flora, and where there were also kitchen gardens.

Elizabeth Gwillim gives an interesting contemporary description of these buildings:[10]

ARRIVAL AND ESTABLISHMENT

They are all like pictures of Italian palaces with flat roofs or balustrades. I hardly know what to compare them to that you know, for they look like marble, and are all built with columns, but it is a lighter kind of building than fine churches in London, and much more beautiful architecture than the inferior ones. Lord Tinley's house is like a great many of them with a double flight of steps outside, but many are only pavilions with nothing above the ground floor, which is the case of the house we live in. They are the prettiest houses, but the upstairs houses as they call them have more air. These houses are built of brick and cased over with the chunam. This is a finer lime than the plaster of Paris and it is made of the small white shells which the rough surf occasions the sea to throw up in great quantities. The stucco made of this lime, and called chunam, bears a polish almost equal to white marble but is I think more like the polish, or glaze, of very smooth white china. The walls, columns and balustrades are all polished. The walls of rooms are sometimes painted, as stucco rooms in England of pale green-blue. Some people colour the chunam for the outside of the house of a light grey, in imitation of the grey granite of the country, leaving the columns, pilasters etc, white. The floors are also of this chunam, coloured according to the fancy of the owner, and here it so exactly resembles marble pavements that I should not have known. Our house has black squares, and white ones for the sitting rooms, and in the other rooms a light tint is much used. Some have dove and black squares, or all dove, which is neat. They mark it in squares so deep that it would deceive anybody. We have folding doors in all the rooms which are, half way, green-painted Venetians. The windows are all Venetians, and no glass, but we can thus exclude the light and yet have air from room to room through the whole house, but they are generally all open, and there are always as many doors as windows.

There are only a handful of these houses scattered through modern Chennai, mostly decaying, and seemingly unloved and unwanted by the majority. The notable exception is the Madras Club, a sweeping white curve of classical beauty sited in extensive grounds; a regular feature. It has been sympathetically restored and cherished; a beacon in a depressing array of crumbling ruin.

The designs of these houses were dictated by taste, local building practices and the desire to impress. William Hickey was very much of the latter ilk, boastfully stating how:

*I derived much amusement from daily superintending the progress of
my new house, in the building and completing of which Mr Robertson,
the proprietor, neither spared his own attention nor his cash, the
bricklayer's and carpenter's materials all being of the best.*

He continues:

*In March 1790 my new mansion being finished and very handsome, I
removed into it. I furnished it in such a style as gained universal
approbation and acquired me the reputation of possessing great taste.
The principal apartments were ornamented with some immense looking-
glasses, also with a number of beautiful pictures and prints, forming
altogether a choice and valuable collection. The expense was enormous,
but as I looked only to pleasant times, having no idea I should ever be
able to lay up a fortune, I was indifferent about the price of things,
purchasing every article I felt any inclination for. When completed my
house was pronounced to be the most elegantly fitted up of any in
Calcutta and, in fact, there was no one like it. Some of my facetious
acquaintances christened it Hickey's picture and print warehouse.*[11]

An important aim in the design of any British house in India was to combat
the overwhelming heat, which most Europeans tolerated poorly, and for
which they were ill-prepared. Clothing was wholly unsuited to the climate,
and women avoided going out in the middle of the day, and for several hours
either side, despite the fact that their light, muslin dresses were much more
suitable than the men's clothes: tailcoats, waistcoats and britches. Sun-
induced ruddiness, or a tan, was nowhere near as fashionable as a pale
complexion. Thus a veranda, often colonnaded, was an important feature,
allowing women to sit or stroll in the shade throughout the day, venturing
out of doors only during the morning and evening. These verandas were often
also at first-floor level, allowing some coolness from a gentle breeze, and
were supported elegantly beneath by further rows of pillars.

In the centre of the house there were three to five rooms, or halls, of equal
size.[12,13] These were only separated by pillars or arches, and were therefore
open to a free flow of air, again helping to keep them cool. The loftiness of
the rooms aided in this. There was a wing on either side containing three
rooms, which would have been bedrooms, and also a library. The windows
tended to be higher, running even from floor-to-ceiling, but were not glazed.
Instead they contained Venetian blinds, which were narrow wooden slats that

swivelled at either end, all being held in a frame, and connected by rods to open or close them simultaneously. They were usually painted a cool green. The doors were half Venetian as well, and when all these Venetian slats were open, a pleasant cooling current of air could be encouraged through the house, but avoiding any direct sunlight. The disadvantage of this arrangement was a disconcerting lack of privacy. It wasn't uncommon to have servants, or even visitors, walk in on one unheralded; even more so than in a Georgian house in England, and who knows what could be heard through the open Venetians. There was an almost complete absence of curtains, which were avoided because they were thought to harbour scorpions, mosquitoes and lizards; this too aided the flow of air, and of course sound, through these echoing halls.[14]

Every room in every house had a punkah. This, according to Emma Roberts:

Is formed of a wooden framework, a foot and a half, or 2 feet broad, hung in the centre of the room and extending nearly its whole length. This frame is covered with painted canvas or fluted silk, finished around the edges with gilt mouldings. It is suspended from the ceiling by ropes covered with scarlet cloth, very tastefully disposed, and hangs within 7 feet of the ground. A rope is fastened to the centre, and the whole apparatus waves to and fro creating, if pulled vigorously, a strong current of air, and rendering the surrounding atmosphere endurable.[15]

The operator who pulled this rope for hour after mind-numbing hour was called the punkah wallah. He was usually relegated to the outside of the room, the rope passing through a hole in the wall. Another neat device was the *tattie*, which was similar in shape and principle to the punkah, but was made of a grass that was wetted, so evaporation from the swinging movement cooled the moving air and, as a bonus, could scent it as well.[16,17] More surprisingly we learn that: 'Most ladies have servants who fan them during dinner, and stand behind their chairs for that purpose.'[18] Perhaps this was no more self-indulgent than today's habit in such latitudes of boosting air conditioning to glacial levels.

The indomitable and intrepid Fanny Parkes arrived in India in 1822, as the wife of a junior civil servant destined not to take the world, or even India, by the throat, but to settle into the humdrum routine of being responsible for ice-making in Allahabad. Fanny, while remaining overtly loyal to her husband, had feminist tendencies, and an irrepressible desire to wander the subcontinent alone, and so she did; the Dervla Murphy of her time, touched with a hint of hippiness. Her journal of these travels makes riveting reading.

She, in fact, adored India from the start: 'On arriving in Calcutta, I was charmed with the climate; the weather was delicious, and nothing could exceed the kindness we experienced from our friends. I thought India a most delightful country.' Nevertheless, even the fervent Fanny found the climate hard to endure at times:

> *The heat is intense – very oppressive. I dare not go to church for fear of its bringing on fits, which might disturb the congregation; you have little idea of the heat of a collection of many assembled in such a climate – even at home, with all appliances and means to boot for reducing the temperature, the heat is sickening.*

She describes a wonderful contraption for cooling a house called a thermantidote – a sort of vast, primitive air conditioning unit, measuring 7ft high, 5ft broad and 10-12ft long. The machine contained four fans on an iron rod, which were constantly rotated, forcing a draught of air through a wide funnel in through the window of the house. The air entering this vast box was cooled by being sucked by the fans through large scented-grass (*khas-khas*) *tattis* placed in wide openings on each side. Water was constantly dripped down the *tattis*, collected at the bottom and recycled to the top. The whole was hugely labour intensive, but remarkably effective, and lowered the temperature of the air in a room by many degrees.[19] Remarkably perhaps, something very similar still exists today in more rural parts of India. The box is smaller, and metallic, and the single large fan is electrically powered. It is fixed into a window space, the two mesh sides containing an artificial grass-like fibre down which water is trickled, just as it was 200 years ago. The main difference today is the absence of manual labour, other than the occasional kick start.

In sweltering temperatures most people enjoy the thought of immersing themselves in water, and a bath or shower is a compelling requirement. The bathroom was by no means unknown in Indian British houses, probably more so than back in England, and perhaps influenced by the prevalence of human contact with water on that subcontinent. Hindus bathed ritually from the ghats of rivers, or in temple tanks, and there was the universal presence of fountains, rivulets and pools in the grander muslim or mughal houses, as well as the baths in the zenanas. Outstanding examples of Muslim aquatic architecture can be found in the remains of the pleasure palace in Mandu, in central North India, or around Srinagar in Kashmir. In Mandu there are spectacular ornate pools with steps and islands, fed by water channels running in whorls or zigzags through gleaming patterned or coloured marble, or by imaginative fountains, waterfalls and spouts. The culture of water as a pleasure, and not just an amenity, was everywhere, and cannot have failed to amaze the poorly-washed European, or at least those who had access to such sights.

So baths and bathrooms were moderately common. Fanny Parkes had one, and proudly describes killing a scorpion there: 'A good fat old fellow', which she prepared and preserved. Elizabeth Fenton's journal of her years in India in the late 1820s refers several times to the bathing room, and the refreshment of a cold bath, albeit momentary. There were other benefits: 'I often go and sit in my bathing-room, which from being in the rear and flagged with stone, is always cool though the window is open.'[20]

Hardly surprisingly, being an almost automatic English preoccupation, concern about the weather was constant. Fanny Parkes succinctly summarises a day in March in Northern India:

At six o'clock it is so cold that a good gallop in a cloth habit will just keep you warm. At nine o'clock – a fine breeze – very pleasant – windows open – no punkah. Three o'clock – blue blinds lowered to keep off the glare of the sunshine, which is distressing to the eyes; every Venetian shut, the punkah in full swing, the very mosquitoes asleep on the walls, yourself asleep on a sofa, not a breath of air – a dead silence around you. Four o'clock – a heavy thunderstorm, with the rain descending in torrents: you stop the punkah, rejoice in the fraicheur, and are only prevented from taking a walk in the grounds by the falling rain. Five o'clock you mount your Arab, and enjoy the coolness for the remainder of the day – such is today.[21]

Later, in June, she notes: 'The weather is more oppressive than we have ever found it; the heat intolerable; the thermometer in my room 93° in spite of *tattis* and punkahs.' Likewise Elizabeth Gwillim, or her sister Mary, often referred to the heat in their letters home.[22, 23]

The land wind is reckoned the most unpleasant. It is a hot dry wind, instead of cooling: when it blows upon you it feels as if a hot iron was passing close to you. It makes ones hair curl like a fuzzy, and ones skin feel like old parchment. When these winds set in, they are quite regular, blowing from four or five o'clock in the morning till four or three in the evening, when it changes to a fine refreshing sea breeze.

RIBBONS AMONG THE RAJAHS

The land wind season does not last above a month or six weeks, in general.

Elizabeth, like most of her kind, was tortured by these hot dry winds that streamed across the land from the baking interior towards the sea. The desiccating effect on the skin and hair was stingingly uncomfortable, and also worrying, as it threatened to banish any bloom of youth, not a welcome prospect. Eventually, the monsoon rains should extinguish the heat and the dry winds, but these had their own surprises:

> *The torrents of rain which have fallen are astonishing. One should have supposed all this would have cooled the earth but on the contrary the heat has been insupportable. The two former winter seasons we were glad to shut the doors of a night and put a blanket on the bed but this year the thermometer has never been below 82 which as far as I remember must be as hot as you ever see it in England. The natives are much pleased with the season for it is the season of plenty. Rain is their wealth and their glory. If we had not had such rains there would probably have been a famine and dreadful calamity everywhere, but these poor people who make no provision for the seasons* [can] *suffer beyond description.*[24]

In general, they found the arrival of the rains to be immensely refreshing, and it is a measure of their concern that Elizabeth, and people like her, were only too aware of the importance of the rains to the welfare and livelihood of the Indian people.[25] Houses were not always up to withstanding it, however, and roofs would leak.[26] Rain was much more common in the hill stations, such as Simla or Mussoorie, to which, in later years, the British fled for relief during the heat of the summer. A whole culture of hill-station life developed during the post-mutiny days of the Raj, but the earliest descriptions by women are from the Eden sisters who accompanied their brother, the Governor-General, Lord Auckland, on his journey into the North-West to visit Ranjit Singh, ruler of the Sikh empire. The Georgians had little concept of retreat to the hills in the heat, and they roasted where they lived and worked. During the winter the climate could be quite cold in the hills, and even in the northern plains, and a fire was often necessary. Sitting around the fire with chintz furnishings, brass fender with typical fire irons, and a glass of Madeira of a winter evening, could only have summoned up nostalgic memories of the winter hearth at home.[27] As the little-known letters of the even less known Sarah Robinson, wife of James Robinson, Assistant Surgeon Bengal army, near Benares reveal, such cosiness was not without hazard. She relates:

The room was dreadfully hot; such a blazing fire was in the grate that the master of the house feared that the thatch (all bungalows are thatched but often have tiles over it) would catch fire and he sent the Maalee [gardener] to the top of the roof with a large pot of water to be ready in case of accidents and there the man was perched all the evening. Speaking of fires, I must tell you a story related by the hero thereof. He had a small thatched dwelling, so ill built that the chimney did not rise above the roof. One night a merry party dined with him and they made a huge fire which got upon the roof of course. He climbed up directly to tear away the thatch and stop its way. Strange to tell, part of the top of the chimney gave way under his feet and he fell down into the fire and put it out! His own weight extinguished all the flames. This story was told to me with perfect gravity.[28]

Candles and oil lamps would have lighted these winter evenings, a dim but flickering light glinting on the glass and silver. Candles were not cheap, and oil lamps were more economical, being: 'Finger-glasses, or tumblers, half filled with water on which they [the servants] pour the coconut oil, always calculating it exactly to the number of hours the lamp has to burn. The wick is made of cotton twisted round a splinter of bamboo.'[29] Sconces on the walls, based on the same principal, added to the light while cylindrical glass bowls, filled with water and oil and holding wicks, were suspended from the ceiling and similarly lit. Emma Roberts notes: 'One of the most beautiful features of the city (Calcutta) at night, consists of the bright floods issuing from the innumerable lamps in the houses of the rich, when, all the windows being open, the radiance is thrown across the neighbouring roads.'[30] Street lighting was of course unknown in those days.

Thus illuminated, the rooms were variously furnished through the decades. In the mid-1700s, Chinese furniture and objets d'arts prevailed, but later during that century it was more common to find furniture from Britain or France. Often this fine Georgian furniture arrived packed flat, Ikea-style, for assembly in India. It was but a short step to copies of it being made with Indian ingenuity (probably under the supervision of European cabinetmakers in the earlier years), especially from the fine range of hardwoods then available.[31, 32]

An interesting reciprocal snobbery existed. In the richest and finest houses of Calcutta, for example, the emphasis was on importing the finest of everything from Europe, whereas in England it was the contrary, with carpets, silks and the other finery being imported from the East, especially from China. In British India this was far too close for exclusivity among the wealthy women of the Presidency towns, who wouldn't have been seen dead serving tea in Chinese porcelain, as opposed to Worcester.[33,34] The grandest houses in Calcutta, such as those along the Esplanade by the riverside, cost a small fortune to furnish in the lavish style prevailing in the Georgian period. William Hickey spent 12,000 rupees handsomely furnishing his house, including the purchase of plate [silver] in about 1781. This would be more than £70,000 in today's money, so his new wife, or rather consort, must have been quite impressed. Out in the rural sticks (the *Mofussil*) the story was different. Relatively humble army officers and planters made do with smaller numbers of fairly ordinary items that moved around with their owners, by baggage-train or boat. Even in Calcutta, the more ordinary houses could be sparsely furnished, as Elizabeth Fenton once noted when staying with friends:

My bed stood in the middle of the floor without curtains, with pillows as hard as the table and about the size of a pincushion. There was only one chair in the room, and I looked in vain for some place to put my clothes, or a basin of water to wash. Furthermore, the room had four windows and four doors, all wide-open and with no means of keeping them shut, so there was no hope of privacy.[35]

Matting on the floor was often more practical than carpets. Sofas were covered with satin damask, but soft furnishings were altogether relatively limited by English standards, including upholstered furniture. This was not just a matter of economy but in an effort, usually vain, to discourage the regular indoor invasion of insects and small animals. Furniture was often placed away from walls or, in order to prevent ant attacks on sweet foods or susceptible humans: 'We put the beds to stand on little square stones grooved and filled with water over which they cannot pass.[36] Tables that contain anything sweet have the feet set in four china basins made strong and shallow for the purpose.'[37] The scourge of indoor wildlife was universal, then as now, but with open louvred windows and indoor lighting, the early Indian British stood little chance of not attracting them. There were snakes, scorpions, centipedes and all kinds of bugs. According to Julia Maitland in 1838, writing from her isolated bungalow on a headland overlooking the river at

Rajahmundry on the East coast, where her husband acted as a Regional Judge, the worst of these were the green bugs:

Fancy large flying bugs! They do not bite, but they scent the air for yards around. When there is no wind at night, they fly round and get into one's clothes and hair — horrible! there is nothing I dislike so much in India as those green bugs. The first time I was aware of their disgusting existence, one flew down my shoulders, and I, feeling myself tickled, and not knowing the danger, unwittingly crushed it. I shall never forget the stench as long as I live. The ayah undressed me as quickly as she could, almost without my knowing what she was doing, for I was nearly in a fit. You have no notion of anything so horrible! I call the land-wind, and the green bugs, the Oriental luxuries. If that were not enough there were also the black bugs: These are not so horrible as the green ones, but bad enough, and in immense swarms. One very calm night the house was so full of them, that the dinner-table was literally covered with them. We were obliged to have all the servants fanning us with separate fans besides the punkah, and one man to walk round the table with a dessert spoon and a napkin to take them off our shoulders. Except Mr S—, who contrived to be hungry, we gave up all idea of eating our dinner; we could not even stay in the house, but sat all the evening on the steps of the verandah, playing the guitar.[38]

Somehow the picture of Julia sitting on these steps, strumming a guitar, seems peculiarly un-Regency, projecting us almost into modern times.

Snakes were often chased around a room until caught, and invariably killed, and Fanny Parkes even witnessed a sleeping baby's foot being bitten by a rat.[39] Worst of all, however, in terms of sheer destructive power was the white ant, better known now as the termite. These live in large underground nests, and create numerous tunnels directed towards any non-living wood. They burrow their way through this, munching invisibly and interminably, creating silent destruction from within. Wooden floors, furniture and other structures could suddenly collapse, having been held up until the last minute just by the paintwork. They were justifiably feared by all Indian British. Fanny Parkes describes once opening a wardrobe filled with tablecloths and napkins, to find the linen was one mass of dirt, and utterly destroyed. Carpets, mats, and any textile on the floors, could also be totally destroyed, as well as the floors themselves.

RIBBONS AMONG THE RAJAHS

If a house in India was very different from that in England, so also was the household within; but to be the lady of that house, one first had to be a wife, unless arriving at the invitation of a brother, or a widowed father. It seems incomprehensible in today's world that an unmarried woman effectively had no status within a household. The promotion to the position of a wife was either preordained by a marriage contracted or promised in England, or a marriage by chance (or design) following arrival in India. Marriage was, after all, a woman's inevitable destiny 200 years ago, and absolutely necessary for any possibility of any independence in her future. India offered rather different opportunities than England.

Chapter 3

The Pioneer Women

After the Indian Mutiny, or the First War of Independence in current terminology, everything changed in India. The horrors and excesses of that event, fought out over many months, have been well described elsewhere.[1,2] The victor was always going to stamp his authority on the country and, as this was Britain, much of the old life was swept away forever. By 1858 the East India Company had been ousted into history, and virtually every aspect of Indian life was taken under British control as part of the British Empire, and directly responsible to government and the Crown. Queen Victoria became Queen Empress, the Governor General became Viceroy, and so started the true Raj. The Indian people were now more or less completely subjugated and, until independence and partition ninety years later, fulfilled the sole function of acting in the absolute interests of the Imperial British, as soldiers, clerks, servants, labourers, railwaymen, and functionaries of every imaginable kind. No longer was there much independence of spirit or estate, apart from what resulted from a token deference by the British to Indian aristocracy, and mostly related to their wealth. India effectively became an exotic oriental extension to the homeland of Britain. In concert with this there was an inevitable social change. Social intercourse with an Indian on a personal level became much rarer, at least publicly, except perhaps the occasional acceptance of lavish hospitality from a Rajah, or Prince. The need of young British masculinity for female company in India could only mean, by then, that a wife had to be brought from home, or British women had to become available in India. So developed a system whereby girls were ferried out to the East to fill this void, and which became rather patronisingly known in later years as the 'fishing fleet'.[3] Needless to say things didn't change overnight, and there was a gradual evolution towards this state of affairs over the preceding two or three decades; it is these earlier pioneering years that are covered here, coinciding with the later Georgian kings, the Regency period, William IV and slipping over into the early years of Victoria.

Although British trade with India, and the existence of the Honourable

East India Company, dated back 250 years to the Charter given by Queen Elizabeth I in 1600, women didn't really arrive from Europe until the mid-1700s, and then only in very modest numbers. The British civilian administrator, trader, or soldier was then a very different animal from his Raj successor following the mutiny. In the earlier years, while focusing on his prime objective of successful trade and a good profit, he was frequently filled with wonderment for that deeply mysterious and subtle continent, as so many others had been before him, and remained captivated for most, or all, of his life. It worked its mysteries on the European intruder to the extent that it was arguable who most influenced whom at this stage.[4] The East India Company then had no licence or desire to invade, indeed its ships were only lightly armed, and that was chiefly for defence, unlike the much more proactive Dutch fleet. The primary British interest was to set up trading posts in what later became the main Presidencies, namely Calcutta, Madras and Bombay with the presence of soldiery mainly being to protect these interests. Therefore, on the surface, the Englishman or Scotsman continued ostensibly British and acted out his role. Less apparently, however, he was slowly becoming Indianized. He started to wear Indian clothes – a good deal cooler than long waistcoat, breeches, topcoat, stock and stockings – and, in many cases, to take on Indian customs of living and eating; he even began to follow a new religion, either Hinduism or Islam. He also had to look elsewhere for female company. In the latter decades of the eighteenth century there were a good number of British men in India, but relatively few women; being outnumbered by about sixteen to one. What is more, a very large number of these young men were still in their teens. These were the writers for the East India Company, who left for India aged 16 on a salary of £5 per year, and had little prospect of return to England inside a decade or two.[5,6] They were trainee clerks, who one day hoped to be factors, or traders with responsibility and power, or they were cadets in the company's army hoping next to be ensigns, and maybe one day a colonel; that is if cutlass or cannonball didn't get them first. Not surprisingly, they had no experience of women whatsoever, but with the arrival of the teens and testosterone it was entirely understandable that they drifted towards Indian girls, with their dark mysterious eyes and colourful muslin saris. There was hardly anyone else, for it was Honourable Company policy to discourage the arrival of women; embodied in the original Royal Charters.[7] The Dutch took the same view, and their resistance to the arrival of women from home led to widespread interracial co-habitation and marriage and, inevitably, a surge of mixed-blood children. This all happened in the heyday of the Dutch East India Company

(VOC), well before the main British arrival, and so very apparent to them. Lord Minto, who was Governor General of India from 1807 to 1813, noted in his correspondence home:

> *The Dutch did not encourage, nor indeed allow freely, European women to go out to their colonies in India. The consequence has been that the men lived with native women whose daughters, gradually borrowing something from the father's side, and becoming a mixed breed, are now the wives and ladies of rank and fashion in Java. The young ladies have learnt the European fashions of dress, and their carriage and manners are something like our own of an ordinary class. Their education is almost wholly neglected; or rather no means exist to provide for it. They are attended from their cradles by numerous slaves, by whom they are trained in helplessness and laziness; and from such companions and governesses, you may conceive how much accomplishment or refinement in manners or opinions they are likely to acquire.*[8]

The Court of Directors of the East India Company became concerned about the morals of their employees with all this temptation around. This is perhaps surprising, until one considers that it may have been induced by alarm at the potential dilution of British blood and, more tellingly, by fear of a tainting effect on religious purity from marriage into the pre-existing Roman Catholic Portuguese communities, which particularly existed around the Presidency towns of Madras and Bombay. They may also have noticed the Dutch experience and so, around 1700, the Company exported the occasional boatload of potential wives who fell into two categories: gentlewomen and other women. Clearly, part of the motive was to assist towards the propagation of a colonising population. The women were given one suit of clothes, and support for a year, in which they were supposed to find a husband. They appear, however, to have enjoyed the Company's generosity too much, and all claimed to be gentlewomen, and would not look favourably on anyone less than a soldier with a commission, or a senior trader (factor). An attempt to bring out women of more lowly origin, who might not be so choosy, was doomed to fail. These women volunteers were not necessarily inclined to succumb meekly to Company will, and often followed their own agenda, behaving with 'dishonourable abandon and notorious impudence'.[9] Marriage was a commercial enterprise for them, and the more profitable the better. These wives looked forward with cynical gratitude to their husband's death, as this enabled them to draw a lifelong pension of £300 a year from the Company (a jointure), and return to England in comparative affluence.[10] Such early attempts at official marriage-making did not last long, and women remained in short supply. There were clear contradictions too, whereby, in 1778, there was some encouragement of soldiers to marry Indian women in Madras. The directors were content to encourage at some expense such marriages, making a present of five rupees for every child of a soldier in the ranks who was baptised. In this instance there appears to have been a deliberate policy of intermarriage in the interests of building up the army.[11]

The relatively small numbers of European women in earlier India were mainly the wives of soldiers or civilians serving in the employ of the East India Company. Not all wives would brave the journey, or risk the climate with its attendant perils to health, even well into the 1800s. When appointed Governor General, Lord Minto (Gilbert Elliot Murray) went to India without his beloved wife, probably to earn enough to retire with her in comfort to Scotland. He was never to see her again. Although he reached England on his retirement, he died there before he could get home to Scotland. Before him as Governor General was Richard Wellesley, or Lord Mornington, elder brother of Arthur Wellesley, later Duke of Wellington. Apart from his reputation as an expansionist spendthrift with Company finances, causing the Directors much anxiety, and later his recall to England, he also had one as a philanderer both before, and particularly after, his time in India. At one stage his brother, the Duke of Wellington, expressed a wish that he were castrated, so flagrant was his behaviour when back in London. Wellesley's wife also did not accompany him to India, and on one occasion he wrote to her in London, saying that if she did not join him in Calcutta it was inconceivable that he would remain faithful, 'as I assure you that this climate excites one sexually most terribly.' He proved true to his threat, it appears.[12] Apart from having marital detachment in common, Wellesley and Minto were otherwise at opposite ends of the behavioural spectrum in other respects.

Countless unattached men would have found feminine comfort somewhere and, in the relative absence of European women, the native women were an attractive alternative. The subject of sexual and marital integration with the local population during the late eighteenth, and early nineteenth, centuries is covered comprehensively elsewhere, and there are a number of well-known and well-researched examples.[13] A notable one was the much admired but, to many eyes, eccentric Major General Charles Hindoo Stuart, who married an Indian woman – his 'bibi'– and fathered numerous children, swam daily in the Ganges and participated in a variety of Hindu rituals and, indeed, encouraged in print an interest in Hinduism among the British. General William Palmer, when just a colonel, and military secretary to Warren Hastings, the first Governor General of India, met and married his lifetime love, Fyze Baksh, by 1779. She was a Muslim from Delhi, and must have been aware that Palmer was already married to a Creole lady from the West Indies whom he had never divorced; but this was not a doctrinal concern under Muslim law. They had a large family, and remained together into old age.

Colonel William Gardner converted to Islam in order to marry a Nawab's daughter, who had totally captivated him at their first meeting in 1798. She was aged 14 at the time, living then in Hyderabad as was he, while in the service of the Nizam. Gardner later entered British service, founding the irregular cavalry regiment Gardner's Horse. He died in 1835, the patriarch of an impressive Anglo-Indian dynasty, and after thirty-eight years of marriage to his Begum. She followed him only a month later, having pined away following the loss of her husband, according to Fanny Parkes.[14]

Sir David Ochterlony was a Scot by origin, and British resident in Delhi from 1804, after an impressive early military career in the service of the Company. Delhi was relatively isolated from mainstream British influence, at that time, Calcutta being the seat of Company power. Ochterlony became Indianized to an extent that amazed the Bishop of Calcutta, Reginald Heber, on a visit during the course of his travels through upper India.[15] His dress was Indian, as was his household and habits, and so was his wife, of which there were said to have been several. His whole demeanour and way of life leant towards Indian culture, which endeared him to his Indian colleagues, such as Shah Alam, the Mughal emperor. Less impressed, however, was the wife of the British Commander in Chief in India, Lady Maria Nugent, on a visit in about 1811. Armed with rigid English certainty, her response was one of shocked prudishness; not the only Englishwoman to react so at this time. She might have been even more shocked by William Hickey, had she known him, but he had returned home four years earlier after two visits to India in which country he had had a successful law practice. This was sufficient to enable him to live in style, and to indulge his liking for high society and all the pleasures that went with it. On his second visit he was accompanied by his mistress, the lovely former courtesan Charlotte Barry, whom he adored, and who styled herself Mrs Hickey. Sadly she succumbed rapidly to the pestilential perils of Bengal, and died quite quickly in 1783, less than a year after her arrival in Calcutta. Hickey, although grief stricken, was too red-blooded to be without female company for long. In 1788 a neighbour of his departed from Bengal to return to England, and in his wake he left an Indian girl, Jemdanee, whom Hickey had often admired. As she was now free, he 'invited her to become intimate with me, which she consented to do.' From then on the relationship deepened to one of mutual respect and love, and she lived with him until her death in childbirth a few years later. She was noted for her intelligence and charm, becoming a great favourite with all his friends. Her loss struck him hard, and he could not return to his court work for many weeks. 'Thus did I lose as gentle and affectionately attached a girl as ever a man was blessed with.'[16]

Colonel James Kirkpatrick was British Resident in Hyderabad by the end of the eighteenth century, with significant influence at the Nizam's court. In 1800 he married Khair-un-Nissa, a member of an aristocratic Muslim family and a relative of Mir Alam, Prime Minister to the Nizam. She, again, was only 14 at the time, and the relationship was attended by a certain amount of scandal, more concerned with her religion and family connections than her age. She bore him two children but, following his death, she eventually formed a relationship with another Englishman, Henry Russell, eldest son of Sir Henry Russell, Chief Justice of the Supreme Court in Calcutta.

These are but a handful of the better known examples of interracial co-habitation. There was widespread evidence of a serious level of intermarriage from the inscriptions on cemetery headstones, mentioning such Bibis, and from the frequency with which these devoted and loyal women were mentioned in British wills. This was until about the 1830s, when this evidence declined rapidly following the near disappearance of the Bibis themselves.[17,18] When Non-Commissioned Officers or Privates retired they had the option to settle in one of the Company's Invalid Battalion establishments, such as on the Ganges, and the cemeteries near these places show evidence of many native women who were married to British soldiers.[19] Alternatively, these men took their wives home to England, which must surely have been a formidable culture shock for the women, not to mention the climate shock.

An alternative for some men was to take a spell of leave in South Africa. To go on leave to Cape Colony counted as service for officers of the East India Company at this time, with full Indian pay and continuation of their appointment. If they went further west, such as back to England, pay was discontinued, extraordinarily, and they lost their appointment. The Cape was, therefore, popular; the climate was attractive, and the Dutch were noted for their hospitality and good food and, above all, excellent wines; the forerunners of today's famous Western Cape wines of South Africa, such as from Constanzia. As far as the younger men were concerned there was, more importantly, the possibility of meeting, and even marrying, a Cape Dutch girl, which was an attractive option in the context of a shortage of European women in India. The girls themselves, and particularly their families, were not unhappy with this result, as they were considered to have risen in their own social scale.

In a situation where writers and soldiers outnumbered European women by so many, these solutions to the finding of a marital partner were a workable alternative. Unfortunately, these men were not a good marriage prospect to any young woman with ambition. It is no wonder, therefore, that these no-more-than-teenagers whored hard around the Calcutta brothels and punch houses being, more often than not, rewarded with something unpleasant in return; even sinister if it was syphilis. As well as this, they could also incur a good deal of debt from the usual run of extravagant supper parties, gambling and yet more women.[20]

The gradual trickle of European women arriving in the mid to late 1700s would have seen all this going on around them, no doubt blanching embarrassedly at a social code far removed from the experience of the majority of them in England. Who were these early women, and what brought them such a huge distance to a strange and climatically hostile land? Many of course were the wives of newly appointed East India Company officials, and soldiers, and inevitably some of these brought daughters or sisters with them. Other younger daughters would be left at home in England to continue their education before joining their families in India in a state of supposed preparedness for marriage. Likewise, daughters born in India would be sent home with the same view in mind. All these girls would have been only too well aware that in Georgian times there was little else in life open to them. They were intellectually banished to an education aimed at suitability for the wifely state; mainly music, drawing, needlework, domestic management, dancing, and perhaps some French or Italian. There might also be an initial grounding in writing, literature, history, or maybe a little geography, but rarely all of these. The teaching would have been at the hands of a governess or tutor, or at least a parent and, for many girls, education would have been much sketchier than implied by this range of possibilities. These nascent Indian British girls would stay with aunts, uncles or grandparents in England where they would be brought up in this way, or they would sometimes be sent to a small boarding school to achieve the same result.[21,22] According to Eliza Draper, all they learnt here was how to be a flirt.[23]

In the eyes of their mothers, an enhanced education at home gave them an advantage over the increasing numbers of mixed race Anglo-Indian girls who were reaching a marriageable age, many of whom were bewitchingly beautiful, but who were seen very much as competition to the growing numbers of young British women in India. This was hardly surprising, as these girls often combined the best of both racial backgrounds, and their fairer skin was much less of an inhibition for those with any qualms about colour. This perceived threat was one factor in the growing tendency, in the early 1800s, to keep the Indian population at arm's length, and increasingly to discourage any form of intercourse, social or otherwise. The age of the supposedly aloof, disapproving memsahib was dawning, paralleled by political moves in the same direction, all to reach full fruition in the post-mutiny Raj years.

No young writer could afford to get married, and the gradually increasing population of young British women were untouchable *until* married, so where else did he turn? Young army officers were in the same category, and were in any case usually forbidden to marry below the rank of Captain, although one found the occasional married Lieutenant. These latter were pitied for their penury, which often put a great strain on the marriage, as the expense of such an undertaking was fearsome: furnishings, carriages, clothes and education all looming alarmingly over the connubial bliss.[24] Inevitably, a proportion of young men continued to turn to the local population, and to the brothels, much as many young men in England would have done, where, in the Georgian era, prostitution abounded: 2,000 prostitutes in a total population of 59,000 in the City of London in 1817.[25] Also, rather depressingly, in the larger houses in England there was the chance of a subordinate, and therefore perhaps available, servant girl. In India, at that time, married women took it upon themselves to protect the young men, with whom they had social contact, from the temptations of the flesh, although the challenge must have been doomed to failure often enough. Many British women of some substance, such as Elizabeth, the wife of Sir Henry Gwillim, welcomed young men from England, who had been introduced to them, inviting them to come and live with the family behind a maternal wall of protection against the possibility of moral wandering. This was the assumed likely outcome of living in a community of their own peers. Some of these women were outraged by what they perceived to be acquisitive and parasitic behaviour on the part of the native female consorts. For the most part this was an undeserved assumption, reinforced by circulating attitudes within the female British community. However, to quote Elizabeth Gwillim, giving the example of one young man:

They waste their health and their money on 'filthy' [to be interpreted literally] *black things whom* [even] *the* [any] *servants of caste would not touch. One son* [of a friend] *was a clever young man and had books to the amount of five, or I think seven, hundred pounds* [a great deal of money then] *but all went to one of these beings and her brats; a disgrace to society.*[26]

It is apparent that in 1804 there was already an emerging resentful prejudice against the ordinary Indian woman, even from a British woman as reasonable as Elizabeth Gwillim, who held a measured respect for the Indian people and their culture. In her case, this resentment seems to be wholly confined to the effects some Indian girls had on young Englishmen. She remarked in her correspondence: 'We are never without one, two or three young men in the house, nor indeed any of the families in Madras, for it is thought both dangerous and disreputable for any young man to live at a hostel, or similar.'[27] One of these young men was Richard Clarke, who was an assistant to her husband in court. 'Richard is very innocent and good, and living with us is a great security, for the young men lead each other into troublesome vices.'[28]

Another young man recently arrived in India was a junior army officer, called Biss, seconded to extensive map surveying work. He also became a guest of the Gwillims, and Elizabeth's young unmarried sister, Mary Symonds, wrote:

He is indeed a very fine young man and a great favourite with us all. I believe, like every other young man who comes out, he does not find India all he expected, though he really does not complain as everyone else does. In England they hear a great deal of the fine pay of Officers here, but nothing of the sad imposition they are obliged to submit to, the very great expense they are at in fitting themselves out with various necessaries which are unheard of in England, and the many hardships they are forced to undergo on their first arrival. When once their establishment is fixed, the pay is certainly sufficient to maintain them very genteelly, but it is impossible for any young man to join his Regiment without considerable assistance from his friends. This is a circumstance very little known in England, but very severely felt by all the housekeepers here, who have numbers of poor young men recommended to them, and whose friends think they have provided for them by giving them a good stock of clothes and paying their passage. Sir Thomas Strange told me he had two or three thousand pagodas

[2½ Pagodas to the Pound] *owing to him, not one of which could ever be paid, for the young man's friends would not remit the money, and he could not find it in his heart to note them for it, knowing it was not in their power to pay it without contracting debts to natives, who would charge them an immoderate rate of interest and keep them in thralldom for many many years.*[29]

Mary appears to have been a pert, amusing girl; intelligently observant, happy to revel in her youth, and in local society, but not to become too drawn into it. She further says about Biss:

I don't know what Sir Henry [her brother-in-law] *has said to you about the young men coming here, but this I do know, that he is always glad enough to see them and most unwilling to part with them. He would fain have persuaded Biss to be sick, or anything else, to have kept him here: to be sure he is a darling etc. etc.*[30]

She could at times breathe small utterances of feminine prejudice in her letters, like her sister Elizabeth, and much like any other girl at the time. However Mary was perhaps more restrained than many, and her correspondence in many ways shows more astute observation. She comments in a letter of 1802 to their sister Hetty in England:

We have a great many more whey faced ladies, for the society here is very large, but at least half the women are half caste, that is they are the children of English men by black women. These girls are sent home to England to be educated, as it is called, that is to learn to dance, to squawk and to strum. I have not met with one tolerable voice in the place amongst the women. ... Most of the civilians have these blackey families: the Misses are sent home to learn to give themselves a few airs and then return here to be provided for by marrying military men up the country. When this work is performed a man of about 60 is at liberty to return to England with a pretty young wife and a family of small children!!! You will wonder why I say the civilians have half-caste children to provide for more particularly than the military men. The reason is that the latter are always moving from one station to another and the children are forgot, or perhaps never known to them at all, besides which the military young men have not as good incomes, and therefore cannot afford to educate and provide for them.[31]

64

One detects here the already prevailing resentment by the recently arrived British woman of her now established mixed-race competitor; an exasperated petulance hovers like a headache over this letter. This was clearly not helped by the realisation that these so-called usurpers, too, were being sent back to England to benefit from better education, so enhancing their competitive edge.

Judging by their diaries and journals from the early 1800s, many such women were struck by the difficulties facing young men at that time, mainly attachment to alcohol and womanising. A number of these men lived in great isolation and were both bored and lonely, to the extent that suicide was not unknown. It was consequently all too easy to turn to these diversions. Some women even went as far as to publish advice to young Indian aspirants back home in England, so demonstrating the degree to which feminine solicitude was possibly aimed at keeping such men for their own kind.[32]

It is clear that there was a growing tension developing. On the one hand there was an increasing number of young men looking for female company, but with insufficient eligible European women, and yet on the other, there was an increasing social pressure to shun Indian, or even Anglo-Indian, women; especially encouraged by the growing population of British married or single ladies, but also with growing political support. In the late 1700s it was common to meet mixed-race women at social events. Fifty per cent was by no means uncommon at a dinner party, and this ratio persisted even into the second decade of the 1800s. By 1827 however, Elizabeth Fenton was moved to remark, 'It seems to me very strange the prejudice existing here against half-castes; formerly when European ladies were rarely met with, they held a place in society which they have now entirely lost.'[33] By then, the prejudice against Anglo-Indians (Eurasians) was absolute.

As early as 1791, Lord Cornwallis, the recently appointed Governor General, introduced wide ranging legislation to suppress the Anglo-Indian population. In particular it excluded the children of British men with Indian wives from taking civil or military office in any branch of the East India Company. Cornwallis, still wincing from his defeat at Yorktown in the American War of Independence, was keen to avoid the development of another potentially troublesome, locally-originated, colonial society.[34] This legislation hardened increasingly, over a handful of years, to an extent that denied most worthwhile employment to young Anglo-Indian men. A culture of haughty disdain developed rapidly among Company officials, and those men from earlier, more equable times were alarmed to see this growing dismissive rejection of Indian dignitaries, initially cultivated under Cornwallis's lead.[35,36]

This emergence of a scornful absence of interest in India and its people was greatly reinforced by the attitude of the vain and ambitious Wellesley. As Governor General soon after Cornwallis, his hubristic ambition was the subjugation of that subcontinent and its rulers, and he strongly reinforced Cornwallis's earlier edicts, even to the extent of banning the entertainment of Indians at Government House. So began for the British, inevitably perhaps, the proprietorial behaviour and off-hand contempt that was going to become the stance of the would-be colonist. Apart from notable exceptions, this was an attitude that would gradually grow within the colonising community over the next thirty years. The Indian British women, or 'the memsahibs' as they famously became known, had a continuing influence on the degree to which their male counterparts, and society in general, mixed with the indigenous peoples of the subcontinent. Initially this was much smaller than in later years, such as in the Victorian heyday of the Raj, but it gradually consolidated with time. Even then it was more likely a parallel attitude to a general progressive change in opinion than a causative influence in itself. The concept of the intolerant, insensitive, vindictive, bored and aloof stereotype of the memsahib became an established description among historians and writers, especially in later years. This was much more evident following the Mutiny, and the subsequent decades of imperial complacency, no doubt contributing to Orwell's famous aphorism from the late 1930s; 'the dull, incurious eyes of the memsahib'.[37] Hyam, though, comments that women were almost certainly too limited by detachment from their surroundings to have had much effect on attitudes generally. In any case, their presence was later encouraged by Whitehall to provide a self-contained society for white men. As he continues, they were:

> *important links in maintaining the structure of white rule. Many were neither idle nor inept, and performed their roles effectively, remaining pleasant and well-balanced people. Only a few turned into dragons, bitter, intolerant and status-obsessed. The stereotype propagated by novelists undoubtedly existed, but such women were in a minority, regarded by other mems as failures, whom they disliked and recoiled from.[38]*

Probably more important than any apparent petulant prejudices of British women, but a force running alongside the political influences of Cornwallis and Wellesley, was the role played by the swelling wave of missionaries arriving in India from the tail-end of the eighteenth century. David Brown,

66

in Calcutta in 1786, was the first of the 'five pious chaplains' and was put in charge of Fort William College, founded by Wellesley who, by this means, had wanted to reduce the prevalence among the young men of the East India Company of 'habitual indolence, dissipation and licentious indulgence', as he saw it – skilfully overlooking his own habitual licence. The evangelical missionary drive was clearly towards conversion of the heathen to Christianity; but neither could it sanction a physical union between the European male and the Indian female. From 1835 the East India Company would not allow intermarriage. By the mid-twentieth century Anglo-Indians numbered some 300,000.[39]

Such changes in attitude did little to solve the problems of the legions of young civil servants and soldiers sculpting their lonely futures in that huge country. The only logical solution on the marital front was to entice out many more young ladies from the home country. In the absence in India of enough daughters of senior Company servants, and soldiers, being available, other possible sources were obviously the sisters, and near relatives, of women who had already married Company employees, and who were therefore encouraged, or induced, to come out to India to join their older sisters in the expectation of finding a suitable husband. Even these would prove to be too few.

At the same time there were many young women in Britain who needed to find a husband as a continuing means of support. They were wholly dependent on their fathers or other male relatives for support, and few received much of a legacy from their parents. Such men breathed an audible sigh of relief when a suitor turned up who could take over the responsibility of care, especially if this was a man of means, and if there were numerous daughters. Those poor girls caught in the middle can only have felt like an encumbrance, or trade goods, even though such a circumstance was clearly the norm. It was all an accepted fact of life, and the pages of Jane Austen novels are dotted with such instances. The more impecunious the parent and the greater the number of daughters, the greater was the pressure. With parents dead, no brothers or other family to give support, and no inheritance, a girl was stranded. Few remunerative occupations were open to her. She could go and live with a distant relative, and make herself useful for bed and board, or advertise her services as a governess, or companion, in the fashion of Jane Eyre. Finally – and not so exceptionally – if gifted with beauty, she could live the, not wholly intolerable, life of a Georgian courtesan, and hope to be kept by a man of substance. Covent Garden was their traditional home, and these women were often well-educated middle class girls who, one must presume, could find no other way out of their economic impasse, or who had been somehow corrupted into this life. William Hickey's diaries give a clear insight into those days from the late eighteenth and early nineteenth century, and indeed his beloved Charlotte Barry, who accompanied him to India, and remains there, was from this background. Not at all dissimilar was Admiral Lord Nelson's paramour, Emma Hamilton.

India was a clear opportunity for many women who were not making progress on the husband front, but the expense of getting there was a considerable disincentive in pre-Victorian days, especially when steamships, which were much faster and cheaper, were non-existent. The first of these didn't arrive in India until about 1837, and was for river use on the Ganges only; a viable steamship passage to India did not come about until the mid to late 1850s, Brunel's Great Eastern being built in 1857 with this in mind.[40] As early as 1829 there had been a preliminary foray, but in those early years it was not a technically practicable solution.

If a young woman was supplied with the lump sum funds for effecting a passage, then India was a proposition to consider, but few women would go so far, and so alone, without any introduction whatsoever; many were unwilling to go at all. They nevertheless often went at the insistence of their family, be this at home or abroad. Most went to join a relative, such as a brother, some of whom lived in great isolation up country as indigo planters, or traders, and welcomed a sister to come and keep house for them. She would hardly find this a hub of social introduction, and most would want to be in Calcutta, Madras or Bombay. Much the same applied to army officers, who generally did not marry until the rank of Major, or had to have approximately fifteen years of service if a Captain.[41] Those who remained single often welcomed a sister to come and live with them, and act as housekeeper. This did not mean the more servile position that it might today, but actually functioning as the lady of the house. Another alternative was for a married woman to invite out her unmarried sisters. Emily Eden writes in a letter of 11 February 1838:

> *There were two Miss ——s come out from England to join a married sister, wife of an officer in the Lancers. She is very poor herself, but has eight sisters at home, so I suppose thought it right to help her family* [by inviting them to India]*; and luckily, I think, they will not hang long on her hands. They are such very pretty girls, and knowing-looking, and have brought out for their married sister, who is also very pretty, gowns and headdresses like their own. The three together had*

a pretty effect. They are the only young ladies at the station, so I
suppose will have their choice of [from] *three regiments.*[42]

Here and there in the correspondence of those times is the odd waspish
assertion that the less attractive girls came to India, there being little chance
of success for them in England. Some desperation must have been mutual,
for both women and men. There was one reported occasion, not necessarily
unique, of a girl coming out to India to marry a much older man, who was a
Captain in the army and had been in India for eighteen years. She was only
18 years old, and it was clear that they had only heard of each other, and had
never actually met.[43] Such was the agonised urgency of the age.

One body of potentially available young women was formed by the
numerous orphans of British residents of India who had been felled by one
of the lethal endemic diseases, or by something more metallic in battle. These
unfortunate girls were often without adequate social connections or financial
resources and were educated, and maintained, in the orphanages of the three
Presidency cities, Calcutta, Madras and Bombay. Almost certainly many of
them were the illegitimate Anglo-Indian offspring of soldiers, often young
officers. In earlier years, social events, such as tea parties, were held regularly
to provide some opportunity for them to meet young civil servants or officers,
but these later lapsed as more puritanical notions of propriety developed. As
a consequence, some Female Orphan Schools (often called Asylums) later
became almost convent-like.[44]

The arrival of young unmarried ladies by ship in Calcutta, Madras or
Bombay occasioned a flurry of excitement among the young unattached
males, who clustered around the church steps before the next Sunday service,
like wasps round a jam jar, waiting to catch a glimpse of the newly arrived
beauties, and greet them appropriately.[45] Some young men managed to
waylay such women in advance of their arrival and, more or less, propose
on the spot. Emily Eden recorded in her correspondence from Delhi in
November 1839 after 'an immense party.'

Several young civilians had really come in from their solitary stations
to look for wives.[46] *Such is the desperation that a gentleman, desirous*
to enter the holy pale, does not always wait until he shall meet with
some fair one suiting his peculiar taste, but the instant that he hears
of an expected arrival, despatches a proposal to meet her upon the
road; this is either rejected in toto, or accepted conditionally; and if
there should be nothing very objectionable in the suitor, the marriage

takes place. Others travel over to some distant station, in the hope of returning with a wife; and many visit the presidency on the same errand.[47]

The whole business could, therefore, be seen as a matter of mutual expediency rather than love. The man needs a woman, and the woman needs a husband. There is a biological imperative on his part, but mostly a social necessity on hers, at least if she was of a young age, which was true of the majority. Her biological imperative could arrive later, as the years ticked by. In her published sketches of Hindustan life in 1835, Emma Roberts further notes how necessity directs a girl's actions. She may have flirted with a number of the young men but then, overtaken by 'more sense than sentiment', she detaches herself from them all and quietly becomes engaged to a worthwhile prospect, leaving 'her butterfly admirers looking foolishly at each other and making a faint attempt to laugh.'[48]

Another example of this fraught marriage market comes from the journal of Maria Sykes, wife of Captain John Sykes, Bombay Army, in 1818:

During my stay in Bombay, I heard of the arrival of three beautiful girls, the Misses G., come out to stay with their brother, a barrister in a good position, and who had invited them to Bombay to see a little of its society. At that time it was thought very little trouble by any gentleman to ride 50 or 60 miles for the first glimpse of any English girls, and especially handsome ones. Accordingly a great number rushed to Bombay but their expectations were doomed to disappointment for the three beauties were all veiled and muffled up, their brother having advised this precaution to baffle curiosity.[49]

The first viewing was at the Governor's ball, and great was the anticipatory excitement. However, these strikingly handsome girls were all soon carried off by the civilians and senior officers. All subalterns were utterly excluded and had not the remotest chance of a dance, let alone of a wife. It wasn't just the men who were under pressure; there was also great marriage competition among the women. The governess of these three 'Misses G.' had been rather shamefully treated by them, by effectively excluding her from society. She satisfyingly upstaged all three by not only getting married first, but very successfully to a wealthy army Major.

Not every young lady's arrival in India was met with such success. Maria Sykes wrote in 1810:

I was much touched at the story of a young girl I met, a Miss H. She had it seems been asked by her sister, who lived in Bombay, to come out and stay with her and, on her arrival in Bombay, she found to her horror her relatives had left for England by the last packet. She knew no one in Bombay till Mr Wodehouse kindly asked her to his house and there, I am sorry to say, she had a good deal to encounter for none of the gentlemen offered to take her down to dinner, and our host himself had to return and bring her down. I was so sorry for the poor girl, and shocked at the breach of politeness she had been subject to and, on her asking my advice on the following morning as to what she had better do, as she hardly liked to return to England so soon, when her parents had been put to such an expense in fitting her out for India, with a complete trousseau, wedding dress included, that I asked her to stay with us for a month or so at our bungalow. Several gentlemen then became very attentive to her, hearing she was soon going back to England, and amongst them a Mr G. who was one of those who had talked the most about Miss H. coming out to be married. He proposed to her while she was playing the piano, and they were married soon after.[50]

As Emma Roberts further commented, the decision of a young woman to travel to India was largely irreversible. Only very rarely in those days did they have the means to afford a return journey, should this become necessary, or if they couldn't any longer face life there. 'Their lot is cast in it, and they must remain in a state of miserable dependence, with the danger of being left unprovided for until they shall be rescued from this distressing situation by an offer of marriage.'[51]

In this climate of hot blooded haste, once a proposal had been accepted there was no hanging about. Engagements were short and businesslike, with marriage sometimes following in a matter of days, and rarely more than weeks.[52,53] To leave it any longer wasted precious time, when the bridegroom might soon have to return to duty, or travel to a distant military outpost. Getting engaged was not always straightforward. In those awkward, formal, days there could be all sorts of hurdles, from obstructive chaperone aunts to parental regulation. An Army officer was constrained by age regulations, and the need to obtain his colonel's permission, and a girl was subject to the will of her parents on the age and choice of partner. Competing proposals added to the complications, with a daughter's choice being less relevant to a mother than the anticipated income of the potential husband. Emily Eden, while travelling with her Governor-General brother Lord Auckland, was entertained by the amorous uncertainties of the several aides-de-camp in attendance. She cites examples with her usual acerbic wit, ending one such with the note that:

> *Above all things Captain P was not supposed to know* [what was happening]. *That is always the end of all confidences, and in the meantime, as Captain P lives in a broad grin, and LE* [the prospective wife] *in a deep sigh, I should think their secrets will be guessed in a week. Thank goodness; now they are all engaged, except Z, who is not likely to fall in love with anybody but himself.*[54]

In many cases love had little to do with getting engaged. Many marriages were ones of convenience, although it seems that most of these continued happily, although in a sense they had to.[55] Divorce was not an easy option.

If the woman wasn't in India for the express purpose of finding a husband, but happened to be there with her parents for instance, then the pressures to conform were great, should they decide it was time she married. As Emma Roberts again remarks:

> *It is no unusual thing for persons who have accumulated a fortune, and who are desirous to spend the remainder of their days in luxury in England, to marry off the females of their family as fast as they possibly can, little caring to whom they are consigned, and leaving them to combat with every sort of hardship, without a hope of their ever meeting again. The condition of girls thus situated is far from enviable; overtures are made to their parents, and accepted by them without consulting the parties who are the most deeply concerned in the transaction; the young lady is simply told that a proposal has been made in which she must acquiesce, and she goes to the altar, if not unwilling, at least indifferent.*[56]

These unlucky women were regularly made to feel a burden in the parental home; there was no way out except into the arms of a stranger. From the man's point of view there might be no retreat either. If the couple were seen out together without a third party, then a contract of marriage intent was presumed, and there could be no backing down without risking a breach of promise action in the Supreme Court.

As the relative lack of available European girls in India meant that they were scooped up fairly quickly, the age at which they became of interest, and also available, became lower. There existed already at that time a younger age for marriage in Britain, as well as the rest of Europe, than would be regarded as acceptable today. In early British India it was lower still, and sometimes there was an overlap. The daughter of one of India's Supreme Court judges, while in England for her education, ran away to Gretna Green and married an army officer widower aged 30. She was herself aged 13, but 'there were no objections to the match, but those which arose from her extreme youth'.[57] She went on to have two sons, and the family later joined her father in Madras. Many such girls had been educated in England and, when this was complete and being mostly single, they joined their parents in India, aged 16 at the most. By then there was little for them to do other than live at their parent's' expense, and so marriage was an obvious alternative to both parent and daughter. Eliza Sclater was one of three sisters born in India and, having been orphaned young, was brought up in Bombay by her maternal grandfather, Charles Whitehill. He was a wealthy man and lived in a handsome house overlooking an expansive green space with a view of the cathedral – hard to imagine today. When Eliza was about 10, the three girls were dispatched home to receive their schooling. Eliza returned to India in 1757, aged 14, and soon after this married Daniel Draper, twenty years her senior and also from a well-known Bombay family. The match was evidently disastrous. There was nothing unseemly about this young age in the Georgian mind. The age of consent was 12 and was only increased to 13 in 1875, and only reached 16 ten years later. In this respect Britain was actually more advanced than the rest of the world, being much influenced by various puritan movements. In the United States 10 had been the usual age of consent, and many of these states now followed Britain, although much of Europe and the rest of the world, on the other hand, remained unchanged.[58] Nevertheless, even in the late 1700s and the early 1800s, the young age at which some girls were married excited a degree of comment. As Emily Eden said in 1839, 'the husband and wife are very fond of each other, but a girl who marries at 15 hardly knows what she likes.' Emily Eden was at the time 42, and unmarried. She presumably knew only too well what she didn't like. She had of course the great advantage of being wholly financially independent, unlike most of her peers.

If the girls in India were even younger when first married than those in England, the men on the whole were older. The disparity was greater because the men were either not allowed to marry until older, such as in the case of the military, or were concentrating too hard on making their fortunes, or perhaps just making hay. More accurately, the general shortage of young

European ladies left the men on the shelf until advancing years, seniority and wealth made them irresistible, if not to the girls, then certainly to the mothers on their behalf. [59,60] As Elizabeth Gwillim noted in May 1803:

The very wealthy matches here are generally girls of 15 or 16 to men of 40 at the youngest, even a 15-year-old to a man of 54, although the latter does not seem to be approved of and, beside that, the lady is past the age to please these gentle youths.[61]

This latter, rather cryptic, comment seems to be uncharacteristically acute cynicism from a normally placid and sanguine lady, although her meaning is obscure. Could it hint at a suspicion of unhealthy, even paedophilic, attraction? Her sister Mary Symonds wrote home later, to an unidentified man, and in a style characteristically blunter and more to the point than her sister's:

I could show you a score of wise men from fifty to sixty years of age who have hitherto known no enjoyment, except what they derived from the hope of spending agreeably the cash they have been scraping together, and in that hope have just taken to themselves wives of about seventeen: they talk continually of the happiness they shall have in returning to England. Good men! They forget what havoc 40 summers have made in their own constitutions, and amongst the friends they are thinking to return to.

But Mary wasn't just critical of the men. She was often disenchanted also with the young unmarried hopefuls, particularly how many 16 or 17-year-olds would, independently of parental influence, willingly attach themselves to much older men. 'Their own sordid dispositions have made them prefer age and riches when they might have married men suitable to themselves in years and with fair prospects, but without much ready money.'[62]

Mary was unmarried herself at this stage, and clearly looked disapprovingly at this sort of attitude. As her own standpoint was one of security, with no particular pressure to get married, she could afford to be judgemental. A mercenary attitude among some of the single girls in India at that time is not altogether surprising. It seems an inevitable sequel to the pattern of marriages of convenience at a young age to some hoary old satyr; a bachelor or widower past his prime. Furthermore, the complete absence then of security and position for a single woman in society can only have encouraged a little gold-digging, although in some cases this was rather more than a little. The Symonds sisters could be censorious in their letters home. From Elizabeth:

> *The girls who are educated for this country either learn very little or, when they come here, they think of nothing but husbands. I do not see anything they do well except dancing and making watch ribbons for the young men, who give them pearls and diamonds in return and many of them have no more decency than to accept of them. I have seen a girl here, whom I have been very slightly acquainted with, sit down and tell me that a string of pearls and a diamond locket she had on was given her by one man who made love to her, her diamond brooch by another, her bracelets by a third, one emerald ring by a fourth, and a diamond ring by a fifth and so on as far as nine or ten. I know that some of the young men who gave them to her are nearly ruined by extravagance and have spoken with regret of the sums they have expended upon this girl.*[63]

And likewise from Mary: 'To be sure, the girls who come out here are for the most part ignorant, pert and bold, and receive all attention as merely what is due to their beauty, though God knows there are not three in the place who have the smallest pretensions to it.'[64] By this time it seems that the gloss had worn off the social excitement of moving to a different country for these two sisters; this, and other general comments, suggest they were becoming disenchanted with their situation socially.

Like Mary Symonds, a few young women in India stayed single and perhaps, like her, had refused a number of offers. As she said in a letter to her sister Hetty in England, emphasising her own choosiness: 'I shall wait patiently and remain ever as I am unless I meet with a man in whom I find those qualities which I think necessary to my happiness, and though amongst my numerous admirers in this country I have not yet met with such a one.'[65] There is a suspicion of smug superiority in this statement, probably reflecting her growing disenchantment with life and society, towards the end of her time in India. In the end she married the Captain of the Indiaman in which she sailed home, and no doubt other girls returned home first, and married there. Others stayed in India, and stayed single, although in doing so they remained dependent on someone else, unless they had means of their own. Emma Roberts was in this latter category, which was a rare circumstance. She had gone to India with her married older sister following her mother's death in 1828. She never married, but was a widely admired writer on life in India, and made a respectable living in this way; something of an accomplishment.

Those who stayed single either had bad luck, or perhaps just good judgement. Some simply decided on a course of remaining single, but this was very unusual for the time, for the clear reasons already noted, that it was almost impossible for a woman to live independently unless she had a personal fortune. An occupational income was exceptionally rare. Others, such as Eliza Fay, eked out a living by dressmaking; she had got as far as getting married, but the marriage had collapsed.

Elizabeth Fenton, a young woman initially married to Lieutenant Campbell of the 13th Foot, a Highland regiment, later married a Captain Fenton following her first husband's death from cholera. She kept a detailed journal, and in it she describes the eldest of three beautiful girls whose fiancé died in England shortly before their wedding. Her mother died soon afterwards; her brother went to India and, not long after this, her father also died. At the wish of her brother the three orphaned girls joined him in India and this eldest, who was avoiding much social contact at that stage because of her bereavement, put all her savings into his business. The two younger sisters got married, and eventually returned to England, but the eldest stayed in India and avoided marriage over the next seven years. After this time, in the style of a true Victorian melodrama, her brother's business failed, he fled home, and she was effectively left destitute. She was quite alone in that country, and had no alternative but to become the companion and assistant of an older woman friend in order to survive. According to Elizabeth Fenton, she was never heard to utter any complaint throughout this time. She never appears to have married; an unfortunate loss to her male contemporaries, even disregarding her beauty.

A wedding in India was little different from one in Britain. As usual there were bridesmaids, and a wedding breakfast with a wedding cake. The main difference was the time of day, the early morning being preferred so as to avoid the heat, and so a wedding breakfast truly was a breakfast. The food would have had an Indian flavour and, just as today, all the trappings depended on financial wherewithal, so that fine Indian brocades, silks and muslins would have predominated only if there was money behind them. Emma Roberts suggested that the likelihood of a lavish reception was somewhat less than in England. Either way, it was sure to be at great expense, as it has been ever since.

As in all aspects of the social history of British India, it is much more difficult to ascertain the details of life among the lower socio-economic groups, for instance from the ranks of the soldiery, and from their wives and daughters. A great deal less was written, due probably to lack of literacy, as well as opportunity. Young ordinary soldiers would very often seek female partners among the Indian, or Anglo-Indian, population or they may have had an introduction to single girls living in the several orphanages of the time, as already described. This was one of the few sources of potential brides for such a man. Many of these girls were half or three quarters Anglo-Indian, and, again a marriage could only take place with the commanding officer's permission. Only a small proportion of men were allowed to keep their wives on the regimental strength. In this situation a wife received half rations, and was permitted a space in the communal barrack room, usually screened off by a curtain. If the soldier was already married before leaving for India, then the chances of his taking his wife with him were only about ten per cent in the early nineteenth century.[66] Those women left at home must have been immensely loyal in the main, just as those that also tolerated the overt masculinity of a barrack room just beyond the curtain, with all its coarseness and pub profanity. For some perhaps, the proximity of so many of her husband's male colleagues may have offered a sense of protection in the more unpredictable parts of India, but others must have become very inured to male behaviour, in all its forms.

A few young unmarried Indian British women, 200 years ago, formed daring relationships with Indian men. Their elders of the later Victorian era would have frowned severely on such unconventional behaviour, but in more laissez-faire Georgian times such things were possible. Thirty years later, however, the thought of a white woman being attracted to an Indian man would have been regarded as impossible, with a prurient incredulity among the women, and a sexual paranoia among the men, such that a forced submission could have been assumed. In these later attitudes lies the essence of popular novels of the colonial era, such as Forster's *A Passage to India*, and Scott's *Raj Quartet*.

Such relationships seem to have been quite uncommon, even in earlier times, although women were clearly attracted to Indian men, much as European girls travelling abroad today can be attracted to the unexpected, and very different, physicality and behaviour of the men from the countries they visit. Isabella Fane was much drawn to a Nepalese General she met in Calcutta, describing him as a beautiful man with magnificent dress. Like the Eden sisters, she was also charmed by the Sikhs for their courtliness and dash. Marianne Postans admired the tribesmen of the North, such as those from Sindh, Rajputana and Mahratta country.[67] In the main, it was rather like being in an art gallery; a case of look but don't touch, and so the admiration was abstract, and detached. In general British women felt very safe among Indian men. If travelling, they were surrounded by them, and sometimes journeyed many miles only in their company, such as Fanny Parkes' voyage of exploration up the Ganges and Jumna, or Mary Doherty returning overland by palanquin from Bangalore to Madras, on her way home. Also, servants were ever present, and usually male. British men seem not to have been unduly concerned on behalf of their women, and this appears to have been a genuine attitude, rather than a defensive reaction to a possible charge of hypocrisy, bearing in mind their own long history of cohabitation with Indian women.

Nevertheless some British women married Indian men. Rosemary Raza mentions Mary Short marrying the ruler of Oudh, Ghaziuddin Haider, in Lucknow in 1817, and that she lived in his zenana as Sultan Mariam Begum Sahiba. In his book, the *Last Mughal*, Dalrymple refers to two Muslim men, Maulawi Abdul Ali and Muhammad Ismail Londini, both of whom married British women at a similar time. The prevailing male dominance of the day, as well as the requirements of Islam, would have ensured these women absorbed Muslim customs and, of course, the religion. Little seems to have been said about these marriages, further implying some liberality of attitude in earlier years. Acceptance gives scant cause for comment, whereas outrage proclaims itself loudly in pen or print.

Chapter 4

Housewife and Household

In India, as in eighteenth and nineteenth century Europe, a woman's place was in the home, particularly a married woman's. Thus it was for the vast majority, and little would change until well into the twentieth century and after at least one World War. Most women needed a husband for survival, or destitution beckoned. Only a minority of women had independent means and, in any case, control of this generally passed to the man upon marriage. She therefore effectively became the possession, or chattel, of her husband. Although, when married, a woman renounced her legal personality in common law, she acquired significant social credit in compensation. She had joined the domestic club; had come of age in the eyes of her peers.[1] Her role as wife was as companion, supporter, sexual partner, admirer (supposedly) and home- and family-maker for her husband. Possibly she was also critic, sounding board, enemy of his enemies, source of social information and family correspondent. Creating and rearing children was a major part of the job description as well, the former at that time often leading to death. Additionally, life was very much a matter of ordering and organising the home, and this included control of the household accounts to a degree, which depended on the trust and symbiosis that existed between husband and wife. Despite all this, women were almost non-persons. Quite often they weren't referred to by name, but as the Lady of Mr So-and-So. In the back pages of the annual *The East India Register and Directory* is a list of all residents for that year in, for instance, Madras. While this list was comprehensive, it contained only men. It seems not to have been considered relevant to include wives, or women generally.

It is fascinating to reflect on how attitudes to the women of those days have changed during the last eighty to ninety years. In his diverting book *The Nabobs of Madras* no less a person than Henry Dodwell, Professor of Asian History at SOAS, and editor of two volumes of the *Cambridge History of India*, wrote:

Perhaps I do them an injustice, but I think their average [the women's]
below that of the men's. Every man had serious work to do; but they
had nothing except to oversee their servants. If the men were in
general of doubtful social rank, they [the women] *were still more*
dubious. At all events the men's motives in marriage was seldom
mercenary; theirs generally was.[2]

This was published in 1926 and, although it may contain much that is
objectively true for that time, it is fair to say that, not only would one be
unable to make a statement of this kind today, but no one would want to, nor
indeed could it be easily justified. The fact that women had no work to do
was hardly their fault. Also, if the women of those days had any tendency
towards being acquisitive, overdressed dolls, it was because the men of that
century placed them on that stage, albeit by tradition rather than individual
intent. It was just a fact of life. More importantly, most women had to be
mercenary because there was no other way to assure themselves, and any
future children, of any security. The men of that era would wonder at the
achievements of women today, equal in all respects in the traditional
professions, except perhaps the Church, and that is rapidly changing.
Although a few women may have taken the responsibilities of marriage and
household lightly, the impression received is that the majority took them
seriously; especially those who were more educated and aware. These were
inevitably the ones who set their experiences down on paper.

The coexistence of husband and wife would have been much the same in
India as it was anywhere else although, compared to today, less based on love
and more on opportunity and convenience. Nevertheless, that great affection,
even love, developed between many couples is reflected in the affection
expressed to family members in private correspondence home, or in the
outpouring of grief in the same such correspondence following bereavement.
This is seen in some of the heartfelt inscriptions found on the many
tombstones of that period. A simple example of the latter, among the usually
more extravagant Georgian epitaphs, is that of Mrs Eliza Green in South Park
Street Cemetery, Calcutta, who died in 1812 aged 37.

This monument is erected by her disconsolate [inconsolable] *husband*
as a tribute to the best of women; a fond wife and a tender mother.

This relatively downbeat statement somehow holds more sincerity and
poignancy, and demonstrates a greater sense of grief, than the more common,
florid outpouring of the age.

The domestic concord of marriage would have been much as always. Revealing descriptions are uncommon, although Mary Doherty wrote in 1820:

My kind husband bought me two beautiful grey horses and broke them in himself for harness. He likewise purchased a little pony, not much larger than a calf, for the children to ride up and down the large park at the back of our house. Every endeavour on his part was made to render one as happy as possible.... No man was ever more truly formed for domestic life in India, where he was in the house from eight o'clock in the morning till half past five in the afternoon, never did I hear an expression of ennui. [Military parades and exercises were in the cool of the morning and evening]. *He drew some figures, I added the ground to them, we read the same books, played with our children and he even seemed equally interested with myself in the shape of the frock I was making or the colour of the ribbon I was trimming my caps with. We breakfasted as soon as he returned from morning parade, dined at three, had generally two or three of the officers to dinner, besides regular parties occasionally. I drove out in the evening and he always joined me after parade giving his horse to the keeper and getting into the carriage to me.*[3]

A siesta in the heat of the afternoon was usual. Elizabeth Fenton refers to putting on her dressing gown, after the time for visiting is past, and lying on the couch while her husband reads. If the heat is not too oppressive, 'We walk about the veranda laughing, singing and talking till about half past two, when we prepare for dinner.' This little description seems almost timeless in its immediacy and charm.

The daytime family routine in India was near universal, and an idea of it is given by Elizabeth Gwillim in one of her letters in 1803:

I rise at eight in the morning. Breakfast, and the accounts, take my time until 10. From 10 till 12 is all the time for writing, learning or drawing. Only two hours out of 24!! And yet more often than every other day people come and take up those two hours. At 12 o'clock comes luncheon time, as we call it tiffin; we are ready to faint for food. Indeed, if I have been detained, I often do in the extreme heat. After this meal, we are so oppressed with heat that it is quite a force to do anything. At this moment I am writing after tiffin, and at three o'clock we dress, and at four we dine. We sometimes sleep a little between

81

tiffin and dinner, but I never do it if I can keep up. Between five and six we go to walk about the garden to see it watered and seeds sown, or else we go out airing, and this is all the exercise we have. If we walk in the garden we drink tea, and go out at eight o'clock to make visits, and as the places are so far from one another we do not get home till about 11 at night.[4]

Sixty years earlier Eliza Draper in Bombay described much the same routine.[5] If the days seemed humdrum, this was partly an escape from the heat, but a woman still had the major task of running the household. If this was thought arduous in England, it was tenfold more so in India by virtue of the much greater number of staff, the variety of languages and customs, and the disparate religious codes.

If there is one subject that the Indian British woman writes about copiously, it is that of domestic staff. This must be partly from constant proximity, but also that it was a major preoccupation, and even anxiety. The sheer numbers are breathtaking compared to the handful in England, except in the grandest houses. As Elizabeth Gwillim comments:[6] 'We live just as we did in England, except we have half a hundred black men about the house, who do not wait upon us quite as well as two maids and a man would do in England.'

Although this sounds like an imprecise number plucked from the air, Fanny Parkes goes into considerable detail in 1831, listing all the household servants, their jobs and their wages, and indicates that half-a-hundred was by no means unusual. Fanny's list follows.[7]

'A *khansaman,* or head man; a Musalman servant who purchases the provisions, makes the confectionary, and superintends the table	Rs 12
The *abdar,* or water-cooler; cools the water, ices the wines, and attends with them at table	Rs 8
The head *khidmatgar,* he takes charge of the plate chest (silver), and waits at table	Rs 7
A second *khidmatgar,* who waits at table	Rs 6
A *bawarchi,* or cook	Rs 12
Mate *bawarchi*	Rs 4
Mashalchi; dishwasher and torchbearer	Rs 4
Dhobee, or washerman	Rs 8
Istree Walla, washerman for ironing	Rs 8
A *darzee,* or tailor	Rs 8

A second tailor	Rs 6
An *ayah,* or lady's maid	Rs 10
An under woman	
A *doriya;* a sweeper, who also attends to the dogs	Rs 4
Sirdar-bearer, a Hindu servant, the head of the bearers, and the keeper of the Sahib's wardrobe; the keys of which are always carried in his cummerbund, the folds of cloth around his waist.	Rs 8
The mate-bearer; assists as valet, and attends to the lamps	Rs 6
Six bearers to pull the *punkahs,* and dust the furniture, etc., at Rs 4 each	Rs 24
A *gwala,* or cowherd	Rs 4
A *bher-i-wala,* or shepherd	Rs 5
A *murgh-i-wala,* to take care of the fowls, wild-ducks, quail, rabbits, guineafowls and pigeons	Rs 4
A *malee,* or gardener	Rs 5
A mate ma*lee*	Rs 3
Another mate, or a *cooly*	Rs 2
A gram-grinder, generally a woman who grinds the *chand* for the horses	Rs 2
A coachman	Rs 10
Eight *saises,* or (grooms), at Rs 5 each, for eight horses	Rs 40
Eight grass-cutters, at Rs 3 each, for the above	Rs 24
A *bihishti,* or water-carrier	Rs 5
A mate *bihishti*	Rs 4
A *Barhal mistree,* a carpenter	Rs 8
Another carpenter	Rs 7
Two *coolies,* to throw water on the *tattis,* at Rs 2 each	Rs 4
Two *chaukidars,* or watchmen, at Rs 4 each	Rs 8
A *darwan,* or gatekeeper	Rs 4
Two *chaprasis,* or running footmen, to carry notes, and be in attendance in the verandah, at Rs 5 each	Rs 10
Total for the 57 servants per month	Rs 290
or about £290 per annum	

During the hot winds, a number of extra coolies, *twelve or fourteen, are necessary if you have more than one thermantidote, or if you keep it going all night as well as during the day; these men, as well as an extra* bihishti, *are discharged when the rains set in. We, as quiet people, find these servants necessary. Some gentlemen for state add an* assa burdar, *the bearer of a long silver staff; and a* sonta burdar, *or* chob-dar, *who carries a silver club with a grim head on the top of it. The business of these people is to announce the arrival of company. If many dogs are kept, an extra doriya will be required.*

This was her own list of servants, hers being a rather ordinary household, and her husband being somewhat below a middle grade civil servant. Other women have recorded similar lists but others made do with only about twenty-five servants on grounds of economy and isolation, but these were in the minority.[8,9,10] It is hardly surprising that some women felt they could barely do anything for themselves, and felt oppressed by the servility and constant attendance, and even by some servant's personal habits, such as incessant *paan* (betel) chewing.[11]

With these sorts of numbers it is no great wonder that household residents kept tripping over their staff day and night. It is difficult to tell whether such quantities of people were all necessary, but it is certain that they were usual, and not entirely the ostentatious extravagance of a household that has become too well off too quickly. The impression received is that many were rather inefficient, and so compensated for by the employment of additional help. Another factor in the large numbers was religion: the Hindus would have nothing to do with the kitchen, even so far as refusing to touch a clean plate, for fear of loss of caste, in case, as Emma Roberts stated, it had been defiled by 'a portion of a slaughtered animal'. The Muslims had different restrictions, and so it became necessary to have some of each religion. Certain jobs could not be done at all by certain castes and therefore, with a large number of servants, the household covered its options in this respect. It is certainly tempting, through contemporary eyes, to consider the employment of so many staff as the unreasonable oppression of the poorest of the population by would-be grandee colonists. Without such large-scale domestic employment, however, much of the populace would have been without work, and poorer still. In a sense the foreign power was unwittingly contributing to a distribution of wealth by employing such large numbers of domestic staff, as well as troops (sepoys), all this being paid for from the proceeds of extracting this wealth from those better off Indians; the Nawabs, Princes, landowners and merchants.

The cost of such a household was prodigious. Fanny Parkes quotes £290 per year for her staff, equivalent to about £15-20,000 today; recognised even then as a large percentage of one's income, but tolerated because of apparent necessity.[12]

HOUSEWIFE AND HOUSEHOLD

British women in India often found communication with their household staff difficult because of language barriers, although the need to communicate was paramount. Some women had no command of their servant's language, which greatly hindered household management, except that the servants themselves learnt English with that remarkable facility the Indian people have for foreign languages, born perhaps of the need to speak two or three of their own in a subcontinent which has several hundred. Often it was a type of pidgin; effective, but amusing to some. Julia Maitland outlines some examples from a written shopping list in 1837: 'Alamoor estoo' for à la mode stew; 'Durkey for stups' (stuffing for turkey – forced up?); 'Eggs for saps, snobs, tips and pups' (for chops, snipes, tipsy cake and puffs); and at the end 'Ghirand totell' and 'Howl balance'.[13] Quaint as this may have seemed to the early Indian British, it wasn't as bad as the patronising distortions they in turn used to their servants, which Julia Maitland called 'John Company's English' and which she felt to be 'silly and childish' (and yet disconcertingly more effective than classical English). The more highly motivated women, like their menfolk, quickly recognised the value of learning a local tongue. Few merchants, or East India Company employees, went to India without some knowledge of an Asian language, and with the advent of Cornwallis as Governor-General following Pitt's India Act of 1784, a professional training was initiated for the Company's administrators. This became focused on Haileybury College, founded in 1809, in which Asian languages were obligatory, along with accounting and political economy. Many men spoke one or two languages, sometimes more, with considerable fluency, and particularly Hindi or Urdu. Quite a few women followed suit. William Dalrymple in *White Mughals* refers to Mrs Ure, wife of the Residency surgeon in Hyderabad at the turn of that century as being fluent in Urdu. So also was Fanny Parkes. In Georgian times a high percentage of women were able to converse with their Indian staff in the local language, with a gradation of capability, but this lessened with lessening interest, motivation and need in the era of the Raj, unless by chance there was a specific curiosity, or a natural ability. In 1802, the intelligent socialite Mary (Symonds), sister of Elizabeth Gwillim, excused herself from the effort by claiming to be poor enough at her own language to justify any effort with Hindustani – a slightly pathetic cop-out in her case. The rest of the household were beavering away, however. Sister Elizabeth was deep in the study of Gentoo (Telugu; a Dravidian language spoken then in Eastern coastal India). Richard Clarke the legal lodger (and Mary's long-term admirer), was studying Malabar, (and no doubt her), and Sir Henry Gwillim was learning Persian.[14] Julia Maitland rather sensibly decided to learn Tamil on the ship north from Madras in July 1837. She was heading for Rajahmundry, just under 400 miles away, along with her husband who was taking up an appointment as a regional judge. Rahahmundry was on the banks of the River Godavari estuary, downstream from Hyderabad, and so of some importance to the British. It was sufficiently isolated to encourage the learning of a language, especially when she and her baby escaped the heat by moving to the coast at Samuldavee, with no native village nearby, and the nearest European station forty miles away. Here she took up Gentoo as well, and in both cases she was assisted by a Munshi; a high calibre teacher of Indian languages to foreigners, who came and went as required. She, like many of the more isolated women in India at that time, was able to communicate readily with their staff, and their Indian neighbours. The British had yet to reach that stage in their history where so much of the world spoke English as to induce apathy in the learning of languages. It was de rigueur for Company employees, and nearly so for those courageous or unlucky women, depending on your point of view, who lived hundreds of miles from civilisation in deep country (the *Mofussil*), for example the wives or sisters of indigo planters. Only by this means could these women speak to anyone, other than their male companion.

Comments about the laziness of servants are dotted through the letters and journals of the early 1800s, such as: 'This one lies under a tree all day asleep, in her rings and pins'.[15] Quite probably they were witnessing the timeless oriental habit of dozing in the heat of the day, and working at a leisurely pace for the same reason. Possibly there was a temptation, with so many staff available, to use the excuse of inappropriate caste to offload a specific task onto someone else, and slide away. More surprisingly, there are regular references to petty theft and monetary fraud. My own experience of travelling in India is quite the opposite and it is one of the safer countries. One may be cheated with charm, by unscrupulous prices in a bazaar, but mugging, and the robbing of hotel luggage, seems exceptional. It is therefore surprising to come across comments such as:

> *I am obliged to keep everything locked up in a storeroom and to give out every day to the different servants a proper quantity for the days use. I cannot trust them with more; they are such pilferers. I must tell you how they contrived to cheat me of the candles. I gave them out a proper number and they cut a piece off each before they set them up. This I should not have found out had a Lady not told me to observe that, and I found they really had done so.*[16]

Also, it seems to have been quite common for more food to have been bought than had been directed, and for it then to be distributed to the other servants, rather than kept for family use. Or else the lady of the house might be short-changed when purchases had been made on her behalf.[17,18] For the less than scrupulous, where a senior servant was given money with which to do all the shopping in the bazaars, this must have been too great a temptation. This senior servant was known as a *Khansamah*, and was invariably Muslim. As his chief means of payment was to take a percentage (*dasturi*) of any purchasing transaction, the opportunities for enhancing this were everywhere. Emma Roberts describes the *Khansamah* as follows:

> *He should be an active and respectable man, for upon his exertions the comfort of a family must in great measure depend. He acts in the capacity of major-domo, purveyor, and confectioner, superintending the cooking department, making the jellies and jams, and attending to all the more delicate and elaborate details of the cuisine. All the other servants are, or ought to be, under his immediate control, and when he is made answerable for their conduct, things usually go on very smoothly. In addition to the* khansamah, *whose place at table is behind his master's chair, there are other attendants of his own class, called* khidmutgars, *one being attached to each individual of the family. Strictly speaking, the duty of these men is merely to attend at meals; but they will cook upon occasion, and indeed are fond of shewing their skill in the art, and also, where economy is considered, act as the* abdar [butler], *who cools the wine, &c, or as the hookah-badar* [pipe-bearer], *and chillum manufacturer.*[19]

The master of the house would have all three, splendidly dressed, and arrayed behind his chair at dinner. In addition to these individuals there would be some cooks, and a number of *mussaulchees* (scullions), and this would complete the table servants. These all had to be Muslim, the Hindus being unable on religious grounds to involve themselves in any way with European kitchens or food. A high proportion of all the household servants were male, excepting only those acting personally for the ladies in the house. The array of other servants has already been listed by Fanny Parkes and she, and Emma Roberts, emphasised forcibly the importance of ensuring honesty and integrity in the *khansamah* and *Sirdar-bearer*, as far as possible. Only in this way could the household be well-organised, firm control passed down through the staff, and the lady of the house be spared considerable domestic anguish. Cleanliness too was essential, or otherwise the house rather alarmingly:

> *Exhibited dusty worm-eaten furniture, ragged mats, dirt and dilapidation of every kind; for a single day's neglect is quite sufficient to allow the multitudinous hosts of insects, which form the grand destructive power to gain a-head. An ill-kept house in India is the most deplorable, comfortless-looking place imaginable; it is overrun with vermin of every kind rats and mice, and such small deer disport themselves over it at all hours; frogs croak in the corners, and bats nestle in the cornices.*[20]

There can be no doubt that some women in India grew quite close to some of their servants, much as happened in England, and it is hardly surprising when one reads the following:

> *We have one great comfort, I feel, by coming from the fancy servants in England, which is the attention and tenderness of these people in illness or difficulties. Even those who beat them and abuse them acknowledge that their care in illness is beyond all things. It is a religious principle with them never to be made angry by anything that an old person or a sick person says. They are patient and forbearing under insults and provocations of all kinds, neither do they bear in mind these affronts.*[21]

A particular favourite were the *Dubashes*, or young men of good caste, who were clean, neatly dressed and literate in two or three languages and acted as interpreters for newly arrived Europeans. They were generally the sons of wealthy parents, and stayed with a particular employer until it was time for him to return home to England. These positions carried prestige, and the opportunity of advancement, and were much sought after. They would also act as personal assistants, but in an advisory capacity rather than performing any menial tasks. As Elizabeth Gwillim observes:

> *They are extremely agreeable in one respect* [in] *that they have no offensive tricks, which they abominate, and have a great contempt for Moor men who always indulge in them* [the tricks], *and for such English as* [also] *do. They never scrape their throats, nor sniff with the nose, nor pick their teeth or fingers, nor make any odd noises, nor*

do they ever scratch their heads or, in short, do any trick that can offend delicate eyes or ears. I own I have been often not a little ashamed to hear one of my [own] country people, who in 10 minutes has committed 10 things that would disgust these people, [and then] swear at them for beasts and dirty devils.

They were obviously a worthwhile example of correct social graces to a newcomer from another country with less than ideal personal habits, and who bothered to notice.

The lowlier servants were of an untouchable caste; today called *dalits*. At that time they were called pariahs. Young girls from this caste, aged 10 years or more, were often sold into service by their families. The proceeds soon disappeared, mainly in food and drink, but the girls could nevertheless end up eventually in steady and decent employment. If they had learnt a little English, usually by being kept by an English soldier, or a young officer, for his personal gratification, they were then regarded as qualified to attend a lady. As Elizabeth says, 'She is no longer an object much to be desired by the gentleman. Such are the maids we have to attend upon our persons.' She herself acquired a girl called Poppa, of whom she was undoubtedly fond, and her description of this girl opens another small window onto the very different life of that period:

She was about 21, at which time the downy fineness of their faces is a little worn, and this is their chief beauty. Her face was plain, but her teeth and eyes very fine and the most delicate form I ever saw, of the lightest kind. I asked if she was married and she said very simply she had been married twice, that her first husband was a Dutch Captain of a ship who had bought her at 200 pagodas when she was 10 years old, that her second husband (the Captain having gone to Europe) was a steward to a gentleman in Madras by whom she had a son, whom she had put into a charity school, but that that man had now taken another woman, the ladies maid of that family. He gave her nothing nor took any notice of the child, wherefore she came to seek my service. After some time I used to question her because she agreed to have leave to see her child once a week. 'I suppose', says I, 'you were very sorry when this man took another'. 'No', said she, 'what should I care for him. I care only for my child and I do not wish to go again to any gentleman.' She has accordingly lived with me two years and 10 months, I believe in perfect innocence. The only trouble she gives me is asking frequently to go to see sild (child), but any refusal occasions no resentment. She is honest in the strictest sense of the word, sober and not guilty of falsehood. She is extremely useful to me in some respects, as all the servants, except one or two who are in a distant part of the house, go home of a night and leave us with all the hundred doors of the house wide open, with jackals and pariah dogs howling round and bats entering at pleasure, and the bed curtains bestrewn with grasshoppers that stun one with their cry, to say nothing of the frogs that in a rainy season prevent all sleep by their croaking chorus. Poppa sleeps upon the hard stucco floor in the room next to mine in the same apparel she wears all day, her muslin dress and her gold necklaces. Mr Gwillim calls three or four times every night [for her] to bring toast and water and she always jumps up in good humour and appears in full dress, as that requires nothing but shaking herself. She never lays even a mat under her: the only indulgence I have seen her use (though there are carpets at her command) is to bring a couple of bricks which she uses as a pillow over her head. But even this is a luxury she seldom takes the trouble to bring in, and at five in the morning she smokes her Saroot *of strong tobacco, and when her work is done reheats it and basks under a tree asleep on the ground in the best clothes I can give her.*[22]

An important part of any household, then as now, was the presence of children. If a woman went to India already married with a family, she faced the exquisitely painful decision as to whether to take the children with her or not. Mary Doherty wanted to leave her two in England, but was overruled by her husband. The reason for leaving them would have been partly to protect them from the health risks in India, and partly to benefit from a better quality of education in the home country. Much would have depended on their age; the younger ones might well be taken abroad, and then later returned to relatives at home for a better standard of schooling than was available in India. If left behind, the agony for the mother could be intense. Lady Nugent departed for India in 1811 leaving four children behind, including an infant son which, during her early months abroad, was a source of considerable psychological distress.[23] On at least one documented occasion, the pain caused by leaving four children behind with strangers, led a broken-hearted mother to smuggle her fifth onto the ship.[24]

Parting from anyone: children, relatives or friends, led to the unspoken, but very real, fear on both sides that they might never meet again. In the case of children, separation was almost inescapable, either by being left at home in the first place or, if taken to India, the agony of a later decision whether or not to return them home. The choice was driven by an understandable desire to protect them from the ever-prevalent danger of disease. Child mortality in Britain was bad enough, but the health horrors of India were enough to force mothers to face the heartbreak of such a parting, knowing full well that they might never see their loved ones again because of the risk to their own lives. At least this way the children stood a better chance of survival. Those children left behind in England, or sent home later, would easily grow apart from their parents, and close family bonding might be sacrificed forever. Strained relations might even develop between husband and wife if she decided to accompany sick children home, or those headed for schools in England, because this could lead to a separation easily lasting two or three years. Mary Sherwood resolved to return to England in 1809, when her third baby was old enough, having already lost two infants in the space of two years. On the point of her planned departure, her husband seems to have had an emotional collapse and, 'Was in a state of the deepest grief, and told me that he absolutely could not bear the thought of my leaving him.' The result was postponement by four years, following which her husband resigned his appointment as Regimental Paymaster, she had another baby, and the family sailed home together.[25] Perhaps his earlier misery could be regarded as self-indulgence, but there is little reason why it should not have been genuine wretchedness. It may have been easier for the women to leave their husbands for a while, than for the husbands to be left behind; the women felt, perhaps, a stronger tie to their children than to their husband.

Women who were married in India often had to face pregnancy without the reassurance and comfort of a mother, or close relative, standing by. Other women became pregnancy machines in the absence of any form of birth control, apart from abstinence, which was essentially ineffective. A woman could face multiple pregnancies; easily numbering into double figures, but then so many of these children died shortly afterwards. Those children who survived often became quite Indianized, because much of their upbringing was in the hands of their ayahs (personal maids), who frequently became very attached to the children, as did the children to them. They often became fluent in the language of their ayah; often more so than their parents were, and certainly more so than in English. Doubtless this allowed them much greater insight into Indian life, and the workings of the servants, than the European adults around them. The bond between those born in India and their ayahs could often be intense and enduring. With the growing evangelical morality of the early Victorian era, however, as well as a parallel encouragement towards greater British hegemony, there was intensifying paranoia that such children would be contaminated by Indian beliefs and attitudes. There even developed a worry that there was a moral and physical risk to them from their female Indian attendants, or ayahs, and that the male bearers were more reliable.[26] By the 1840s, however, there was even horror expressed at the notion of leaving children to the care of native men.[27] One extraordinary first-hand report cites the poisoning, by their ayah, of all four children of one family, because she resented her mistress's rebuke for giving them *paan* (betel).[28] Such stories might underlie the existence of these anxieties, but could equally be delusional paranoia resulting from a growing racial prejudice. The increasingly powerful desire that children should be brought up with a strong and dutiful sense of Britishness, uncontaminated by Indian influence, became another major motive in sending them home to England, especially by the 1830s. As mentioned, the third compelling reason for sending children home was for a good education. Although schooling was available in the Presidency towns, such as Calcutta and Madras, the standard was variable and the inmates tended to be from poorer families, other ranks in the army, mixed race children and orphans. The better-off would despatch their children to England, where standards were higher and formed the proper path to a good career, and where the girls could acquire that particular European polish which would help them stand out among their Anglo-Indian mixed race competitors back in India. Both sexes learnt their mother tongue, sometimes rather patchy up to that point, and acquired the refined British accent that distinguished them so readily from anyone brought up in foreign parts. These children tended to go home from the age of about 4, and at the latest perhaps 8, although Elizabeth Draper (née Sclater) went home aged 10 in 1754. The cost was considerable, as there was the passage price for the child, and some sort of carer, and then the cost of maintenance and education. The greatest cost, however, was to the peace of mind of the child's mother.

Lady Maria Callcott wrote in 1810 from Point de Galle, Ceylon, close to the old Dutch fort:

> *I walked to the beach this morning to see the last of the homeward-bound ships; two-and-twenty sail got under way at daybreak, and many an anxious wish went with them. Many a mother had trusted her darling child to the waves, nay much more, to the care of strangers, in the conviction that, depriving herself of the delight of watching over it, was to secure its permanent advantage.[29]*

Sarah Robinson, wife of a Bengal Army surgeon, wrote from Secrole near Benares, four years later:

A number of families are now away from Secrole. They are gone down to Calcutta to send their children to Europe. Everyone urges me to beware of keeping my Alexander so long. Hitherto he is well.[30]

She was in an agony of indecision about this nearly inevitable event: 'I think to part with him will almost cost me my life. I shall need every assistance that an absolute sense of duty can give me.' Her letters home to her sister are shot through with this anxiety and, later, with the despair at not having heard anything long after he had sailed. In the end her fears were justified, but ironically for the wrong reasons. She died of cholera in 1818 aged just 34. Her husband died less than a year later, and they are buried together in South Park Street Cemetery, Calcutta. Alexander will have never seen them again, and it is unlikely he ever saw their tomb.

Not everyone sent their children home, but the great majority did, especially if they had the means. In 1794 Eliza Macpherson sent three boys home at the same time to go to boarding school (Eton), but certainly thought she would never again be happy in India.[31]

Once the children were settled with relatives in Britain they tended to make their own lives, and perhaps missed their parents less than the parents missed them. They wrote dutiful letters outlining their progress at school, and an example remains from Mary Wimberley's son, Douglas, to his father, which gives an unusual insight into the rigours of the almost entirely classical education of the early 1800s; no mention of Mathematics, English Literature or British History.[32]

July 14, 1841
My dearest car.
As you wish me to give you a long account of all my school affairs, I think the best and most correct way will be to give you the plan of a week's work.

On Monday we are questioned on about eight or 10 pages of 'Tomline's introduction to the study of the Bible', then we construe and parse about half a page of Xenophon, next we are examined by the headmaster (week alternatively) in Tomline's, Xenophon, Virgil or Sallust, next two chapters of Goldsmiths Roman History, abridged by Pinnock.

On Tuesday the Eton Latin or Greek Grammar (week alternatively) Virgil or Sallust, about 20 lines, eight lines of Bland's verses. Goldsmiths modern geography.

On Wednesday, Latin or Greek Grammar, Ellis's Latin exercise, and Xenophon.

On Thursday the Latin or Greek Grammar. Translation of the old Xenophon, Virgil or Sallust, two chapters of Roman history.

On Friday Latin or Greek Grammar, Bland's verses, Xenophon and geography.

On Saturday, 20 lines of Virgil, by heart; Ellis's exercises.

I must now tell you all about our games

My favourite game in summer you may easily guess; namely cricket. The others are marbles, leapfrog, fly the Garter, which is something like leapfrog, only you have to fly a great distance, and various others of no consequence.

I hope that you are all well. Give my kindest love and many kisses to Mama, Eddy, Florry and Dual, and tell them I long to see them and you too dearest Papa.

Tell Eddy and Florry I will answer their letters as soon as I can. I have been most happy at Drum, riding and fishing; in short I was never idle.

One day I caught half a dozen fine trouts which, with four that my cousin John Ogilvie caught, were fried for supper and were very nice.

I must now bid you goodbye and believe me dearest Papa

Your most affectionate son
Douglas Wimberley

PS. I am exceedingly obliged for your most kind present and I'm sure that never children had such kind and affectionate parents, and I hope I shall make a good use of it. I will try and get Charlie to learn his lessons and help him as you wish.

The form of this letter will resonate with anyone who has spent some time absent from home during their school years. Writing home was a duty, mostly tiresome, but driven by conscience, and perhaps also by a nearby adult. Padding the letter with routine facts takes up the necessary space. What is remarkable to us today is the content of the teaching week. The almost entirely classical focus may have been a useful prelude to learning other languages, and was probably a worthwhile introduction to philosophy, logic and ethics, but there was an amazing lack of anything practical, other than sport and extracurricular activities. Nevertheless, rote learning, and crammed events from ancient texts, will have trained a good memory. Hopefully this could then be put to better use at a later date.

In a society where marriage was, to a great extent, a contract of convenience, arrangement or even enforcement, it is inevitable that one must ask the question as to how successful it was. In the main, married couples remained together, but it is unclear whether this was always happily. This seems unlikely when so many were either semi-arranged, or spur-of-the-moment decisions, but a sense of duty and religious conscience was a strong cement, and a particular feature of that time. Less-than-happy couples will have contrived to find a compromise position that maintained equilibrium. Those couples deep in the *mofussil*, and isolated from all European social contact, may well have discovered a mutual appreciation, and a consolidation of their relationship, as a consequence of sharing the arduous and isolated lifestyle. Otherwise in India the common situation of a large age difference will have led to some disparity of interest and energy. Also, the husband's occupation may have been intensely distracting or, if in the army, he might be away for weeks or months on manoeuvres, or at war. Elizabeth Gwillim writes about her husband, Sir Henry Gwillim, Supreme Court Judge in Madras:

> *This is Wednesday night; he arrives, or so has done, at nine o'clock*
> *tired and drawn and goes fast asleep. With difficulty he is encouraged*
> *to go to bed; wakes at 5 o'clock in the morning and mounts his horse.*
> *He comes up on Saturday night at the same hour, in the same state.*[33]

She saw little of him therefore, and perhaps it was not just by unfortunate chance that she was childless. At the other extreme of interpersonal relationships, William Hickey describes an unfortunate woman who was persuaded by her only relative in India, her sister, and a number of friends to marry a man she detested, on the grounds that it was a beneficial match. She swore to him, at the altar, that she would never allow him to touch her, upon which he promptly beat her up. She died at sea en route to Madras a few days later; a merciful escape perhaps, and in those days one of the very few escapes available to her. Not many marriages were made in heaven at that time.[34]

In the context of Georgian courtship and marriage, to what extent was infidelity a reality? Eliza Sclater we have met before. She returned from England to India in 1757 aged 14 and married Daniel Draper, a man twenty years her senior. The marriage was not a success, with a growing coldness and estrangement. Nevertheless, Eliza made every effort to get closer to her husband: 'Whose humour I am now resolved to study and if possible conform to him; if the most punctilious attention can render me necessary to his happiness, it shall be so.'[35] Whether she later entertained thoughts of straying is uncertain. In a letter to her unmarried male cousin, Thomas, she said: 'Nothing can be more difficult than the management of illicit attachments … India abounds with fewer temptations to frailty than I have yet seen.' This perhaps suggests that the subject was at least in her thoughts. She had certainly had the opportunity. The family had returned to England in the hope of alleviating Daniel Draper's poor health, and also to arrange the education of their children. He eventually returned to India, but she stayed on another two years during which time the already celebrated writer Lawrence Sterne, author of Tristram Shandy, fell head over heels in love with her. There has been much speculation about the matter in the years since, but there is nothing at all to suggest that she yielded to him, despite his eloquently expressed ardour. Ironically, several years later and back in India, her husband had a scandalously open and unexpected affair with a woman living in their home. This was clearly a factor in Eliza's later elopement with a Naval Officer. This did not last long, and she went to live with her grandfather and thence returned to England. It seems possible that, in the light of these later developments, she may have regretted her earlier faithfulness in the face of persuasive temptation; but by then Lawrence Sterne was dead.

Perhaps it is inevitable that stories of constancy and restraint do not survive as well as tales of lost honour, but infidelity undoubtedly occurred among women, although it will have been much commoner among the men. Marriage, especially a semi-arranged one, was almost an excuse for making it possible for either party. What would have been social suicide before marriage became much easier within its framework, provided great caution and discretion were exercised. Even an accidental pregnancy could be attributed to the marriage itself, as probably many women have experienced down the centuries. Nevertheless, as Eliza Draper noted, the domestic arrangements in India were hardly conducive to even a brief liaison in a dark corner. As like as not, one of the myriad servants would dart out of the shadows at just the wrong moment.

Paradoxically one has the impression that marital fidelity was somehow greater in the more liberal eighteenth century atmosphere, where social enfranchisement flourished to the extent that men could live openly with Indian women; whereas in the nineteenth century, when Victorian prudery and secrecy prevailed, infidelity became more commonplace. One factor that encouraged this in India was the development, from about 1820, of the hill station. These were highly popular refuges from the roasting temperatures of the plains in the dry season, so that women took themselves off for respite, and their husbands stayed behind to continue their responsibilities. Unfortunately – for the husbands that is – there was a fair sprinkling of young army officers, and other ranks in the hills, and contemporary reports by women give a clear indication that some married women indulged in more than just playful dalliance.[36] The same applied in military encampments when a regiment was away at war. As Robert Waterfield wrote, with reference to the married women in a particular camp:

The regiments to which their husbands belonged was up the country with Sir Walter Gilbert, and not having anyone to watch over them, or to keep them within bounds, they came out in their true colours, and proved false to their plighted vows. There were some few exceptions, and I am afraid but few, and the scenes enacted by the false ones was, in some cases, disgusting in the extreme.[37]

It is always hard to find explanations for these indiscretions, in either sex, but various factors must have been at play. Immaturity, unhappiness, loneliness and a need for comfort would have been among them, or sometimes perhaps just uncompromising wilfulness, or a wish for excitement in an otherwise humdrum life. Many of these soldiers' wives were barely out of childhood, and their crude barrack room lives would have greatly coarsened them. There were complications too. Mary Wimberley and her husband, then Chaplain to the Governor-General, met a young woman who had just discovered her husband's unfaithfulness. It seemed to her that her husband no longer wanted her, and she wondered whether to leave him. They promptly confirmed that if she did, she would have no backing from the law, which would not oblige any continuing financial support from her husband.[38] The dice were severely loaded against women in this situation, and they had little choice but to try and resurrect the marriage. Men, on the other hand, had the full weight of the law behind them.

Theodore Tanner, senior merchant in the Company's service, prosecuted his wife for divorce in 1790 as a consequence of her adultery with a third party by whom she had a daughter. Mother and daughter received from him just one shilling, 'and no more'. An aggrieved husband, by contrast, would obtain a hefty sum in damages from the other side.[39] Not entirely surprisingly, the cards were always dealt well for the men. Richard Holmes quotes the case of a subaltern who was court-martialled, and on the point of being cashiered, for disrespectful behaviour to his commanding officer. This would not have been so unusual, until one learns that the disrespect shown was to sleep with his CO's wife. General Sir Charles Napier, Commander in Chief, India, overturned the sentence however, on the grounds that 'The tree from which the young officer had stolen the fruit had not required much shaking.'[40]

One of the more celebrated of such episodes during the early nineteenth century was the 'criminal conversation', that opaquely coy expression of the day for adultery, of Lady Barlow with a young army officer called Captain Pratt Barlow, who was a distant relative of her husband. This was none other than Sir George Barlow, who had been elevated somewhat above his social rank to Acting Governor-General of India upon the unexpected death of Lord Cornwallis in 1805. This leap in rank rather went to Lady Barlow's head, and she conducted a lengthy affair with the well-named Pratt Barlow, a cynically ambitious younger man who ensured that he profited financially from the relationship. There were at least two children resulting, although she seems never to have been quite sure who the father of one of them was. Sir George undoubtedly turned a blind eye in both Calcutta, and later Madras, over several years. The likelihood is that he wanted to avoid the disgrace that was so much a feature of divorce at that time, as well as all the attendant publicity and embarrassment. Once they had all returned to London, however, there was no such retreat, especially after the governess came across the couple *in flagrante*. She had entered a drawing room to witness her Ladyship on her knees, with a hand inside Pratt's trousers. Sir George had no alternative but to take the matter to court, upon which the newspapers made hay of the story, and no doubt revenue too, as did Sir George himself. He received damages of £2,000, at least £70,000 now. In this instance the disgraced wife was settled with a modest annual income for life.[41] This episode was a *cause celebre*, and rather more exotic than the usual instances of marital failure, although it is impossible to give any numerical idea of the incidence of the latter in India. Scattered through the newspapers published in the Presidency towns, however, are occasional notices such as the following:

> *I, William Maughan, late Captain of the Armed Marine of Bombay, do hereby give notice that having made a suitable provision for the support of Elizabeth Maughan, my wife, now living apart from me at*

*Malacca, in the East Indies, I will not be bound or answerable for any
contract or engagement, or debt whatsoever, to be contracted, entered
into, or incurred by the said Elizabeth Maughan.*[42]

Needless to say, separation and divorce was in those days a great deal less
common than a marriage finishing as a result of premature death. The
incidence of widowhood in India was inevitably high. For a woman this was
more than just devastating. It was potential destitution. If her husband had
left her any capital she could return home to England. As Elizabeth Gwillim
noted: 'Here (in this place) is a beautiful young woman of 25 going home
now with five children, from magnificence to poverty.'[43] Many could not
afford the journey, although it was usual practice to auction all the husband's
possessions down to his britches, stockings, shirts, snuff boxes, uniform,
harness and so on, in order to provide the necessary funds. Such sales were
common practice; often to brother officers or colleagues privately, although
the saleroom was another outlet. Where this didn't raise enough funds to
purchase a passage home, it was equally common for a subscription to be
raised for the assistance of the widow. This was especially so in the army
where the camaraderie of brother officers induced a greater emotive
generosity in a social circumstance where widows had little to fall back on.
Mary Doherty, wife of Major Doherty of his Majesty's 13th Light Dragoons,
wrote in 1820:

*In the beginning of November Major Blankley expired. His widow was
pregnant, and had two little boys. She lost the baby they brought from
England sometime before. We took her to our house, and Major
Doherty with that kindness of heart, and so peculiarly his own, set on
foot a very advantageous sale of her property; each officer allowed
her five days pay and allowances, and other regiments also subscribed
handsomely.*[44]

Within months, Mary found herself in an identically distressing situation and,
likewise, was a recipient of a generous subscription from her dead husband's
colleagues, which enabled her to get back to Madras and find a ship home
for her and her two boys. The widows of East India Company employees
could expect a modest pension. Similarly, the widows of Company army
officers also received one, the level of which was relative to their husband's
rank. The pension for a colonel's widow was 238.6 rupees for every year
spent in India, and for a Lieutenant's, 71.3 rupees.[45] In other words the widow

of a colonel who had served ten years in that country received the current equivalent of about £10,000. On the other hand, widows of officers and men in His Majesty's regular army received no statutory pension. Nevertheless, this was discretionary, and something might be offered in response to a petition on grounds of great poverty. In subsequent years this situation was sometimes more likely where the husband had been killed in action, especially if there had been considerable bravery. If a widow remarried, such pensions were forfeited after a grace period; a practice that still exists today.

There was inevitably a worthwhile practical alternative in the struggle to find funds to support oneself, and that was to find another husband towards the same end. This was the outcome for very many widows left stranded by disease or war. The situation was exacerbated by the fact that so many men were considerably older than their wives, and thus more susceptible to a fatal illness. Their greater age might at least mean they were wealthy enough to leave sufficient for a widow to be independent. In the army, remarriage by widows was strongly encouraged; the widow of an ordinary soldier had to find a new husband, or else new quarters. This was not a problem. There was no limit to the numbers of single men around and, as Richard Holmes reports, many of these soldiers' wives were engaged two or three deep on the off chance.[46] After the First Sikh War (1845) there were some fifteen widows in the 3rd Light Dragoons. Most of these were remarried within a month, and some of these women ended their marital careers having had three or four husbands.[47] Such hasty remarriage was not uncommon; there is one well-documented case of a widow who attended her husband's funeral the day after he died, and was proposed to that same day by the Regimental Colour Sergeant, upon which she burst into tears. The chastened man, thinking he had been a bit quick off the mark, apologised and said he would return in a few days. She exclaimed, through sobs, that her tears were not as he supposed, but a result of having already accepted the Corporal of the burial firing party; he was by no means such a good prospect.[48] Likewise, Marianne Postans wrote in her memoirs (1838) about a gunner who had died of fever and left an attractive widow:

An hour after her husband's death three of his comrades proposed to her, and before a week expired, her weeds were laid aside. The woman's second husband also died and she again married with similar promptness. A third time death severed, and Hymen retied, the mystic knot; and last of all, but again a widow, the woman died also.[49]

These examples of swift remarriage do not at all reflect any callous flippancy, or intemperate voracity, on the part of the widows. They simply emphasise the desperation they faced in a country far from home, with no continuing means of support, no relatives and no income apart from what they could eke out of cooking, sewing and washing for their dead husband's soldier colleagues. Remarriage was an entirely pragmatic solution. Love was irrelevant; the new partner wanted someone to cook for him, and share his bed; the new wife wanted survival and a roof over her head.

This pattern of behaviour was not confined to the ordinary soldier. Officers' widows faced the same desolation, although the response tended to be more considered, and less precipitously practical. Also, as we know, many were able to raise funds to return home. Elizabeth Fenton had been married to Neil Campbell, a young officer from a Scottish regiment who died of probable cholera in April 1827. His best friend, also a soldier, was Captain Fenton who was solicitously helpful and attentive from early in Elizabeth's bereavement. Within six months he was pressing her to marry him, both to her face and in lengthy correspondence. In this he was abetted by a number of her women friends who made their own independent case. Elizabeth's older and close friend, Mrs Grant, expressed her concern about her young friend being so alone and unprotected: 'As a single woman you must be miserable; whereas as a married one, if you were not happy you might be tranquil.' These few words convey much of the attitude to marriage of the Georgian period. Elizabeth, however, was not so sure: 'The more I thought of marrying in such indecorous haste, the more I revolted from the idea.' But soon after she continues: 'The time for hesitating was past, and all I had then to do was to get through my part as firmly as I might.' Not the most enthusiastic or passionate reaction, but she was remarried to her late husband's best friend within twelve months of being widowed; quite slow by the standards of the day.[50] The marriage proved happy and long-lasting, and the couple moved to Australia where they lived for many years.

The pressure to remarry may have been less in civilian life for the reason that so many widows retained the financial means by which they could return to Britain. Nevertheless, early remarriage was common here as well. A young woman by the name of Hannah Butterworth was married three times in eleven years. The seemingly inconsolable Mr Keighley, within fourteen days of his wife's sudden death in 1788, married a Miss Peach; presumably a living example of her name.[51] This was an event 'of whose delicacy I could not entertain a very high opinion,' said William Hickey, with surprising censure, given his own reputation, and echoed elsewhere by the much more straitlaced

Emily Eden witnessing a very similar situation. The carping quips of shocked opprobrium lie ever in the wings.

Although just a handful of examples from the few surviving contemporary accounts, they serve to emphasise the social reaction to marriage, and its sudden end, in the late eighteenth and early nineteenth century. One is left with the strong impression of the isolation and vulnerability of all these women, who had lost everything for which, and by which, they existed, other than any children. Desperate they could only have been.

Chapter 5

Society and Propriety

In common with many cultures that find themselves transplanted to some other environment, such as any migrating population, the British in India attempted to live a life that mirrored the society they came from. Georgian social life for women in England is well described by several writers, and Indian British social life by a few.[1,2,3,4,5,6] There were some concessions necessarily made to the fact that this life was in India, dictating adjustments in food, address, house design and the management of cohorts of domestic staff. The core features for the women nevertheless remained the same; household management, entertaining, attending social functions, visiting and receiving, and attending to their appearance and that of their domestic surroundings.

Even more than in England, social life in India was entirely governed by distinctions according to rank, occupation, salary and position, and this precedence was rigidly prescribed, being eventually set down in 1841 as a set of strict rules on 'Precedence in the East Indies'.[7] The Governor General was the overall supremo, following Pitt's India Act of 1784, before which it was the Governor of Bengal (Calcutta), followed by the governors of Madras and Bombay. This Presidency order applied to those lesser mortals in each, who were, in turn, the Chief Justice, the Bishop, Commander in Chief (Army), Council members, Puisne judges and, lastly, the Commander in Chief, Naval forces, presumably because his domain was the sea and not the land. After this came the civilians; the East India Company's servants, who took precedence over the company's soldiers who, in turn, took precedence over those regiments that served the King directly – a cause of some bitterness. His Majesty's soldiers had a greater social prestige however, and were better paid, although the officers needed to be because they often bore the burden of considerable debt, having purchased their commissions. They were 'gentlemen' however, whereas East India Company officers were an eclectic crew who had no status west of the Cape. For everybody, rank surmounted everything and birth, ability, intelligence, and even personal wealth, took second place to one's appointed position and salary. The status of the woman exactly followed that of her husband, or senior male family member, and woe betide anyone who stepped out of line and forgot their place. John Low mentions an example: 'a Miss Hunter of Blackness, an aunt of the present family, thought fit to marry a common soldier, and consequently was thrown over by the family.' As Miss Hunter's daughter became Lady Panmuir, the unfortunate rejected mother was able to snub her peers in the end.[8]

This reflected status of women in India could be fragile. Isabella Fane acted as hostess when travelling in the company of her father, the Commander in Chief and while she did so, she carried all the prestige and pomp associated with that position. When returning to Calcutta with a mere aide-de-camp, however, there were: 'No official receptions, and hardly a nod from the ladies in up-country stations who had clamoured for introduction when she had passed their way before.'[9]

There was no occasion where precedence was more determinedly and exactly followed than dinner, be this a formal occasion or just a domestic gathering. Ladies could not wander into the dining room of their own accord but had to be led by hand, or 'handed', according to the strict protocol due to their rank; inevitably that of their consort. Their place at table followed the same stringent formality. Often a woman would be accompanied by two men who would then sit either side of her, reflecting the excess of men over women and, as Sarah Robinson says, this was 'often very fatiguing' although, intriguingly, she doesn't quite say why. She also adds:

> *Though it is polite, yet I believe everyone but the vain and coquettish would dispense with a good deal of it. It must astonish the natives much to see the wonderful civility and respect with which European dames and damsels are attended.*

Mary Doherty was quite surprised at the routine compared to England, commenting soon after her arrival at Madras, and when staying with the Ogilvys:

> *The mode of life in Madras was to me very fatiguing. Breakfast was ready soon after eight and from that time until past one the family sat in the breakfast room receiving morning visitors. The room was so dark and you could not see to read or work. If you went out to pay visits you first changed your dress putting on what you would wear at*

a public dejeuner in England. At about two came what they called Tiffin, the real dinner, after which the family separate and lay on the sofas [during the heat of the day] *till the carriages are ready at half past five o'clock...we then dressed for dinner, either at home or out at seven. These dinner parties were the most formal things imaginable generally about 30 or 40. When you arrived at the stranger's house two gentlemen came down the steps and hand you into the drawing-room. If at a general officer's, they were his aides-de-champs* [sic]; *if at a civilian's, the younger sons or brothers of the family. The ladies were dressed as for a ball, the gentlemen, if officers, in regimentals. At dinner the master or mistress sat opposite each other in the middle of the table with the fish and soup before them. The aides-de-champs at the head or foot with the joints of meat. The lady of highest rank was handed in by the master; the mistress of the house by the gentleman of highest rank, each succeeding lady by the highest gentleman present. Everybody in Madras is supposed to know the gradations. There is a book for the information of strangers for it is not like in England, as an Earl's wife or daughter has no rank but what she derives from her husband's situation in the company's service. The civilians rank first, then the company's officers and, lastly, the King's officers.*[10]

With such formality the opportunity for a social slip-up was significant. What we would laugh off today as a minor misunderstanding could then have laid a chill cloud over proceedings for the rest of the evening. When Isabella Fane was acting as hostess for her father, when he was Commander in Chief, India, she took this leading role at a large Calcutta dinner in the 1830s. By mistake she arranged for a certain lady to be accompanied into dinner by her father, the senior man present, only to realise that there were at least two other women who should have taken precedence. Inevitably, one of the senior ladies who had been overlooked was the sort who stood on her rights, and made sure the atmosphere was poisoned, to the great discomfiture of Isabella Fane's unfortunate first choice. Added to this, part of the rigid protocol was that no person should leave to go home until the senior lady present had made the first move. Isabella Fane found that her senior choice was confused as to whether she should take this step, or leave it to the true top dog. She, in turn, didn't budge, probably out of pique, and so the occasion proved unforeseeably long, and embarrassing.[11]

Such ritualistic inflexibility was a good opportunity for a snub. When Sir

Edward West was Chief Justice of the Supreme Court in Bombay he crossed swords with the then Governor, Mountstuart Elphinstone, on a variety of matters, one of which was Sir Edward's suspension of five barristers for alleged libel. As a consequence he found himself seated at dinner in a place well below his station on at least one occasion.[12] On another, the governor did not allot a lady for him to escort to dinner, and he found himself descending the stairs to the dining room alone, and having to wedge himself between two male friends. We might now laugh this off as an oversight but, unless Lucretia, Lady West, was unduly sensitive on her husband's behalf, the situation as recorded in her correspondence was taken as a serious insult.[13] An apology was firmly expected. According to Emma Roberts, that arbiter of Indian social practice, a lady who found herself 'handed' to dinner by a relative or, worse still, walking alone was said to be 'wrecked'. Whether this means stranded in the sense of a shipwreck, or that her social status was destroyed, is unclear, but probably the latter. However, she generously, and wisely, goes on to say: 'A mark of rudeness of this nature reflecting more discredit upon the persons who can be guilty of it, than upon those subjected to the affront.'[14] From all such rigid attitudes the concept of etiquette was gradually born, and polished to perfection in the Victorian era. Such strict formality was well known in French circles a good hundred years earlier.

Protocol, with a dogmatic inflexibility of this sort, seems curious to modern minds, even bewildering. However, it seems likely that it was a necessary adjunct to that stratification of society designed to clarify to the world who was the leader, and who were his deputies. In other words, who it was that held a deservedly special station in life reflecting his occupation, or responsibility, under the ultimate controlling authority – parliament and the king. This would have been particularly true in Indian British society, where position in life was a result of struggle and effectiveness, and the devil take the hindmost. The winner would reap the rewards, and with them an appropriate lifestyle, and it was just bad luck on the runners-up. There was not much deference to those with power and responsibility, except when absolutely obliged by this social structuring, much like the gradation of rank and uniforms in the armed forces. It made clear to all which of those persons were in charge, and in what order, and to whom due deference should be paid. This social orderliness was seen, in abstract terms, in many aspects of life in the Georgian and Regency periods, from the geometrical beauty of the neoclassical architecture, to the mathematical complexity, and yet purity, of baroque music. There was even an impressive orderliness of the military activities of the Army and Navy, to an extent that made them some of the best fighting forces in the world. In this age of enlightenment an organised framework for social behaviour, and a similar framework for its context, seemed to move forward hand-in-hand, creating gradual order out of chaos.

Dinner parties were frequent; certainly two or three a week in the larger establishments, or among those of greater status, and perhaps more at times. The modest household, such as that of a doctor or clergyman, might have eight to twelve people, but a Presidency Governor, Chief Justice, or Commander in Chief would have thirty to fifty. The relentless round of entertaining was an embedded structure in Georgian life, and the local European society tended to be invited in turn, especially if of some social standing.[15] Such dinners were *de rigeur*, and occurred despite possible disagreements, animosity and even confrontations with the hosts, and woe betide anyone who failed to reciprocate such an event in their turn, whether they felt inclined to or not. Occasionally an invitation would be refused on grounds of indisposition, or impending absence, but sometimes as a result of a more arcane social code. Sir Edward West received an invitation from the sixth Regiment and its colonel in Bombay, but declined as they had not previously called on him, and he had not therefore had a proper introduction. Such was the formality and rigidity of that society. The correct people had to be invited, at the correct frequency, and if someone had stepped overtly outside the correct formula for behaviour, they wouldn't be invited again. Sir Edward West's wife, Lucretia, had occasion to write to the Governor of Bombay, the scholarly and ageing bachelor Mountstuart Elphinstone, on the verge of retirement, to complain that she 'Had met several times at his house ladies of spotted reputation, and who are not visited by anyone. Of course I had a polite answer pretending ignorance of the subject.' Elphinstone later told her that his enquiries had confirmed that the two lady's characters were indeed so bad that they would not be invited again. Frustratingly, we are left to guess what they had done to incur such disapproval. Lucretia West was slightly unconvinced of his sincerity but seems to have primly regarded it as her duty, in her position, to avoid meeting such people again, or at all. She continues:

> *I am rejoiced that I did it, as one of the ladies, Mrs Hawkins, has had the* [self-] *assurance to come and call upon both Mrs Heber* [wife of the celebrated Bishop Heber] *and myself. I luckily called out not at home, and we shall not return the visit, but this is the consequence of her being invited by the Governor.*[16]

There seems little doubt that Elphinstone's apparent gaffe was another calculated attempt at snubbing her husband, the Chief Justice, she being the first lady of the Presidency because Elphinstone was unmarried. Probably today's rough equivalent would be seating someone of importance at the bottom of the table at a state dinner.

This rigidity of protocol was reflected, too, in the very Georgian and Regency practice of visiting, or calling, a necessary social practice of remarkable complexity. This was really an intricate means of achieving mutual introduction within British society, but particularly so in British India, and therefore of social networking on a very personal level. It was in essence a necessity of the era, there being no other way of easily cementing relationships within a loose structure of civil servants, merchants, the military, lawyers and others. It was the Georgian precursor of the telephone or, in today's world, email, Facebook or Twitter. However it was a great deal less instantaneous, and the time and energy committed to it was immense but, without it, a collection of foreign individuals in a strange country would have a good deal of difficulty in getting to know each other, or what was happening in their community.

Unlike in Britain, the Indian British custom was that the male representative of new arrivals would call on the already resident families.[17,18,19] Failure to do so caused great offence, and might mar all future relations in that local society. Following the primary visit, there would then be a return visit by both husband and wife to the home of the newcomer, but only if the newly arrived wife was considered socially acceptable. If the unfortunate lady had a slightly sullied reputation, or if she was Indian (later, even Eurasian), then this return visit would not take place, and the social future for that couple became rather clouded; clearly some pre-judgement here. In her early time in India, Elizabeth Gwillim appears to have enjoyed the visiting process, but it is clear from her later letters that she soon recognised it could be a demanding business. One might have had a list of visits numbering into the hundreds and, as homes tended to be scattered, a great deal of time was expended on the exercise.[20] On a random and unexceptional day, Lucretia West recorded seven received visits in the first part of the morning, and then having to cope with nine return visits before lunch.[21] It is no wonder that many people found themselves falling behind on the commitment. Her correspondence indicates that she had little good to say about most of her acquaintances, except a chosen few, and that consequently she was rather retiring in Bombay society. It isn't any wonder, therefore, that she found the whole business tedious, just as many others did.

'The returning of visits is a great bore as all the people I have yet (so far) seen are unpleasing and vulgar and wishing to be true ladies'.[22] Distant return visits could, amazingly, involve arriving for breakfast and staying until the time for the evening carriage drive, at about 5 pm. Many trips of this sort, and a woman's time would be heavily occupied.

The requirement to travel several miles during the day for this purpose could be an unattractive prospect, especially in May and June because of the intense heat that beat down on the carriage roof, gently roasting the occupants. In addition, there were swirling clouds of dust, and spine-shuddering jolts from the unmade rocky and rutted roads. Relief from the heat came with the onset of the monsoon in July, but with this also arrived sheeting tropical rains, flash floods and endless mud. There would also be the repetitive tedium of trailing over the same old tracks, visiting yet another newcomer, or responding to a visit already made to them. One probable consolation would have been the endlessly fascinating and colourful people seen in their villages and hamlets scattered on the way, and the rich unspoilt scenery of that time. Unlike the endless acres of cultivation today, there would have been great tracts of forest and undergrowth containing a range of trees and shrubs quite unknown to these foreign visitors. Some might have borne fruit, such as the mango or papaya, and others such as the stately banyan, and the esteemed and useful neem, would have appeared strangely alien. At the same time that Lucretia West lived in Bombay, there also lived Elizabeth Grant, a rather younger woman, whose father was a colleague of Lucretia's husband Sir Edward in the Supreme Court. To combat the inconvenience of the blazing sun, Sir John Grant had rather ingeniously designed a carriage whose open sides were shaded by venetian windows, and which had a double roof holding a gap between the outer leather one, and the inner one of cork. This provided useful, and much prized, insulation against the blazing sun, much like the tropical roof in the early Land Rovers.

The visiting ritual was a pleasurable opportunity for creative gossip, and also some splendidly sarcastic invective. As Lucretia West remarked in 1824:

[There are] *always morning visitors, and this is the very most gossiping place I ever met with; one cannot blow ones nose without it becoming a discussion whether one has done it properly or not.*[23]

Sarah, wife of Assistant-Surgeon James Robinson, says a few years later:

After breakfast I went out to pay two morning visits. The ladies I visited had no beauty of either person or manner, but each had a lovely child.

No real consolation there.[24] Elsewhere one reads:

Went in the palanquin and called on Mrs Jennings (a disagreeable effort of politeness) where I was well cross questioned.[25]

Not surprisingly, an excuse was often made not to see someone, by feigning illness for instance. This was quite a common practice that did not necessarily cause offence, probably because it was often genuine.[26]

Despite these instances, the practice of visiting nevertheless fulfilled a wholly useful process of social communication and bonding, and Elizabeth Grant remarked with some perception:

It is the most sociable country in the world, truly hospitable. Everybody is acquainted, every door is open, literally as well as figuratively, there is an ease, a welcome, a sort of family feel among these Colonists in a strange land that knits them altogether very pleasantly.[27]

A number of insights into social history can be derived from the correspondence and journals of pre-raj British women in India, although limited in quantity. These day-to-day observations of local society, and the men and women that formed it, reflected life in India generally, and were uncluttered by the cares and distractions of official duties to which a man might be subject. Much of it is anecdotal and, inevitably perhaps, superficial, but women would have had a different perspective on the events surrounding them. These accounts could be derived from personal experience in any of the three large Presidency towns, or a small military or civilian station up country, and from those people within it, and also from the constant ebb and flow of Indian British visitors. Some of the comment is adulatory, but much is critical, and both men and women of any rank come under the microscope.

In general, local society took its lead from the senior individuals present. These, in turn, would be the Governor, the Chief Justice and the Commander in Chief in the Presidency towns; in towns up country, the persons of greatest status might be senior military officers, the Resident, and perhaps his closest entourage. Women, as we know, mirrored the status of their husbands. The

Governors could be very different individuals; the sisters Elizabeth Gwillim and Mary Symonds in Madras wrote numerous letters home that survive, and they were contemporary with two Governors of Madras, both well-known names.

The first was Edward Clive, 1st Earl Powis, who was Governor from 1798 to 1803. He was, needless to say, the son of Robert Clive of Plassey fame. He must have been under some pressure to live up to historical expectations; no doubt a personal burden in the light of Robert Clive's already existing reputation for Machiavellian behaviour. This latter was with particular reference to the East India Company's relationship with the Bengal Princes, as well as his duplicity in ensuring personal financial gain, meanwhile considerably restricting the means of achieving the same by his colleagues, especially those that were younger, or more junior. Edward Clive nevertheless appears to have been a distinguished Governor, who earned the thanks of Parliament on his return to England. The sisters knew him well on the social circuit; indeed Elizabeth seems to have exchanged presents with him; he sending her 10yds 'of the finest flannel from his estate near Welshpool', and she sending him some garden flower seeds received from England. He was a keen and devoted gardener.[28,29] She particularly admired Lady Clive, commenting: 'It was a disappointment that Lady Clive and her two daughters had left this place, as they were also very free and agreeable.'[30] A year or so later she said farewell to Lord Clive, who sailed home on the *Castle Eden* in September 1803. She wrote to her mother the following month:

It is a most wonderful thing that he should, with his immense fortune, have chosen to stay so long from his wife and children, his native land & fine estates, filling a place of great emolument so much to be desired by many noblemen of smaller fortunes and fondness for public business. He was extremely good natured as a private gentleman but his whole time was given up to his garden and the [raising] of veal and beef leaving other matters to the care of a few people who contrive to hold him in a sort of thralldom [sic] and lead him to their purposes, worse people than many of them you cannot conceive. Lady Clive is said to have greatly desired his return. I imagine from what I hear on all hands that she must be a very clever woman, and could not but see with pain that he was losing that credit which the name of Clive ought to claim in India.

William Bentinck was the other Governor whom the Symonds sisters knew, in the early 1800s. He held that role from 1803 to 1807, leaving little mark on Madras because his term of office was overshadowed by the disturbing sepoy mutiny at Vellore, for which he was held partially responsible by the Court of Directors of the East India Company, and so recalled to England. There was little sign yet of the man who would become Governor General of India twenty years later, brimming with cost-cutting measures, and reformist zeal in matters of Indian education, and long-held rituals such as suttee.[31] In a sense he was the initiator, unwittingly perhaps, of attitudes that later found fruition in the detached, overweening behaviour of the post-Mutiny Raj. To Elizabeth Gwillim, however, he was a taciturn, restrained individual:

Our Governor lives very quietly and Lady Bentinck, his wife, is as plain in her dress and as simple in her manners as possible. On state occasions she wears a great number of jewels, and he has a fine service of plate [silver], but in other respects they seem to set an example of economy that is followed by all the settlement.

Perhaps his then economy was an early indicator of his later application of this quality when in power. No doubt every subsequent Governor General was encouraged to avoid the excesses of the Wellesley era.

It was a couple of years later that he contradicted her earlier impression of him, by challenging the power of the Supreme Court and so crossing swords with Sir Henry Gwillim.[32]

Although complimentary about those Madras governors that they knew, Elizabeth, and her sister Mary, were rather less so about Elizabeth's husband's colleagues, the other judges. The Chief Justice at that time was Sir Thomas Strange with whom they were on rather friendly terms at the outset. After all, he and Sir Henry had read law at Christ Church, Oxford, together. Gradually, however, the two developed a growing difference of opinion about the jurisdiction of the Madras Supreme Court over the rights and welfare of the Indian people and as a result their relationship became increasingly strained; a sanguine and urbane Londoner of great ambition versus a passionate Welshman, conscious of the rights of the underdog. When Sir Thomas later took ship to England, purportedly to fulfil a long-held plan to travel round the USA[33] she, and Mary, separately, wrote home with acid emphasis:

Sir Thomas Strange has taken his passage in this ship, he having some very urgent business to transact which requires his presence in

England. What his business is, he and his family keep a profound secret, but his sudden departure has put Madras into a general consternation.

Later she adds:

He had universally the character of being intriguing in spirit and utterly deceitful… . One thing was always apparent, that he was ambitious of grasping all the power and all the patronage belonging to the others… . Sir Ts father was, as you know, an engraver; a profession which nobody in high life falls into. However, he rose to great honours in it, and some wealth. At the same time there can be no pretence to family [ie social status].

This has the hallmarks of defensive pique, and thence sour snobbishness, born out of fears for her husband's position where she senses he is being outmanoeuvred by his immediate colleagues.[34] The sisters' collective view appears to have been that he had gone home 'to solicit for himself some higher employment', using the influence he might have with Lord Melville, Henry Dundas, President of the Board of Control of the East India Company, and a close friend of William Pitt, whose daughter had just married Sir Thomas Strange's brother, considerably raising the social profile of the Strange family. Their other gripe was that Sir Henry Gwillim had to cover the court work in Strange's absence, not helped by the chronic illness and absence of the third judge, Sir Benjamin Sullivan. The sisters' attitudes deteriorated in parallel with their growing disenchantment with Madras life. Mary writes:

Sir Thomas, having quitted his employment [in Madras] *most dishonourably, in hopes of regaining the wealth his brother had wasted, became the tool of a weak government whose paltry all-wicked vices he intended to forward by Lord Melville's interest.*

She continues a paragraph later:

He now seems to be running headlong into all the follies he can think of. He is going to be married to a girl of features ugly enough, God knows, but he being 52, she has persuaded him that his resistless [irresistible] *charms have won her heart, and she had fallen in love*

with him during a month she had been staying at his house, that he is
obliged to take compassion on her young heart and marry her.

This is spite, which one must remember was aimed at the man who was once a family friend. Caught in the crossfire is the young lady in question, a Miss Louisa Burroughs, daughter of Sir William Burroughs, a judge in Calcutta at the time, and no doubt a useful contact for Sir Thomas. Although one can assume Mary Symond's description arises from personal malice, albeit aimed primarily at Strange himself, it is pertinent to note that the Burroughs family had excited comment elsewhere in the correspondence of the time. William Hickey, in his characteristically brazen fashion, did not restrain himself in his memoirs.[35] 'On the 29th October that disagreeable and offensive coxcomb, Sir William Burroughs, arrived in Calcutta, being accompanied by his eldest daughter, as odious an animal as himself.' This latter lady was, in fact, the sister of the girl who had just married Sir Thomas Strange but, between the two of them, they had not made a big impression on Indian British society.[35]

The early reaction in the Symonds sisters' letters home, to the strangely curious range of people to be found in Madras at the beginning of the 1800s, was amazement and amusement. Later, they became tired of Madras society, and so became retiring as well, and their comments veered towards the peevish. Much of this arose from the increasing disapproval that Sir Henry Gwillim experienced from the Madras Governor, and his Council, and also from Sir Thomas Strange, about the rights of the Indian people under English law, as well as the deliverance of this law in respect of the activities of British society in India, in matters of litigation, taxation and trust fund administration.[36] These issues were enshrined in the Charter of Justice, brought from England to the Presidency towns, under which the law was supposed to operate fairly and beneficially to all. This Crown directive was at odds with the East India Company's own judicial network that was inclined towards an interest in Company matters only. Sir Thomas Strange took a rather treacherous line, in supporting Governor Bentinck's attempt to undermine the royally appointed Supreme Court in favour of Company courts, largely to further his own ambitions. It eventually became apparent that his journey to England had been to obtain an extension of office, to which end he had made it clear to those in London that the blame for the difficult relations between the Madras government and the Court lay with Sir Henry Gwillim. Consequently this unfortunate judge was recalled home in 1808, a scapegoat, and it isn't really surprising that the two sisters' feelings towards

Madras, and its people, had moved from excited curiosity to disenchantment. By the time he left India his wife Elizabeth was dead, having succumbed suddenly to some unknown illness, and was put to rest in a rather dour tomb, inscribed in Latin, in the nave of St Mary's Church, Fort St George. Possibly the stress of recent events had compromised her health, but it is more likely that there were hazards of a more prosaic nature in that climate.

In Georgian Britain, rank was the yardstick by which society operated. To a very large extent this was inherited, and thus one's life was defined at birth. It was only the exceptional person with great skill, or a large amount of acquired money, who could slide from a third class seat on the 'Flying Stagecoach' of life, to a first class one. Even then, a sidelong glance of disdain from the established upper class would keep such people in their place; parallel but somehow lesser. This was particularly so of the wealthy merchants who returned from India and tried to lever their way into society with ostentatious mansions, grand balls and other displays of wealth; not always well received. These were the nabobs, who were most apparent in the eighteenth century, and who bought their way into the Court of Directors of the East India Company to continue their influence in India, and their income, in absentia.

This bipolar culture was wholly different for the British in India. Here it was easily possible to jump up the class ladder if one had made enough money, and this was of course the reason why many went there in the first place. This was not just a matter of survival, because of a lack of opportunities at home, but an actual chance of self-improvement. In India there were unimaginable opportunities. As a merchant the move towards betterment was straightforward; for a civilian (civil servant) it was more a matter of gaining seniority by using influence at the Court of Directors at home, either with one of the old India hands, or a family member. With newfound wealth, stock, and thus position, could be purchased in the East India Company, giving a possibility of influence even in England beyond that already achieved in India. Elizabeth Gwillim, and sister Mary, saw signs of preferment everywhere. They refer to it independently in their letters. From Elizabeth in 1803:

In this place one's acquaintances consist of God knows who. There are some very fine folks who talk very magnificently, and hold their heads vastly high yet, those who have been in England and made a point of enquiring, tell such curious histories that you would be much surprised to hear them. Some of the great men have been shocking

115

*players and some have run away from their creditors and some, I
believe, have run away from something worse. Here have been
parsons who were never ordained, and some of the barristers came
out common soldiers, and these are the sort of people who give
themselves the greatest airs and puff most about their families. One
of the ladies who is at the head of society is the daughter of a tailor,
another who gives herself the greatest airs in the place came forth
from a gin shop and, I do assure you, their manners are not at all
superior to their former state.*[37]

Mary, in 1802, also comments on this daughter of the tailor in Charing Cross.
'She is rather pretty and at least twenty years younger than he is.' The
implication clearly being that a woman could advance herself socially, if she
was good-looking, and not too choosy about whom she married, as long as
he had the important prerequisites of money and position. In the same letter
she relates:

*Another of our acquaintances is a Mrs Chinery, who may be a relation
of your friend of that name for aught I know. I am told she is the
daughter of an innkeeper on the road near Stamford Bridge. She is,
however, one of the finest ladies in this place. They give splendid balls,
and it is observed of the lady that she wears the most expensive dresses
of any body and seldom appears twice in the same.*[38]

In that year the celebrated portrait painter George Chinnery had arrived in
Madras, but without his wife or children. He went on to paint the great and
the good of India, and later Macau, including at least two Governors General.
He had come to join his brother John who had been in Madras ten years
already, and it is possible Mary is referring to John's wife.

Elsewhere in her correspondence Mary refers, with further asperity, to the
background of some of the other great ladies of Madras, two being the
daughters of a hosier in London's Lombard Street. Also:

*Here are five sisters, all well married, in the eyes of the world at least,
daughters of an inferior Customs House officer who lives on Tower
Hill. Two more great ladies are the daughters of an innkeeper at
Hounslow; two more, daughters of a slop shop at Portsmouth.*[39]

(A slop shop was where cheap ready-made clothing was sold. The term slops

116

is still used for clothing issued in the Royal Navy). Judging by the rise to social eminence of these women, it is clear that India was the land of opportunity for women as well as men. It is also clear that snobbery ever prevailed in such a stratified society.

At about the same distance as from London to the Shetland Isles, lay another social microcosm of the British in India. Bombay was 800 miles away on the west coast, across territory that was then partially hostile and virtually impassable. It was generally visited by a two-week sea trip, this being by far the quickest and most comfortable means of getting there. It avoided the steep and rocky mountains of the Eastern, and then the Western, ghats with nothing more than local tracks that were rock strewn, seriously uneven and, in the wet season, pitted with deep muddy ruts. Progress was at a walking pace on horseback, bullock cart or palanquin. Equally far away was Calcutta, the senior Presidency town situated to the north in Bengal, and a good 1,000 miles distant. Although the British were represented in intervening cities such as Hyderabad, Bangalore and Indore, these were mainly military personnel, or senior civil servants, such as the Resident and his staff. British women were mostly to be found in the three Presidency towns, although there were numerous exceptions such as the wives of army officers, regional judges, residents and up-country growers and merchants, such as indigo planters.

In Bombay Lucretia West, wife of Sir Edward West, the first Chief Justice of the Supreme Court there, kept a detailed journal of the voyage out, and the years after their arrival in early 1823. In many ways she faced the same problems in Bombay that the Symonds sisters had in Madras, in that there was smouldering resentment of the implicit power of the crown-appointed Supreme Court over the autonomy of the East India Company, its regional civil courts and the civil Governor, in their jurisdiction respecting local and Indian affairs, and the traditional role of Hindu law. Mountstuart Elphinstone in Bombay, and his successor John Malcolm, were determined to suppress the power and existence of the Supreme Court and, in Elphinstone's case, bring the aspirations of Sir Edward West to heel. This situation was, therefore, much the same as that in Madras had been a few years earlier, between its Governor, William Bentinck, and Sir Henry Gwillim; except that the latter had an enemy within, in the shape of his colleague, the Chief Justice Sir Thomas Strange.

Sir Edmund Stanley had a similar experience, at a similar time, while Recorder in Prince of Wales Island (Penang), with the then Governor there, William Phillips, and his council.[40] As already indicated, the motive of these judges, and the reason they and the Supreme Courts were in existence, was to operate a judicial system under the terms of a Royal Charter of Justice, which should be dignified, honest, fair and equitably inclusive of the Indian people, as well as objectively balanced. It was felt essential to root out corruption, as well as extortionate fees and neglect, among even the barristers. The East India Company senior civil administration, especially the Governors, resented this intrusion upon their position, and what they perceived to be a migration of legal influence away from the European community. There was a fear that it would be increasingly available to Indian society, which could then possibly use it to undermine governmental power.[41] As a consequence, West, like Gwillim, was kept at arm's length by the central components of the Bombay British, and his involvement socially was the minimum required by protocol as the second most senior person in the Presidency. Although deeply disappointing professionally, this suited both he and his wife personally, neither being well disposed towards the way of life in Bombay.

Lucretia, unusually, seems to have enjoyed the voyage out more than her existence subsequently. At first there was some pleasure to be had in the newness of it all:

> *The heat very great but we all occupy ourselves & feel well & we do not mind it, sleeping on the Esplanade (in a borrowed bungalow) is the greatest delight, drinking tea on the beach & lounging about till bed time, usually a 1/4 before nine o'clock.*[42]

She settled into a reticent and antisocial pattern surprisingly early in her time in India, which became gradually worse as the social tensions increased, much as was the experience of the Symonds sisters in Madras.[43] She became resentful of the pressure from frequent visitors, and the constant need to attend dinner parties and theatre productions, many of which she avoided. Although she was obliged to hold large dinner parties for thirty to forty guests, these were endured with reluctance, no sense of pleasure, and some bitterness at the cost. As she said at the time: 'We do not feel inclined for gaiety.' With growing disenchantment, she again writes in the same letter, referring to the composition of another party:

> *sad vulgar women, but there are very few lady-like ones to be found, the men are also moderate, the high military are certainly the best...*
> *A party of 32 at dinner, dull as I think they all are here.*

118

Although she had a handful of close friends, her life was really woven around her husband and his work. His judicial role was time consuming, and physically exhausting; sitting all day, wearing full judge's robes, in a very hot and crowded courtroom cooled only by punkahs. In addition to this, while in India he had written a very well received, and globally applicable, work on political economy.[44] Many of Lucretia West's friends in Bombay had died, or returned home, leaving her feeling even more isolated. Eventually, after five years in India, she watched her beloved husband die after just a week's illness, leaving her desolate and distraught:

> *The last week I have seemed so lost, and my nerves so shattered I have scarcely the power to do anything, and seem as if I must close my eyes to the future.*[45]

Sadly, of a future there was none, and her own eyes were soon closed forever. Throughout her husband's illness there is no mention in her letters of the fact that she was pregnant. Within three weeks of her husband's death she too died, during childbirth, leaving only their 2-year-old daughter, Fanny Anna, to mourn them all.

Lucretia was not alone in her reaction to Bombay Society. Maria Graham (later Lady Maria Callcott, then wife of the well-known Victorian landscape artist Sir Augustus Callcott) was the wife of a young Lieutenant RN whom she had met on the voyage to India in the company of her father, he having been appointed to the Commission of the Navy in Bombay. She became a popular travel writer and her first book, *Journal of a Residence in India* (1812), gives an account of her stay in India from 1809–11, just ten years or so before the arrival of the Wests. Early in this she observes:

> *I shall endeavour to describe our colonists. On our arrival we dined with the Governor and found almost all the English of the settlement invited to meet us. There were a good many very pretty and very well-dressed women, a few ancient belles, and at least three men for every woman. I found our fair companions, like the ladies of all the country towns I know, under-bred and overdressed and, with the exception of one or two, very ignorant and very grossière. The parties in Bombay are the most dull and uncomfortable meetings one can imagine. Forty or fifty persons assemble at seven o'clock, and stare at one another till dinner is announced, when the ladies are handed to table according to the*

119

*strictest rules of precedency, by a gentleman of rank corresponding
to their own.*[46]

Other women in Bombay, however, were rather dazzled by the people and
events of this Presidency town. Maria Sykes, wife of Captain John Sykes,
was there at the same time as Maria Graham (Callcott), and not too far
removed in rank. She too attended a grand evening at the Governor's house
in Parel in 1810, one of the original islands of Bombay and still in existence
as a district of Mumbai, the old Governor's house now being a medical
research institute. She was impressed by the 'delightful gardens' and the
height of the six fountains: 'One cannot imagine the beauty of falling water
in this climate.' She met the Governor, who was a 'Short, thin old man,
stooping very much, wearing a very rusty-looking coat, his hair reaching to
his shoulders, and came straight down; he has a small squeaking voice; I
never saw such an object. He is above seventy – he looks a hundred.'[47]

Although one might not think it from this comment, she was inclined to
sycophancy, being much impressed by a ball given in honour of Lady
Malcolm, the wife of Sir John Malcolm, a late ambassador to the Court of
Persia, and future Governor of Bombay. She was especially impressed by the
cost – 'near £10,000.' She revelled in the company of the great and the good;
well-known Indian British names such as Mountstuart Elphinstone, then
resident in Poona (before he became Governor of Bombay), Sir James
Mackintosh and Sir John Malcolm, Bombay's successor to Elphinstone.
There was nothing she enjoyed more than engineering a conversation with
some such worthy. Of Elphinstone she said: 'I would say his character was
perfect, for no person ever discovered that he had a fault.' And elsewhere she
wrote: 'it was said of Mountstuart Elphinstone that, had he been Governor
General, there would have been no Indian Mutiny.'[48] As the latter event was
in 1857, and over forty years later, one must suppose that this was a later
addition to her journal; her admiration undimmed, and doubtless also her
regret that Elphinstone had turned down the Governor Generalship. Quite
clearly she would not have had a great supporter in Lucretia West on her
overall assessment of the man.

Being the wife of a soldier, she was as conscious as her peers of the
manner in which civilians (civil servants) regarded themselves as superior
to the military. On one occasion she wrote to Mountstuart Elphinstone, in
Poona, to ask for the loan of an elephant, saying that she wished for once to
look down on the wife of a Bombay civilian. Her request was granted, with
the added apology that the elephant had not been a few inches higher.[49]

SOCIETY AND PROPRIETY

It was perhaps inevitable that many women, in the absence of other regular diversion, would jot notes in their journals or letters about the people whom they met or entertained. Today we might call this gossip, and inevitably opinions about a person or event could vary, depending on the source. The same Mary Sykes who had adulated Bombay society was very taken with Lady Hood (1785-1862), wife of Sir Samuel Hood and daughter of Baron Seaforth. This could not have been the more famous Viscount Hood, Admiral of great fame, but a rear-admiral cousin whose last employment was on the East Indies Station, and who died in Madras in 1814. According to her, Lady Hood:

> Would have shone pre-eminently in any country as a person of most accomplished mind and charming manners; she understood and conversed in several languages; she had travelled a great deal in various countries of Europe, and had profited much by all she had seen and observed.

Two years later, in 1814, Lady Hood appears in the journal of the less star struck Sara Robinson, wife of assistant surgeon James Robinson of the Bengal Army, who lived in Secrole, the military cantonment adjacent to Benares. It is unlikely this could have been another Lady Hood and, although her abilities were well-recognised, she nevertheless became here the source of some amusement, related mainly to her size. 'Lady Hood amazed us by her masculine manner and singular appearance; she was not young or fair, but seems well-informed.' She went on: 'Lady Hood was so fashionable that it made me uncomfortable. She has something not unpleasant in her originality.'[50] Sara Robinson's journal, like those of many of her kind at that time, is studded with verse of a typically florid Georgian style, gushing with hyperbole, and trying to emulate the style of Scott or Byron, writers much admired by women of the era. She inflicted this verse on anyone who was willing to listen – or even if they were not, but were within range. Lady Hood became a subject of this verse but, sadly, history doesn't record whether she was aware of the fact. She was observed to be a rather large lady, exciting Sara and her friends to a brief descriptive flourish:

> Send us the Lady of the Lake to see.
> What's there about this fair obesity.
> All nature might be made a simile,
> To body forth her huge enormity.[51]

Despite this malicious wit, she was more than happy to receive Lady Hood's compliments on the arrangement and decoration of her drawing room. Later in Sara's journal, which was written in chapters to be sent home for her sister to read, she describes an incident emphasising the poor woman's bulk. This underlines both her inclination towards derisive gossip, and a desire to express it in writing, in someone with more time on their hands than desirable:

Did I tell you of poor Lady Hoods mishaps? During that night of storm and darkness (on her way home after dinner) the bearers fell twelve times with her palanquin, and one came howling to James [the surgeon husband] *with his shoulder dislocated. Probably her ladyship had caught hold of him in one of her overthrows, and her weight was no trifle!*

One can imagine only too easily the unpleasantness suffered by the unfortunate woman, or indeed her bearers, falling repeatedly into wet glutinous mud on a pitch-black night, from a height of several feet. Sarah continues on her caustic way through her writings, but within them, and within others, lies a defining fact about the social existence of women in the late eighteenth and early nineteenth century:

Mr Yeld left us on the seventh to go down and meet his wife and the ladies I before mentioned, and they all arrived on the 10th. The damsel is wonderfully deficient in personal attraction, but seems quiet and unpretending. The widow is plain in person and face, but looks really the silent picture of melancholy and as if she had vowed never more to smile. She is I believe in a very pitiable situation. A widow in India must be so, I think in many respects, for even the natives will if possible show her how happy they are to show disrespect to a woman who has lost her natural protector.

This fact is the enforced, and complete, dependence of women on this natural protector, which was to an extent that could not help but expunge most independent originality of opinion, so tending to make some women's commentary on their world nothing more than a superficial, cynical disdain for other women, and many of the men, within it. Their education was so restricted, and their life outside the domestic hub so narrow, that most would have been unable to comment in any depth on matters of a political, economic or military nature, and they were more or less confined by circumstance, and by repression, to discussion on personal minutiae, which included each other. Eliza Draper (nee Sclater) wrote on this subject, as early as 1769, to Thomas Sclater in England, a much cherished cousin, and her chief correspondent:

As to the women, they are in general a set of ignoramuses, or at best pretty triflers, and I do not covet their society much from my dislike of hearing the subjects of scandal and dress perpetually canvassed, and such are the only topics that enliven a female assembly in India ... India, my dear cousin, is I believe the very last country that an agreeable woman should expect to live uncensured in[52]

An occasional, but heartfelt, comment one comes across in the women's correspondence of pre-Victorian days, is a resentment of what they took to be Scottish preferment in the appointment of positions in the Honourable East India Company. There is no doubt that there were very large numbers of Scots coming to India from the mid-eighteenth century onwards. In 1707 the Union of Scotland and England gave the landed families of Scotland access to the East India Company, and this proved to be a godsend to the impoverished second, and later, sons of the well-educated and able Scottish gentry. They emigrated in droves as teachers, merchants, missionaries, tea and indigo planters, and soldiers. By 1785, almost half of the company's writers in Bengal and Madras were Scots.[53]

The high calibre medical schools of Scotland provided a large percentage of Company medical officers throughout India, both military and civilian. The very successful Scottish and Westminster politician Henry Dundas (1742 to 1811; later 1st Viscount Melville) became the first President of the Board of Control following Pitt's India Act of 1784. Dundas had always been interested in India, although his family didn't make a huge success there; three of his brothers went out, two of whom died. He was instrumental in ensuring that Scottish aspirants were given opportunities to go and, by the late 1700s, sixty per cent of the free merchants' residence permits issued by the East India Company, were to Scots. By 1813 there were thirty-eight prominent private merchants houses in Calcutta, of which fourteen were dominated by Scots.[54] There were similarly high percentages of Scots among the military, largely explained by the high preponderance of Scottish regiments in India. Of the Royal regiments (as opposed to Company ones), seven of the fourteen were Scottish in the latter part of the eighteenth century. All these figures become even more impressive when one recognises that

Scotland had about ten per cent of the population of the British Isles at this time.

These partialities offended the supposedly unprejudiced scruples of those non-Scottish ladies who commented. They were certainly meeting large numbers of Scots in their daily lives, although it is less clear that there were so many in positions of great importance. From the time of Warren Hastings's appointment as the first Governor General of all India in 1773, as opposed to just Governor of Bengal, there were in total fifteen holders of this title up to the time of the Great Uprising in 1857. Only three of these were Scots. There were slightly more in the provincial Presidencies; about six of the twenty-three Governors of Madras are identifiable as Scottish over the same period, but rather more in Bombay: nine of twenty-four, or almost forty per cent. These are still quite high figures in the context of the low Scottish population relative to all Britain. In both Madras and Bombay they predominated between 1815–40, which was about the time these women were recording their observations, and a good five or more years after Dundas's death. It is probable that their reactions were often just an expression of personal prejudice, relating to the unsuccessful appointment of a disappointed husband or brother. When referring to a Dundas brother, and other Scotsmen, being appointed to Prince of Wales Island (Penang), Elizabeth Gwillim commented: 'The whole is to be composed of Scotch. I really do wonder how such a thing could be borne by the English. It is a complete Scotch job, as I hear it was called.'[55] She remarks elsewhere, however, that: 'There are good members of every country, and among the Scotch highly commendable and virtuous persons but, they being so together, and have so much the command of this country, and are so numerous here, that an Englishman has no chance.'[56] Sarah Robinson in Benares states, with her usual tendency to social hyperbole: 'I have told you of the immense number of Scotchmen in India. They are in proportion of 99 in 100 to the English.'[57] Many hundreds of miles away in Bombay even the urbane, if taciturn, Lucretia West was moved to write: 'Sir Charles and Lady Chambers came yesterday [a judge colleague of her husband's]. He is a plain man and I am sorry to say connected with all the Scotch as his wife was never out of Scotland till she married.'[58] Four years later her husband welcomed another Scottish judge, Sir John Grant, as a new colleague. At the opposite corner of the country, in Calcutta, the writer of *Scenes and Characteristics of Hindustan with Sketches of Anglo-Indian Society*, Emma Roberts, cast a gentle sideswipe at Scottish religiosity in writing:

Sir Elijah and Lady Impey and family surrounded by their staff; Johann Zoffany *c.* 1784. Sir Elijah looks on with indulgent cheerfulness while his wife gazes directly at the artist with an expression of resigned weariness. (Thyssen-Bornemisza Collection)

The *General Harris,* a typical East Indiaman perhaps somewhere in the Dover Straits. (Private Collection)

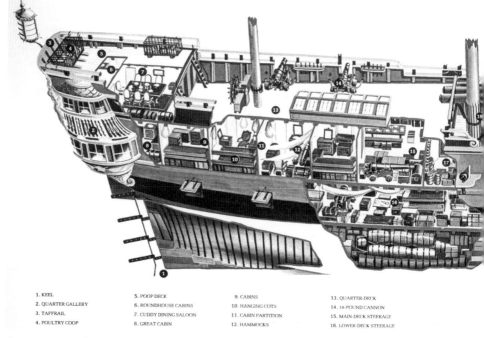

1. KEEL	5. POOP DECK	9. CABINS	13. QUARTER-DECK
2. QUARTER GALLERY	6. ROUNDHOUSE CABINS	10. HANGING COTS	14. 18-POUND CANNON
3. TAFFRAIL	7. CUDDY DINING SALOON	11. CABIN PARTITION	15. MAIN-DECK STEERAGE
4. POULTRY COOP	8. GREAT CABIN	12. HAMMOCKS	16. LOWER-DECK STEERAGE

A cutaway plan of an East Indiaman showing the limited accommodation for passengers below the poop deck. (Courtesy of John Batchelor)

An Interesting scene, on board an East-Indiaman, showing the Effects of a heavy Lurch, -after dinner. —

A Cruikshank cartoon of dinner aboard an East Indiaman in an immoderate sea. The likelihood is that most people would absent themselves from the table during heavy weather. Also, the space allocated for dining covered only half the width of the ship and was sometimes in two sittings. (Library of Congress)

An amusing illustration of the method by which passengers and crew came ashore from ships anchored well offshore at Madras. See p. 40–1. (Author's Collection)

Esplanade Row & Government House. The resplendent view of Calcutta that would have been first seen by newly arrived voyagers. This must surely have given them confidence and reminded them of home. William Wood, early 1800s. (Author's Collection)

Another view of the riverside esplanade in Calcutta. (Author's Collection)

Loll Bazaar, Calcutta. James Baillie Fraser 1826. More 'downtown' Calcutta in 1826. This view is interesting because of its depiction of various forms of transport, including several palanquins, a tonjon, a buggy and a hackery. See p. 41–2. (Author's Collection)

The style of an upmarket private country house in the late 1700s and early 1800s. (Author's Collection)

A Garden House in Madras today, with little garden left. One of the very few such houses remaining. (Author's Collection)

Colonial architecture of the peri-1800 period that remains today and is well preserved. (Author's Collection)

Colonial architecture of the same period in danger of further deterioration and a slide into nonexistence. These are barrack blocks from Fort St George in Madras. (Author's Collection)

Indian British domesticity; a rather formal view of breakfast. (Author's Collection)

Indian British domesticity; a lady being attended to by her maid, among other servants. (Author's Collection)

Women's attire showing some concession to Indian fabrics, in the earlier years (1810). A dress made from a Kashmiri shawl. (Mary Evans Picture Library)

A Dhobee or Washerman

Other familiar household servants: the dhobee, or washerman. (Author's Collection)

A Syce or Groom.

Other familiar household servants: the syce, or horse groom. (Author's Collection)

Other familiar household servants: the dharzee, or tailor. (Mary Evans Picture Library)

The quadrille was an inevitable and frequent sight at balls. For many, the intricacies were complex and required practice, as here, in Cruikshank's depiction of lantern-jawed ladies and balletic young men going through their paces. (Author's Collection)

Mount St Thomas, Madras, in 1804, after James Hunter. This view coincides with the time that Elizabeth Gwillim and her family lived there. It is particularly interesting because of its depiction of an all-black family in western dress, and especially of the trio of a white male, black partner and mixed-race child (in the right foreground). (Author's Collection)

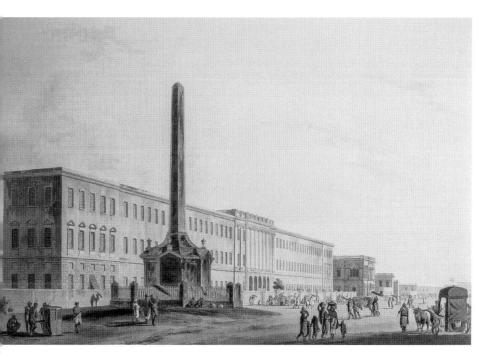

The *Writers' Building Calcutta* by Thomas Daniell, 1798. This is where the teenage writers from Britain worked, and were housed, hoping eventually for advancement and riches. (Author's Collection)

The Writers' Building today. (Author's Collection)

An Indigo Factory. William Simpson 1863. Where many a young woman found herself alone, deep in the up-country *mofussil,* except for husband or brother. (Author's Collection)

A watercolour of Indian birds, here a Purple Sunbird, painted from life in Madras by Elizabeth Gwillim, between 1801 and her death in 1807. (Courtesy of the Curator of Manuscripts, Rare Books and Special Collections, McGill University Library, Montreal, Canada)

A watercolour of Indian birds, here a Red Bulbul, painted from life in Madras by Elizabeth Gwillim, between 1801 and her death in 1807. (Courtesy of the Curator of Manuscripts, Rare Books and Special Collections, McGill University Library, Montreal, Canada)

A watercolour of Indian birds, here a Jacana, painted from life in Madras by Elizabeth Gwillim, between 1801 and her death in 1807. (Courtesy of the Curator of Manuscripts, Rare Books and Special Collections, McGill University Library, Montreal, Canada)

A watercolour of Indian birds, here a Pondicherry Vulture, painted from life in Madras by Elizabeth Gwillim, between 1801 and her death in 1807. (Courtesy of the Curator of Manuscripts, Rare Books and Special Collections, McGill University Library, Montreal, Canada)

South Park Street cemetery, the famous British burial ground in Calcutta, which effectively operated until about 1850. (Author's Collection)

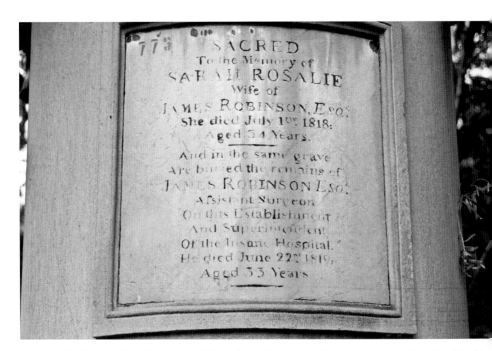

The tomb, in South Park Street, of Sarah Robinson and her surgeon husband, who died a year apart in their thirties. Her letters are frequently referred to in the text. (Author's Collection)

SOCIETY AND PROPRIETY

*The Cathedral and the Scotch Church are the two principal places of
Protestant religious worship: the latter is the handsomer edifice of the
two but, strange to say, notwithstanding the preponderance of the sons
and daughters of Caledonia in the European population of Calcutta,
it is very thinly attended, while the Cathedral is always full to
overflowing.*[59]

Another victim of national criticism was Holland. The Dutch had been in the
East Indies for as long as the British, but undoubtedly more successfully in
the seventeenth century, and certainly more forcibly, having better armed
ships and men, and an encouragement to use them in their quests. British
traders, on the other hand, were at that time only supposed to use force as a
defensive measure under the terms of their charter. The Dutch only ever had
a toehold in India, having favoured the Spice Islands, such as the Moluccas
and the Banda Islands, lying further east in what is now Indonesia. From here
they dominated oriental trade throughout the 1600s and the early 1700s. The
British and the Dutch crossed paths, and also swords, over almost 200 years,
until Dutch power in the East waned in the eighteenth century with increasing
decadence, and even corruption, in their eastern colonies. This may have been
largely because of an overstretched line of command all the way from
Holland, without the advantage of effective absolute power and control
locally, one of the great advantages for the British in having a Governor
General in a single contained land mass, as the British had in India. There
was, in consequence, too much power in the hands of regional officers, who
ruled unrestrained and became tempted to enrich themselves at considerable
cost to the VOC (Dutch East India Company), which eventually collapsed,
bankrupt, at the end of the eighteenth century. In these later years Dutch
people, as individuals, were often friends with the Indian British. A number
of these men had Dutch wives: 'Col Mackenzie of the Madras engineers; his
wife was a Dutch lady who scarcely speaks English.'[60]

As a people they were not always seen in a favourable light by the British;
certainly not in some of the women's correspondence. Elizabeth Gwillim's
comments are a particularly censorious example, as when commenting on
the development of Prince of Wales Island, and elsewhere 'further east':

*The Dutch settlers are such a depraved, cruel, set that the natives
would everywhere receive us with joy. The present race of Dutch on
the eastern islands happily join the rude manners of two or three
centuries back; the licentiousness of the East and the cruelty of slave*

125

drivers. They are a disgrace to humanity, and the women are neither more chaste nor less cruel than the men.

In another letter she says: 'I am told that the Dutch women in their settlements exceed even the Moor[ish] women in cruelty.'[61] Something had certainly excited her acrimony. Although she may have heard rumours spread by gossip, there was a general impression among the British that Dutch occupation was oppressive, with little regard to the welfare of native peoples, and with continuing torture and slavery well into the second half of the nineteenth century. Lord Minto, who was Governor-General of India from 1807–13, had something to say about Dutch women, arising from his observations of them in what had been Dutch-controlled Java, following the British conquest of that island in 1811. This annexation had resulted from fears that it might become a French base in the East during continuing French control of Holland from 1795, under Napoleon's brother, Louis Bonaparte, especially when war was resumed between England and France. To retain other seized Dutch East Indies territories from earlier years had seemed unnecessary at the Treaty of Amiens in 1802, and they were handed back to Holland. Napoleon rose again both before, and again after Trafalgar, and with the resurgence of a French threat in the East once more, so Britain became nervous of its interests there. Lord Minto spent some time in Java after the invasion, having masterminded this in company with Stamford Raffles, and continued to write frequently and lengthily to his wife at home in Scotland. In one of these letters he noted:

The chaperons and older Dutch ladies are a class not yet described in Europe. The principal mark to know them is by their immense size. The whole colonial sex runs naturally to fat, partly from over-feeding – partly from total want of exercise. The morning air is the grand pursuit of the English Orientalists; the Dutch of both sexes have a horror for it, and prefer their beds. In the rest of the day nobody can go out; and in the evening they think a drive in a carriage too great an effort. They pass their time as follows. There is a canal opposite to every door on the other side of the road. Each house has a little projecting gallery supported by posts in the canal. The lower part of this, that is to say, from the level of the road down into the water, is made in some small degree private, by upright bars at a little distance from each other, and with this bath the road communicates by wooden steps. Here the lady of the house, her relatives, and female slaves, lave

126

their charms, and here you may behold the handmaids of Diana sporting on and under the wave in sight of all passing Actaeons. This is the morning scene. They have chairs brought out in the gallery above, and sit with their beaux in conversation and repose. Suppose an immense woman sitting behind a stall with roasted apples, and we have an old Dutch lady of the highest rank and fashion. Her upper garment is a loose coarse white cotton jacket fastened nowhere, but worn with the graceful negligence of a Scottish lass, an equally coarse petticoat, and the coarsest stockings, terminating in wide thick-soled shoes; but by standing behind her you find out her nobility, for at the back of the head a little circle of hair is gathered into a small crown, and on this are deposited diamonds, rubies, and precious stones often of very great value. It is well with this if they can speak even Dutch, many know no language but Malay.[62]

While under British control the island was governed by Raffles, who strove to reform the monopolistic mercantile trading system of the Dutch for one that was of more benefit to the Javanese population, while simultaneously providing an income stream for government through taxation. Although the principle was commendable, the outcome was not successful in the eyes of the Company. He also abolished slavery, and released all those he could, the slave trade having been abolished in England in 1807, although not actually existing slavery. That came twenty-five years later. Raffles and the British developed a good working relationship with many of the Dutch but, after only four and a half years, and the end of the French wars at the Battle of Waterloo, the Directors of the East India Company, and the Board of Control in London, could see no point in holding on to what had proved to be a rather unprofitable territory. It was returned to the Dutch by Treaty, along with Malacca, although not that remote town of Bencoolen in Sumatra. This is where the unfortunate Raffles found himself posted at the same time. The Dutch returned to Java in gloating triumph, according to Wurtzburg, and were not overwhelmingly received by the Javanese, who had rather appreciated the more liberal way of conducting business under the British.[63] In the hurly-burly of Anglo-Dutch politics there was much to-ing and fro-ing of territory, but the growing concord between the two countries was marked by this gradual return towards the starting point. The main exceptions in the rather later Anglo-Dutch Treaty of 1824 were that Malacca was returned again to the British, and Bencoolen to the Dutch. This was not a bad exchange; there must have been many Britons glad to see the last of Bencoolen, with its reputation as a hostile, disease-ridden backwater.[64]

The other nation that was well represented in the East was France, which had always coveted a greater presence and control in India and was, in fact, close to permanently overwhelming the British on at least two occasions. One might have expected more remarks about French individuals in the correspondence of Indian British women but it is surprisingly absent. This is probably because they were rarely likely to have met any French, as the two nations were at war for much of the latter part of the eighteenth century, and the early nineteenth. Political comment was not really the domain of the British female correspondent. There is mention in their letters of English ships being taken by French privateers interspersed between important items about 'jam pots losing their tops' and 'two grand balls that week'.[65] That the ship *Admiral Aplin* had also been taken by the French was definitely noted and in particular that: 'By an unusual act of kindness the private letters were given up to Captain Rogers who arrived in Bengal about a fortnight ago from whence he brought them to Madras'.[66]

More than a year later, having doubtless already regretted her earlier compliment to the French about the return of their letters, the writer noted with some indignation that some of the personal and political correspondence from the *Aplin* had been copied by them, before it was returned to the British, and was later published in French newspapers. The embarrassment of having their personal comments aired in the enemy's press was considerable. Such actions were calculated propaganda moves, and each country studied the other's newspapers closely. Mary Symonds noted a little later, in 1804, that: 'Our troops have completely succeeded in driving all the French out of Maratha country which is a great thing for us, as they are a mischievous deceitful set.'[67] That was all she said: thus was a proud nation felled by a single sentence.

In their letters, further concerns were expressed about the vulnerability to the predations of the French fleet of British ships trading in India and China, but within a few years this powerful fleet was rendered toothless by the loss of its base, Mauritius, in 1811.

After Waterloo, and with the cessation of hostilities, the invasion of India by the French was aimed more at women's purses than men's territories. Shops selling French goods started to open, exciting interest in fashion-conscious minds. Lucretia West in Bombay in 1824 recorded: 'I went with Mrs Baker to a French shop which is just opened; she bought, but I never do useless things.'[68] And again, later the same year: 'I have been with Mrs Baker to the French shop and suffered more from the heat than I can express and was not tempted to waste any money in useless ornaments.' These are typical comments from her, and again reflect her tendency to primness and social reticence. Within three years however, she had succumbed to its temptations, notably after the birth of her second child. 'In the evening Miss Webb and I drove to the French shop to look for some toys for baby.'

After the Anglo-French wars it is surprising how quickly any hostility, or even animosity, to France settled, especially in the East. Lucretia West soon noted various occasions when French ships anchored in Bombay harbour; sometimes bringing newspapers and post, and sometimes just news. Nevertheless it was exceptional to actually meet a Frenchman, and certainly no women.

Much of the chatter and small-talk about acquaintances in all this correspondence tended to be deprecatory, as if it were a way of letting out feelings that were repressed in an ordinary social context. There was one section of the community, however, which rarely came in for criticism, and which was generally described with admiration. This consisted of the young men: officers, civil servants and others, with whom they came into contact through their husbands, brothers or friends, and for whom they held a maternal, or sisterly, concern. This was based on the constant risk of disease, or from injury or death in battle, or from worries incurred by a fondness for the bottle – or for local women – than was desirable, and even from concern as to whether or not they would make the grade in their chosen careers, or take pride in a job well done. These were natural maternal concerns among the older women; the younger ones would be dipping a toe in the hot spring of matrimonial exploration. A married woman might feel this responsibility towards a young man as a consequence of his lodging with the family, following his arrival in India after an introduction from friend or family. In Elizabeth Gwillim's house we have already heard about Richard Clarke, who was the son of a close family friend, and who worked as a clerk in the Supreme Court where her husband sat. Elizabeth, being childless, half regarded Richard as a surrogate son. Her unmarried sister, Mary, became a particular friend of his, and they would go to dances together, although as she commented: 'To be sure Richard has a little lead in his heels and we can't often persuade him to dance, but he is very fond of going amongst mirth of that sort and is a great beau at handling the ladies.'[69] The two of them would go out walking, 'almost every evening; sometimes on the beach', but walking in the soft deep sand she thought too much effort in the heat and, inevitably, inappropriate footwear. For quite some time they had a riotous social life, but in due course we know that Mary lost interest in this, following the alienation of the Gwillim family from Madras society. Richard grew increasingly fond of Mary, but she was quite a lot older than him and eventually he had to give way, disappointed but always chivalrous, to an older man: the captain of their eventual homebound ship. Richard too was on that ship and, over the months of their journey, had to bear with fortitude the discomfort of witnessing the blossoming romance.

William Biss was another young man who lived with the Gwillim family on and off for two or more years, and on whom they doted. He was a 20-year-old army cadet, introduced from their home town of Hereford, and who became a good friend of Richard Clarke. The two sisters grew rather fond of him, especially the unmarried Mary, no doubt to Richard's irritation. About William Biss she said: 'To be sure he is a darling, so mild, so modest, a thousand times too good for this country. I own I am half in love with him.'[70]

He spent quite a lot of his time with the family in Madras, having been selected to join a specialist group of military surveyors and map makers. He proved to be: 'Such an admirer of the ladies that we call him beauty-hunting Biss. He is such a beau, and languishes at the ladies and sighs like a Romeo. He is certainly a very pretty young man.' One can almost see the smile of indulgent pleasure from the older woman at the 'beloved' younger man's boyish playfulness. Notwithstanding his levity in company, he appears to have been very effective and hard working in his career.

From time to time there might be several young men about the place, all of them viewed with approval by the ladies of the house, who were regularly amused by their collective antics. Elizabeth describes one occasion with relish, when Richard and another friend secretly left the house to replace a much-valued ceramic pot which had been given to her as a present, but which they had inadvertently broken. In attempting to avoid her seeing them leave the house, they climbed a spiked 20ft gate and, in doing so:

> *Richard was caught by the back of his small clothes* [ie the seat of his close fitting knee breeches] *and hung till the nankeen* [cotton twill] *gave way. The other, determined to be wiser, mounted the hedge which was higher but, as he is a Cavalry Officer, he hung by his spurs and could not be liberated without much difficulty.*

The image of anyone trying to climb over a hedge, wearing spurs, verges on the farcical.[71] Having freed themselves, they went in search of the woman who had been the source of the original pot but, owing to a misunderstanding, were shown into her bedroom where they found her 'in her undress'. Following stammered explanations, all was quickly forgiven, and much Rabelaisian mirth resulted, although one wonders if a Victorian household would have been quite so unruffled.

An enduring feature of military life is the stop-go existence. The oscillation from frenetic activity to listless indolence was striking in the Georgian-Regency army, and when a young officer was not on parade, nor on exercise (then called manoeuvres), nor at war, he was lounging about looking for diversion. Inevitably a minority would have applied themselves to their books, but many were out hunting game, or perhaps women. Remarkably, given the conventions of the times, young officers, in pairs or even alone, would regularly visit married women in the cantonments, and these women were more than happy to entertain them to breakfast, tiffin or tea, sometimes for long hours. Sarah Robinson describes in her journal how young officers would sometimes come to tiffin and stay until sunset, despite her husband being out on his medical duties. 'The morning of the 13th was rendered very pleasant by Mr B reading to me a new book: *Dr Syntax's Tour to the Lakes*; after proceeding through a hundred pages, much amused and gratified, our pleasant party was broken up by another officer Mr H who stayed for tiffin.'[72] There is no reason to suppose there was any impropriety (unlike in later years in the hill stations); there were far too many servants around, and their husbands were very well aware of these visits. Any suggestion that this was likely may reflect more on male prurience than on the actual morality of the day.

At other times, couples would entertain these young men together, for breakfast or dinner. The young men themselves were thousands of miles from home, had minimal contact with women, and were fearfully inexperienced. The indication appears to be that these women were happy to offer advice on day-to-day life to these young innocents, provide an introduction to young single women, or give tips on the best way to gain their friendship. Almost certainly some young men would have regarded these older women as surrogate mothers, and others would have seen them as a good opportunity for developing their drawing room skills. Doubtless the women enjoyed a little matchmaking as well. Married women were a safe option for conversation; such approaches to a single woman would have been socially inconceivable.

Maria Sykes (wife of Captain Sykes of the Bombay Army) often received letters from single men, and as she wrote in her journal:[73] 'A married woman is a safe recipient of news and commentary outside the political, military and administrative and which would not be of interest to another man perhaps, and not possible to a single woman without attracting comment.' The reverse situation, that of a single woman visiting a single, or married, man without an accompanying person, would have been very rare. If she were to go as far as to stay at the house of one, a tsunami of scandalised gossip among the neighbouring European population would have followed. It is no surprise that in 1835 Mary Wimberley, wife of the Rev Charles Wimberley (and later Chaplain to the Governor-General) commented in her diary:

> *Wimberley and I dined at Captain Johnston's, who called on us six days ago. We were very much annoyed to find a Miss Sandiland is staying with him. It is highly improper for him to have any female protégé in his wife's absence. His own friends were annoyed at it, as it had given rise to a good deal of talk and scandal in Calcutta. She* [a Mrs Wyatt] *was sure his intentions were good but it did not do!*[74]

It seems clear that through all the major Indian cities a proportion of young men, perhaps the most fortunate, found themselves the informal wards of established families. These nurtured their ambitions, and protected them from the perils of daily life, and the women of these households would undoubtedly have been the champions of propriety and restraint.

Chapter 6

Dine and Wine

As all Georgians knew, one of the most enjoyable forms of self-indulgence was eating. They made the best of every opportunity to fill their stomachs pleasurably, especially at someone else's expense. While the men usually won this race, the women were not far behind. A generous table demanded adequate financial resources, which was not beyond the reach of middle class civil administrators, merchants or the military, but was more of a struggle for young writers or junior army officers; they often had meals provided for them in their messes or residences, albeit plain. Much of a woman's responsibility in running a house was to put food on the table, and plenty of it, and India was no different from England, apart from the type of food, and its availability.

The general pattern of meals was universal, and was a compromise between English and Indian habits. Breakfast was inevitably the first meal, although did not necessarily mark the start of the day, because military manoeuvres were often carried out before daybreak, and also many private individuals would go out riding for leisure at this cool time of day. All those taking part would return home to break their fast in princely fashion. There are many descriptions of what constituted breakfast, but Emma Roberts, in her handbook about Indian British life in the early years of the nineteenth century, describes an example during the events constituting a grand military review, or field day. The ladies mostly arrived in carriages, but some would go by horse or even turn up on an elephant. After witnessing the proceedings from a discreet distance, no doubt tittering like schoolgirls behind their fans at the antics of the military, they would retire to one of many large tents, really nothing less than marquees, which were specifically reserved as 'Dressing tents for the ladies, who shake off the mornings dust and repair their charms, by re-arranging the hair and re-smoothing the drapery.'[1] They would then find their way along intricate passages connecting these tents, aiming for breakfast, where they were met by:

Fish of every kind, fresh, dried, pickled, or preserved, or hermetically sealed in tin; delicate fricassees, rissoles, croquettes, omelettes, and

133

curries of all descriptions; cold meats and games of all sorts; pâtés, jellies and jams from London and Lucknow; fruits and sweetmeats; with cakes in endless variety, splendidly set out in china, cut glass and silver.

And a final, very English, touch: 'The guests providing their own tea cups, plates etc.'. While food was readily available in a military cantonment, hardware obviously wasn't.

Feasts such as this were not at all out of the ordinary; for the majority, breakfast was not so lavish, but still generous in proportion to the numbers present. In 1827, Elizabeth Fenton, when still married to her first husband, Neil Campbell, describes a morning in Dinapore when they both rose at the sound of gunfire, the official mark of the start and the end of the day. They strolled along the banks of the Ganges admiring the lifting dawn light brushing an apricot tint over the distant mountains, and revelling in the throng of local people ritually bathing at the ghats. Rather less ritually, many were also rhythmically beating the life out of their clothes on the wet, grey stones, in ancient traditional fashion. The river was busy with boats setting out on the day's chores as the couple wandered homewards, completed their morning's ablutions, and settled on the verandah to a typical everyday country breakfast of *gurram panee,* fish, rice, eggs, cold meat, fruit, preserves, curry and so on. Somehow a modern breakfast cereal seems totally inadequate. Breakfast at that time being a social event, there were always visitors to share it, and talk the time away.[2]

At around one o'clock there would be tiffin, which equated to lunch and could be anything from a light meal (Elizabeth Fenton would have *pummelo –* a citrus fruit not unlike grapefruit – and bread), to a full middle-of-the-day dinner. The word derives, not from the Hindi, but from the obsolete English word, tiffing, which means a snack between meals.[3] Mrs Jameson in 1820, in Bombay, wrote:

At one o'clock Mrs Grant [wife of a Supreme Court judge] *sent down to me to come upstairs and take tiffin, or what we call eleven hours* [elevenses?] *or lunch. Here we had as much at tiffin as we used to have every day at dinner at home, along with tarts, fruit, bread and cheese, with wine and beer. After that was over, had a little conversation for an hour.*[4]

This could hardly be described as a snack between meals, and one suspects that not much conversation passed before stupor intervened.

So the day wound on to its culinary climax, with dinner at seven to eight o'clock. This was truly the main meal of the day, and it could be spent, then as now, with the family alone, or be the occasion for inviting guests to continue the endless reciprocating social tide within the community. Family dinners might involve guests who were staying, or lodging, and would have been attended by all the servants, as listed earlier. When there were invited guests, the numbers would depend upon the wealth and status of the host. A mere Assistant-Surgeon in the Bengal Army (James Robinson, and his wife Sarah) might have had only twenty or so but, even then, the table must have creaked under the weight of the contents. As Sarah wrote to her sister Ann:

There was no great redundancy [!]. *Most of the things are the produce of our own farmyard. Soup, fish, turkey, ham, suckling pig, a saddle of mutton, fowls, rabbit pie, boiled leg of mutton, pickled beef, fillet of veal, mutton steaks, carrots and vegetables in great variety.*[5]

As she remarked elsewhere:

A large income is necessary… . I have not mentioned the number of guests which we must entertain, many are patients of James's and many come to us who have no other place to go, for you know in India are no inns or lodging houses and people entertain each other. Hospitality is doubly a duty in India.[6]

At the other end of the social scale the numbers of guests were unimaginable by today's standards. When Sir Thomas Stamford Raffles, as Lieutenant Governor of Java, held a dinner there to celebrate peace with France in 1814, as well as the birthday of the Prince of Orange (partly a diplomatic flourish to their Dutch predecessors); the number of guests was 500.[7] The choice of food was always gluttonously gargantuan. Emma Roberts describes a dinner for sixty as consisting of an overgrown turkey, 'the fatter the better', in the central place of honour, an enormous ham likewise; at the top of the table a sirloin, or round of beef; at the bottom, a saddle of mutton; legs of roasted or boiled mutton down the sides, along with fowls, 'three in a dish', geese, ducks, tongues, 'lumps', pigeon pies, mutton chops, chicken cutlets, curry and, of course, rice. The biblical text that evidently governed Indian British life at that time is to be found in Isaiah 22:13. 'Let us eat and drink for tomorrow we shall die'. Many of them did, and all knew its potential imminence.

In the hot weather of India, and especially with sauna-like humidity on the coast, dinner would usually be served on the verandahs. The layout was glittering, literally so, the tables being strewn with silver and glass, even down to silver covers for the glasses to keep out the flies and, in the light of candle sconces and hanging oil lanterns, these would all have shimmered enchantingly, like a river in sunlight, as would have the polished marble, or *chunam*, floors and columns. Potted flowers were placed on the balustrades between these columns, their vivid colours contrasting with the spotless white of the muslins and turbans of the attendant servants, 'waiting with such extreme stillness'.[8, 9] As Elizabeth Grant wrote in her memoirs: 'Their bare feet made no sound on the matting, they never spoke, they were machines divining wants, and supplying them magically'.

Many of the cleverly attractive lighting ideas were learnt from traditional Indian practices. Elizabeth Gwillim describes occasionally seeing the large rectangular and water-filled Indian temple tanks, illuminated with great originality and effect by placing small pottery oil lamps on the multiple inclined steps (or ghats), down to the water's edge. They were arranged up and down these ghats in a continuous zig-zag pattern giving a reciprocal reflection in the water, the whole producing a glimmering chain of diamonds centred on the water's margin, forming an encircling necklace around the tank edge.[10]

At a dinner there were servants by the score. Each guest brought one or two, who stood behind their seats, outnumbering those on whom they waited. They had to ensure that their respective charges were passed all the dishes that he or she might have wanted. These could be anywhere, especially on a large table, because in pre-Victorian days the fashion for dining was à la francaise, whereby all the dishes were put on the table at once, around an impressive centrepiece, and would then be changed later for a similar pot-pourri of joints, pies and fowls which somehow a servant had to get to his charge in a manner that was fit to eat. Inevitably the food was cold (but this probably didn't matter because the weather was hot), the spectacle dazzling, and the ostentation yet another way in which the host could impress those around him by his wealth, success and largesse. It wasn't until much later in the nineteenth century that dining à la russe was introduced, where courses were prepared in turn, dished up in the kitchens, and brought to each individual at the table ready to eat, with less chance that the servants standing behind the chairs would trip over each other in a scrabble to meet the whim of their charges. Other servants behind the guests would attend to the punkahs, or gently waft fly-whisks (*chowries*) made of 'peacocks' plumes or fleecy cow-tails mounted upon silver handles'.[11] There must surely have been a press like a football crowd in the rear ranks around a dinner table.

In addition to the table servants, there would also be a palanquin per person at a formal and sizeable dinner party, each with nine to nineteen men, and two *lanthorn* (lantern) bearers.[12] A party of sixty guests might therefore see 200 to 300 servants, all impeccably dressed in white muslin, and scattered among their palanquins around the gardens under the neem and mango trees, murmuring quietly to each other, or just enjoying a tranquil doze. When the personal servants left the house after dinner: 'The door-keeper takes especial care to search each one who passes out, so that none of your spoons or forks may disappear with them.'[13]

There were hookahs at intervals around the dining table for the use of guests, and also the little pipes called chillums for any guests who wished to smoke, which, not uncommonly, included women. As rarely happens after a dinner these days, the ladies would have withdrawn, so that the men could chew the fat and draw on their cigars, or chew their cigars and draw on their reminiscences.

A regular unwelcome guest at dinner was the mosquito. This was inevitable in the evening when eating out of doors, and the only protection was clothing which, fortunately for all present, then tended to cover the exposed skin fairly comprehensively. Long dresses and long sleeves for the women left the legs and neck vulnerable, whereas the breeches and hose for the men, and their long sleeves, left only the head and neck exposed to the predations of this murderous insect. Murder it often was, for the evening Anopheles mosquito was the very one that carried malaria, quite unknown to those on the receiving end at the time.

There were other unwelcome guests by day. Opportunistic birds were apt to scavenge daringly at the breakfast table, as Elizabeth Gwillim wrote to her mother:

The crows here are of the sort called hooded crows, and so familiar that they come to the rooms and take biscuits off the sideboard. If the breakfast is laid, and the servants go out of the room for a minute, they are on the table eating the butter and the rolls, and loaves they take [but] not being able to fly with them they drop on the floors. A hundred times I have come to breakfast and seen the loaves carried out and lying on the pavement and 20 or 30 of these miscreants flying away in a dreadful fright.[14]

Although scaled down in size, family dinners would be surprisingly similar in formality and duration to the larger gatherings. Eliza Fenton remembers them as: 'Very, very long, at last terminated by cheroot smoking.'[15] As one would expect, special family meals were held for major events such as Christmas, but also at other religious festivals, such as Michaelmas at the end of September, and Candlemas in early February. Lucretia West in Bombay commented at Michaelmas in 1826: 'I have ordered a goose, as I like to keep up English customs, and I hope feelings also, as much as possible.'[16] In Madras, a number of years earlier, Elizabeth Gwillim was encouraged by her husband to think of Candlemas as the last day of Christmas, even though it was more than a month later, and so they would have a large Norfolk turkey and some mince pies.[17] Whether such a turkey gobbled its lengthy way from Norfolk to India, or whether it was bred locally from transported stock, is unclear, but probably the latter.

Clearly the Christmas period was as popular 200 years ago as it is today, although a good deal less commercial. This Welsh-English judge's wife was clearly enchanted by the way the native Indians entered into the spirit of Christmas, in the early years of that century. Although an alien feast to their own religions, the Indian people have always enjoyed any opportunity for festivities and jollity. As always in India, flowers played a central part:

Christmas in many respects is kept in Madras as May Day is in England. At daybreak the arches (or opening, if it be a colonnade) are dressed up by the servants. A plantain tree is set on each side of every arch. These trees are stripped of the lower leaves and each forms a white ivory-looking column like a very large elephants tooth [tusk]. It may be about seven or eight feet high and, so far, it runs straight. Here therefore, very much resembling a capital, are fastened on large bunches of the plantain fruit: above these the long leaves, springing out, bend over and, meeting each other at the keystone of the arch, are then bound together with strings and bunches of flowers. These columns are then bound round with narrow wreaths of flowers, of which they provide at least 100 yards, and the tops of the arches are filled up with them by hanging them in festoons, crossing each other in various ways, so as to produce an agreeable open blaze of lines. The floors of the verandas and halls are strewed with flowers and small leaves, so as to make almost a carpet.[18]

The Nabob send us a letter of congratulation on the return of the season, and a large present of the finest fruit with wreaths of flowers.

Even the family servants and their children came into the house at breakfast with presents of fruit and flowers, often bound into stiff, formal nosegays. The impression is of a colourful, happy, noisy occasion, like a children's party, enjoyed as much by those who had no concept of the nature of Christmas, as by those born to it. Of course, the whole episode was an excuse, then as now, to bring out the best of the food and drink, and think not of tomorrow, but to revel in the pleasures of today.

Much of the food that was to European taste could be obtained locally. French beans were a staple, as well as wild ones from the hedgerows, and were eaten complete, or shelled and boiled like broad beans. Potatoes were available for half the year, new ones coming from northern India. Turnips and carrots were always to be found, as was cabbage, but not broccoli or cauliflower. The endives were large and white, according to Gwillim, but beetroot and lettuces small. Onions, cucumber, spinach, mustard, radishes and mint were all available, and sage and parsley grew well. Many of these would be home grown, but were often grown from seeds brought out from England. Several herbs could not easily be obtained, such as thyme and marjoram, and so existed the paradox that, although the British were initially in the East to obtain spices to send home, when they started living there, the need for certain herbs caused an unexpected shift in the opposite direction: 'I forgot to tell H... to send me bags, from Covent Garden, of herbs constantly ... thyme and marjoram I have not tasted since I came here.'[19] There were also local vegetables that were unfamiliar to the European; among them were sweet potatoes, numerous strange green vegetables, tamarinds, gourds, coconuts and, of course, rice. Fruit was plentiful, and new arrivals to the country were assailed by an abundance of astonishing flavours. Oranges, pineapples and melons were everywhere. French grapes could be obtained from Pondicherry. Elizabeth Gwillim particularly liked *pumple moos* [sic – obviously grapefruit], which she likened to the shaddock of the West Indies. Plantains, of the banana family, were prevalent and popular, but nothing could beat the mango for sheer delight. There were many varieties, and some Indian British cultivated them seriously, becoming distinct connoisseurs in the art. One of these was the very Indianized General William Palmer, Resident of Puna at the onset of the nineteenth century, who studied the fruit seriously, cultivated and wrote about them, until his career was effectively ended by Wellesley for being too influenced by Indian culture.

Most Indian British houses outside the fort walls of Madras were called garden houses, and lived up to that name. There was major cultivation of all those vegetables required by the household, especially those held dear by the

British but difficult to obtain from Indian markets. Thus cauliflowers, celery and artichokes were successfully grown, being largely unknown to the local people at that time. Fish were plentiful in the coastal towns and available in deep country where there were rivers. There are descriptions of the fishermen on the Coromandel coast, near Madras, going out in hundreds, surging through the surf right out to the horizon. One or two men sat astride a catamaran – no more than three or four slim, tapered, buoyant tree trunks bound together – who paddled furiously, with the water washing between the logs and over the occupants, and the net folded and ready in front of them. Little has changed today except that the boats are now occasionally made of fibreglass, and the numbers are fewer. Elizabeth Gwillim at one time stated by explanation, in a letter to her sister, that *catty* means a bundle, and *muram* means wood, noting further that a mutual friend, Mrs Edward James, 'Is very fond of calling old maids old cattimarans, and you may tell her that when she has a mind to be affronting she need not use a foreign language but say at once – you old faggot.'[20] An unexpectedly earthy remark from a refined Georgian lady, but one that would not even be unfamiliar today.

She would often travel to the beach in a palanquin and, if a boat was coming in, send the palanquin boys off to buy enough fish for the family and for all nine of the boys:

> *Many of them* [the fish] *are very nice and more to my taste than the other kinds, but they are smaller sorts of fish much like little trout and lasprings* [old term for smolt], *and there is a small kind the same as whitebait, about a penny a plateful. These they dress very nicely: they stick them on bents through the head and then fry them quite stiff, and they look excessively pretty and eat the same as whitebait. There is another kind much more like an anchovy than our sprats are, and I think they are anchovies. Mr Gwillim has not failed to eat fish above one day in twenty since he came here. We have no lobsters here, but we have prawns as large as the tail of a middling lobster, and exactly the same, but there is no inside to them but we mix some crab with it and it makes very fine lobster-like sauce.*[21]

As for meat, there was a ready supply of beef and mutton, and plentiful fowls such as chicken, geese and turkeys. Meat was very difficult to keep in a hot climate, and hence the universal interest in the disguising properties of spices at the time. 'Wishing to take advantage of a fine sheep killed yesterday, we had another dinner [party] today but the weather is so hot (near 100°) that it

was quite bad at 10 o'clock, so we had to kill a lamb for our company.'
[guests][22]

In addition to these meats there was plenty of game, although mainly in
hunting country, and mainly where the military were to be found, who were
rather handier with a gun than the average merchant or lawyer, and certainly
a lot readier to use it on hares, wild duck and quail. The latter were often
domestically husbanded in rural communities, as Fanny Parkes implies:
'Through the stupidity of our servants some animal got into the quail house
last night and killed seventy-nine fat quail; very provoking – but as this is
the season for them it is not of much consequence, we can replace them.'[23]
She elsewhere remarked on how efficient the native people were at hunting
wild duck:

*We used to send out men into the jungle to catch them, which was
performed in a singular manner. The man, when he got near water on
which the wildfowl were floating, would wade into the stream up to
his neck with a kedgeree pot upon his head; beneath this mask of
pottery the birds would allow him to approach them without taking
alarm, they being used to the sight of these earthen pots which are
constantly to be seen floating down the stream, thrown away by the
natives. When close to a bird, the man put up his hand, catches its
legs, pulls it instantly underwater, and fastens to his girdle. Having
caught a few, he quits the river, and secures them in a basket.*[24]

According to Fanny, these ducks were always in beautiful condition, and
were thereafter kept in tanks, or ponds, until needed.

In keeping with the Georgian penchant for luxury, if it could be afforded,
some foodstuffs were exotic. This was mainly because they were hard to find.
In a letter written about the Queen's Ball in Simla, soon after Victoria's
accession, Emily Eden commented how, twenty years earlier, no European
had ever visited the place, but that on that date in the late 1830s they were
all there celebrating, the band playing Puritani and Masaniello: 'and eating
salmon from Scotland and sardines from the Mediterranean, and observing
that St Cloup's *potage à la Julienne* was perhaps better than his other
soups.'[25] This again hints at the rarefied existence of the upper echelons of
British expatriate society; a sort of Indian *Downton Abbey*.

Although there is an amusingly wicked condescension about Emily
Eden's writings, one must remember that she came from an extreme of this
society, being a sister to the Governor-General Lord Auckland, and having

arrived in Simla after travelling overland in a baggage train of immense size, in a sort of royal progress through Upper India. There were many hundreds of horses and bullocks, some hundreds of elephants, 850 camels and 12,000 people such that it took three days for the whole cavalcade to pass one spot, much like an army on the march to war.[26] Little did they all know that war was to be the eventual outcome of Auckland's stately regional visits; the disastrous first Afghan campaign.

Ordinary people, below the salt, also had access to the finer foods. A favourite delicacy in season was dressed turtle soup. At regular intervals this was advertised in the local newspapers such as the *Madras Gazette*, as being available at a given time in a particular hostelry. It could be enjoyed on the premises, or a servant could be sent round with an empty tureen; a forerunner, as it were, of the modern take-away[27] There were surprises as well. Sarah Robinson wrote about having a roasted leg of porcupine for tiffin in her journal to her sister, the meat of which was said to be sweet and reddish, commenting: 'I shall feed the fair Mrs A with this, whereby she will remember us.' Mrs A was not one of Sarah's favourites. There is no record of the reaction, but one is left with the impression that porcupine meat might not be that sweet after all.[28]

One item which all those thousands of British people really enjoyed eating, however, was food from home. Remarkably, this was not such a rarity. Such treats could be bought at auction, the sale dates again being announced in the Gazettes. These sales often represented a major investment by East India Company Officers, the goods having been solicitously brought all the way from England in expectation of a fat profit to supplement the ever meagre salary:

> *Mr King, Purser of the Harriet, begs to inform the Ladies and Gentlemen of Madras that he intends to retail the whole of his Investment, in which are the following articles, on Saturday 11th inst. for ready money only, as his stay in Madras will be very short.*

Doubtless he couldn't wait to sail home with a hold full of silks, cotton goods and shawls from Kashmir to sell to curious Londoners, further gratifying his bank balance. The listed foods included bottled pale ale, hams, pickled tongues in firkins, sheep tongues in kegs, hung beef, Bath chaps, dry smoked tongues, double Gloucester cheese, salted salmon, or white herrings, cases of pickles, salad oil, essence of anchovies, mushroom or walnut ketchup, capers, white wine vinegar and mustard.[29] These would have been truly succulent delights to the confirmed English palate in India, something akin to the Marmite or HP sauce on sale to British expats in French markets today, although a touch more exotic.

Apart from auctions, food and other goods could be obtained from shops in the main towns, or from one of the several Provisions Merchants to be found around the country, especially in the more provincial areas. Mr Havell in Patna ran his own scrupulously well-ordered farms to supply all kinds of foods to the British public. Pork was especially popular, and was regarded as clean and wholesome, being of both Chinese and English stock; much to be preferred to the local pigs. These lived on the very worst offal, and were regarded as unclean by everyone, regardless of religious sensibilities. Prices were appropriately high, and only the well-heeled could shop there. Emma Roberts wrote that such goods cost about ten times as much in Calcutta as they would in England; at the very least five or six times. By the Victorian age, and into the Raj, the choice of food from Europe was far greater, and the processes of canning and preserving had advanced significantly. Journey times were also shorter because of the growing use of steam, and particularly the opening of the Suez Canal in 1869.

Commonly, and rather more cheaply, the longed for foods from home were sought by request in the regular correspondence:

If you can get some mushrooms at any time, a little ketchup, or of your preserved apricots, we shall be much obliged to you for them. The two gammons of bacon Ned was so good as to give us have turned out very fine. One, and half the other, have been dressed to different companies here. They were much admired and eaten at luncheon clean to the bone.[30]

And elsewhere:

I now have the pleasure to say that all my pickles and ketchup came in perfect order. The ketchup is as fresh as a mushroom from the field and we eat it every day with our fish.

Some English eating habits have lasted well through the centuries. As for pickle, this was everybody's favourite, including the servants, who had difficulty in resisting the temptation to help themselves to a portion. Casks of excellent English beef and pork were occasionally received, and were highly valued and greatly enjoyed.

Confectionery was a weakness for the British, just as it is now, and was always in demand. Candied almonds, sugared plums or carraways, tolu lozenges, blackcurrant drops and mint seeds were, among others, all sent for with fervour from home; 'from Tringham's by the pound.' It was a challenge to pack preserved foods well enough to survive four or more months at sea, with the constant movement and shipboard damp: 'Three Gammons of bacon appeared indifferently, being so much rubbed as to have nearly lost the outer rind, but on cutting two of them we have found the meat perfectly good and as a red and white as ever.'[31] Elizabeth Gwillim clearly adored the sweets and, in a startlingly modern expression for the early 1800s, declared that 'They are super excellent all.'

Often these sweet things would dry out, or not survive the journey wrapped only in paper; 'the candy is gone from the orange chips' – disaster. There developed a considerable experience in packing all kinds of goods and, given the conditions in the ship's holds, an amazing amount floated through unscathed, occasionally literally. Glass jars, and early hermetic sealing of tins, assisted greatly. Marmalade was ever popular; a conserve that spread throughout the far reaches of the Colonies as a banner to British taste and eccentricity. Mary Wimberley wrote with glee on 7 September 1827 that, 'Mr Burnett sent me a large jar of marmalade made by his cousin Miss Fanny Grant in Perthshire.'[32] On the assumption that it was made from Seville oranges, these would have travelled all the way from Spain to Scotland, by sea and land, and then the finished product would have wound its way again by sea to India; an enormous effort to please the British palate.

In the Georgian era particularly, it would have been unthinkable to contemplate food without wine, or indeed beer, port or Madeira. In fact, these beverages were drunk more commonly than water, even by women, who often drank beer during the daytime. As Elizabeth Grant recorded in 1827: 'The bitter beer, well frothed up and cold, was the favourite beverage, especially with the ladies.'[33] There was no concept of danger from the water at that time; it was simply that beer and wine were enjoyable alternatives to the often foul taste, and appearance, of such water as was available. To quote Fanny Parkes:[34]

> *In Calcutta* [in 1830], *the tank water being unwholesome to drink, it is necessary to catch rain water, and preserve it in great jars, sixty jars full will last a year in our family. Here* [in Cawnpore] *we drink the Ganges water, reckoned the most wholesome in India, whereas the water of the Jumna is considered unwholesome.*

Given the religious and social practices even then, it seems unlikely that Ganges water was actually safe. A European would regard it unwise to go too close to this river even today, let alone drink from it. Wine, as with Madeira and port, was sometimes mixed with water to disguise the latter's taste, not to make it safer; an unknown concept at the time, quite apart from being ineffective in any case. Virtually all alcoholic drinks came from Europe, mainly with an origin in France or Portugal. Arrack was the main indigenous beverage, a spirit distilled from palm tree sap, or sometimes rice. It was cheap, fairly unsubtle in its flavour, and certainly in its effects. It was the local drink consumed by the soldiery, and the poorer Indian British, and the cause of much alcohol-related morbidity. Higher social classes came across it as a component of punch, a very old Indian drink that was in widespread use in the seventeenth and eighteenth centuries. The arrack was mixed with sugar, citrus juice, water and spices and was popular with all-male groups, especially young writers, but also, to a lesser extent, the women. Cherry brandy was a particular favourite with the latter, who also drank wine in greater quantities than would have been seen at home.[35]

In the early years of the East India Company, wine came to India from Shiraz in Persia, but this ceased in the mid-1700s as a result of political difficulties, and thus the source moved to Europe. The wine was then shipped in the holds of the East Indiamen; the port and the favourite, Madeira, were shipped in pipes. One still occasionally hears today of a pipe of port. The word originates from the Portuguese for a barrel – *pipa* – which was equivalent to an English half tun. Today this amounts to 550 litres, but in former times it was 534 litres or 60 dozen bottles, and no small amount when it came to bottling and delivery. Several of these pipes would be carried in a ship's hold, and could become lethal if they became loose and rolled about during a storm.[36] Mary Wimberley describes her husband, with his bearers, drawing off and bottling a pipe of Madeira:

I assisted a little after receiving visitors. The wine has turned out very fine, of a beautiful colour, and is as clear as crystal. Drew off about 32 dozen but could not finish it for want of dry bottles. When finally finished there were 40 dozen quarts and 15 dozen pints.[37]

No mean supply for a humble chaplain, even if he was the Governor-General's.

The annual supply of wine to India, shipped under the responsibility of the Company, amounted to 6,260 pipes in 1805, according to Parkinson.[38] This equated to nearly five million bottles and, bearing in mind the size of the Indian British wine-drinking population, indicated that individual consumption was quite high. This population reached about 40,000 in the 1820s; so would have been less in 1805, but more than three-quarters of these would have been ordinary soldiers, who didn't drink wine.[39] Therefore, fewer than 10,000 civilians and officers consumed this amount, indicating a substantial weekly consumption per head, especially given the greater strength of Madeira or port. Claret was sometimes doctored with brandy to make it last longer, but also making it more expensive than unsullied French claret, which was about 3s 4d (around £5.50 today).[40] Certainly Eliza Fenton found the family's annual liquor bill for 1768 to be rather high, but this may have had as much to do with the amount consumed, and the need for frequent entertainment, as it did with the cost per bottle.[41] In a context of high alcohol consumption, there seems to have been little realization of its dangers at that time; in fact wine was usually regarded as having good medicinal properties, and even that 'People using perpetual exercise require a good deal of wine. This must be Madeira in general, for light wine will not bear the climate.' This declaration comes from the informed opinion of a medical family of the time.[42]

Some indication of the level of alcohol consumption can be obtained from tavern bills. In just one and a half days in a fairly ordinary punch house in 1770, Joseph Shearme got through eight bowls of punch, one bottle of arrack, four bottles of wine, one each of port and Madeira, some beer, grog and cider. One must presume that he had a little help with this.[43] In a more gentlemanly household, such as that of a certain Mr Francis, examination of his wine book for 1774 showed that in one month he and his guests imbibed seventy-five bottles of Madeira, ninety-nine bottles of claret, seventy-four bottles of porter, sixteen bottles of rum, three bottles of brandy and one bottle of cherry brandy. If aspirin had been available, doubtless they would have got through a good deal of that as well.

All-male dining groups drank copiously. 'Pushing the claret about', as William Hickey succinctly expressed it, meanwhile piling the tables high with empty bottles as a mark of their prowess. The women were not so far behind, especially at formal dinners where they too drank the wine, and perhaps a cherry brandy when they withdrew at the end of the meal. This custom at least allowed them to escape most of the endless round of toasts and songs that followed. Many of these toasts were formal and statutory, such as to the king, the Governor-General, the governor and council of that particular Presidency, the Commander in Chief etc. This would often be followed by toasts to the Navy, the Army, the Ladies and so on, ad infinitum depending on the mood of the occasion, and on who was presiding over the dinner. It seems to have been almost a contrivance, designed to ensure the consumption of even more alcohol. The president for the occasion would also decide on whether the toasts were in bumpers. This effectively meant draining the whole glass, and Hickey records a dinner in 1797 where he drank twenty-two bumpers in toasts, after the usual imbibing at dinner, followed by a rollercoaster of glassfuls until 2 am. It is hardly surprising that he wrote, 'a more severe debauch I never was engaged in in any part of the world.'[44]

Some of the behaviour at the dinner table became rowdy, doubtless fuelled by the alcohol, and Hickey, who never shrank from an explicit discourse on some of the less decorous aspect of his lifestyle, described a dinner party where:

> *I first saw the barbarous custom of pelleting each other with little balls of bread, made like pills, across the table, which was even practised by the fair sex. Some people could discharge them with such force as to cause considerable pain when struck in the face. Mr Daniel Barwell was such a proficient that he could, at the distance of three or four yards, snuff a candle, and that several times successively. This strange trick, fitter for savages than polished society, produced many quarrels.*

One such incident was taken very badly by a recipient, who then responded by hurling a leg of mutton at the offender, which struck him hard on the head. A duel resulted; the injury by leg of mutton was followed by injury by pistol ball, resulting in the unfortunate victim being laid out for months; so ended the practice of pelleting. Inevitably such chaotic behaviour was commoner in a youthful male domain, steeped in alcohol. In the normal household, or at formal dinners held by the dignitaries of any presidency, the behaviour would be entirely contrary. Soon after her arrival in Madras in 1819, Mary Doherty was clearly unimpressed by the conduct at a dinner for thirty to forty people in the house where she and her husband were staying:

> *Conversation there is none, either at dinner or afterwards, and the formalities are great. Tea is then served* [after dinner] *and the greater part of the company sit down to brag, a gambling game in which large sums are lost. Some unfortunate young, old, lady (for the girls are too busy husband-hunting) plays the Bluebells of Scotland or perhaps sings 'Oh Nanny wilt thou gang with me', to a piano, not tuned since it left England.*[45]

At much the same time, on the opposite side of the sub-continent in Bombay, Maria Callcott commented:

40 or 50 persons assemble [for dinner] *at seven o'clock and stare at one another till dinner is announced. At table there can be no general conversation, but the different couples who have been paired off, and who on account of their rank invariably sit together at every great dinner, amuse themselves with remarks on the company as satirical as their wit will allow.*[46]

Back in Madras Julia Maitland (1837) wrote similarly:

After dinner the company all sit round in the middle of the great gallery-like rooms, talking in whispers, and scratch their mosquito bites.

I am sure India is the paradise of middle-aged gentlemen. While they are young, they are thought nothing of – just supposed to be making or marring their fortunes, as the case may be; but at about 40, when they are high in the service, rather yellow, and somewhat grey, they begin to be taken notice of, and called young men. These respectable persons do all the flirtation too in a solemn sort of way, while the young ones sit by, looking on, and listening to the elderly gentlefolks discussing their livers instead of their hearts.[47]

Elizabeth Gwillim, in her turn, remarked:

At these [dinners] *one always meets the same set of people who do not care one farthing for each other, and the one half of them are wishing each other hanged. One hears the same scandal of all, and in general one sees the same fine clothes, and here are some ladies on whom you would think it snowed pearls and rained diamonds, yet when you learn their secret history you find their husbands are over head and ears in debt, and that they have half a dozen children at home* [England] *unprovided for, rather than avoid some ostentatious extravagance which all their acquaintances know they cannot afford.*[48]

These rather jaundiced views reflect the tedium of repeated social events in a small community, from which there was no escape and where every person knew everyone else's business. Nevertheless, such comments show some indication of the wit of these women writers, one of the few intellectual talents they were able to nurture in a completely male dominated society, and in which they clearly took pleasure. Nevertheless, there is always a fine margin between wit and sarcasm.

In the perpetual heat of India, and the East Indies, the greatest desire was for coolness. Apart from cooling one's body, which wasn't always easy, there was inevitably a strong urge to chill one's water or wine, or indeed milk and butter. Unfazed by what might have seemed impossible, the Indian British of the eighteenth and early nineteenth centuries set about the task, proving yet again that necessity is so often the mother of invention. An early device was to place a cloth petticoat around each bottle which, when wetted, cooled its contents by evaporation. According to Emma Roberts this fanciful arrangement was colour-coded, Port, claret and burgundy being clothed in crimson, 'with white flounces', while Sherry and Madeira were dressed in white.[49] In addition to this, there was an enterprising return to a practice as old as the Roman Empire. Adding saltpetre (potassium nitrate) to water causes it to cool as the crystals dissolve. By immersing a long-necked pewter flask full of water into this dissolving solution, the water within was allowed to cool appreciably in just a few minutes. Saltpetre was readily available in India, being an important export for the manufacture of gunpowder, but it was an expensive process, used only on grander occasions.[50] A simpler technique was to hang bottles inside a cage covered with a permanently wet cloth. This contraption was suspended outside in the breeze, and the resultant evaporation again created a cool interior within which the bottles were suspended, perhaps later to be dressed in their moist petticoats. This age-old process survives even today, as anyone will know who has driven in desert conditions with a goatskin of water suspended from the wing mirror.

The Holy Grail was, of course, ice. Never daunted, the colonists set about making ice in large quantities, especially in the northern regions. Fanny Parkes gives a detailed account of the process, her husband having been a civil servant who oversaw the ice-making in Allahabad in the 1830s.[51] In January and February ice was made almost every night, the process being very weather dependent. The person in charge, the *abdar*, would judge whether or not a cool, crisp night was due and if so, he would beat his hand-drum summoning all the available men from the bazaar, who would arrive to fill with water the hundreds of shallow pans laid out on a flat surface. In the correct conditions about an inch of ice would form on the surface of the pans and, when the *abdar* judged the time right, perhaps at three o'clock in the morning, he would return to his drum, calling everyone back to harvest the ice. They would then hurriedly carry this in a basket to an ice pit dug into the ground. Each of the latter contained about 80lb of ice, and over each one was built a house of thick mud walls and thatched roof. The single entrance was sealed with a bamboo frame covered with straw. The gathered ice was beaten into a solid mass in the pits, by teams of men who had to be changed regularly before they succumbed to the cold. Here it would stay, covered with mats and straw, until the hot weather in April or May when it would be chipped out and distributed as arranged. The process was very labour-intensive, and therefore expensive, and was paid for by subscription from the members of the ice club that formed for that particular region. Fanny Parkes recorded that each member was allowed 24lb of ice every other day, and that it lasted that year until 20 August. Theft of the ice was a problem. Not surprisingly it was as popular with the Indians as it was with the British.

Before the days of refrigeration, initially with clumsy evaporation machines in 1870, and later with conventional electric refrigerators in the early 1900s, the making, or obtaining, of ice was a regular anxiety. Champagne, after all, had been available in India since the eighteenth century, and one could not possibly contemplate drinking it un-chilled. Elizabeth Fenton wrote in 1828: 'I was thankful to accept of some iced champagne as a momentary stimulus.'[52] Fanny Parkes herself remarked, in a very hot June in 1832, and rather more prosaically. 'Our only consolation, grapes and iced water.' In 1786, William Hickey, no stranger to champagne (or ice) in prodigious amounts, made the surprising comment on how he had sat down: 'To an excellent dinner, with a bottle of capital good claret, made cold as ice.'[53]

The real breakthrough came in 1833 with the first shipment of the much better, and longer lasting, block-ice from America. The arrival of the clipper *Tuscany* in Calcutta on 6 September, carrying 180 tons of ice, caused great excitement. This ice had survived the four-month journey, without melting, having been covered with the ingenious and effective combination of pine sawdust and felt. The concept was the brainchild, some years before, of Frederic Tudor of Boston, then only a boy. Along with some friends, he built up a trade taking ice to the West Indies. With his partners he developed a company that harvested blocks of ice sawn from frozen ponds in New England, and stored in local ice-houses before being loaded onto ships. Tudor and Rogers' shipment to India proved very profitable, sufficient to allow the formation of a branch of the company in Calcutta. Within a few years branches were formed in Madras and Bombay as well. The large ice-house near the beach in Madras was leased to Tudor and Rogers for storage of their shipments, and the building still stands today (although now a Ramakrishna museum), a monument to man's ingenuity and industry. Eventually, this enterprising ice trade collapsed, an inevitable victim of the march of technological progress, as electricity and refrigeration slowly rolled across the world.[54, 55]

The ineluctable culmination of all this obsessive interest in food, dining, and chilled wine was that zenith of Georgian social entertainment, the ball. These glamorous events were far from uncommon; almost weekly according to Elizabeth Gwillim in Madras, and even more for some, and they could be held anywhere, and by any person, with one proviso. They had to be able to afford it. Therefore, just to host a ball was a ticket to grandness and respectability in India, if not at home in Britain. Everyone then knew automatically that you were in a league of your own, supposedly wallowing in riches. Unfortunately, history is full of individuals who have spent lavishly on entertainment in order to give a great impression, while concealing behind the scenes the real truth – that the cupboard was bare.

The ball was, not unexpectedly, combined with a grand dinner, and the whole event could be extraordinarily lavish. Guests would arrive by carriage or palanquin; the arrival area and avenues leading to it, would be lit by a myriad earthenware oil lamps on bamboo poles. The ballroom itself rarely had a wooden floor because of the potential damage from termites, but was always wonderfully decorated. In Cawnpore however, the floor was wooden, and there were two rows of pillars either side, with sofas placed between them. Various descriptions attest to the extravagance of it all, referring to delightful gardens, and fountains 'flinging water to a great height', according to Maria Sykes, who writes about a ball at Government House in Bombay (1809) in which she describes:

> *The ballroom hung in pink silk covered thickly with silver stars; sofas, armchairs etc. all of the material. The supper room was equally rich but in blue silk and gold stars... . The ladies held a fancy fair in the grounds, booths being erected where they sold confectionary, toys, jewellery etc.*[56]

She met colourfully dressed Parsees, and was witness to an astonishing firework display, with rockets, wheels, airborne model ships firing at each other, and waterborne fireworks ejecting birds and flowers etc. Elsewhere there are descriptions of private balls where the supper table could be 300ft long, set on carpets in the garden, and decorated with coloured awnings supported by bamboo trunks heavily decorated with flowers. There would be overhead lighting with 'an hundred of wax lights all burning in cut glass shades', casting a flickering golden light over the richly dressed guests below.[57]

Sometimes a ball would be thrown by a wealthy local Indian, such as one of the Parsees of Bombay, and all the great and the good of the British community would be invited. Doubtless this was good political networking, and perhaps favours could be called in at a later date. On Prince of Wales Island (Penang) in 1812, Toonko Syed Hossein hosted an event that was reported in detail in the Island Gazette:

> *The extensive premises belonging to the Toonkoo, as well as all the approaches to it, and the avenues around, were illuminated.*
>
> [The guests] *were conducted to a pavilion, brilliantly lighted and elegantly fitted up in the eastern style, with Chinese and other paintings, beautifully executed. The dinner consisted of every delicacy that the most liberal and extensive hospitality could procure; the wines were excellent, abundant, and delightfully cooled. The utmost conviviality presided.... Toasts were drunk with enthusiastic applause, each toast being accompanied by an appropriate tune from an excellent band...the health of the Honble the Governor was drunk by the company, standing, three times three, with warmth of feeling.*
>
> *After the conclusion of the dinner, the company was entertained with Malay, Malabar, and Siamese exhibitions of Nautching and Dancing, and also Siamese and Chinese Theatrical Performances; and at intervals, with choice fireworks.*[58]

Syed Hossein was a rich and influential Muslim citizen of Arab descent, who came from Aceh in northern Sumatra but was then living in Penang. He had been invited by Francis Light, founder of Penang in 1786, to help develop the island's economic growth.

Not all such events proceeded smoothly. At one ball the guests were startled by a loud noise, which they assumed to be the start of the firework display in the garden. Everyone ran to the doors to discover a violent storm in progress, with torrential rain, thunder close by and great bolts of lightning:

> *All the fireworks were extinguished and, what was still worse, the supper and the building which contained it were washed away. There was poor Mr Cochrane* [the host] *at the head of about a hundred black*

servants trying to save something from the wreck, but they gathered up custards, whipped syllabub, sandwiches and bunches of flowers, all mixed together. At last it was discovered that a great deal more supper had been prepared than the tables would hold and with that, and the first which was not injured, they made one handsome table inside the house which was quite enough, for all these things are just for show because nobody ever eats, and they stayed until about four in the morning and they finished the evening, or rather the morning, very gaily.[59]

In the late eighteenth and early nineteenth centuries, the main dance at a ball would have been the quadrille. Like most dances of the time, its origin was French, and it superseded the arcane intricacy of the minuet, which few of the gentry mastered to any degree. The quadrille was in sets of four or eight, with the corner pairs dancing with each other in turn. It was sufficiently complex that it demanded some preparatory instruction, certainly for many of the less urbane and socially refined men, although others 'danced away as if their lives depended on it.'[60] Women, of course, were more formally educated in such matters. The retiring, and slightly haughty, Lucretia West often mentions dancing the quadrille at various balls, apparently with some pleasure, but invariably she limited the number of dances, and declined invitations, 'Begging to adopt my matronly character and, after supper, at half-past twelve slipping away unobserved.'[61] She was only in her thirties, whereas Emily Eden mentions a Mrs C who: 'Is past fifty – some say nearer sixty – wears a light coloured wig with very long curls floating down her back, and a gold wreath to keep it on, a low gown, and she dances every dance'.[62] As an event, the ball was inevitably a marriage market, and thus very popular with single women and men, as well as with the mothers. Every effort was made to get there and, to quote Raza: 'In the remote *mofussil* ancient finery was dragged out of storage, and fashions not seen for years in elegant circles were enthusiastically paraded on the dance floor.'[63]

Apart from the quadrille, country-dances are mentioned in the correspondence and, finally, the waltz arrived to great approval in the early 1800s. To be actually able to hold a partner around the waist was the very essence of excitement for most, especially the men; but there was also tut-tutting and not a little apprehension among a few of the ladies. Lord Minto described a dance in Batavia, Java, in a letter to his wife in 1811, in mixed British and Dutch company:

Mrs Bunbury, the wife of an officer, a young pretty English-woman, stood up in the dance; but seeing, when the first couple reached her, the Dutch gentleman take his partner fairly in his arms and hug her, as it appeared to her as a bear does his prey, she fairly took to her heels, and could not be brought back again by any means, to see or share such horror.[64]

Interestingly, in the earlier years of the British in India, there were no qualms about wives being seen by Indian men dancing at a public event. By the time of the young Queen Victoria, however, this possibility was very much more frowned upon, and regarded as highly improper and unsuitable. This was all to be expected in a culture that was increasingly defining its own prejudiced identity in India, moving steadily away from that of the indigenous population, and where European women were finding themselves in a climate of refined isolation, increasingly distanced from their Indian counterparts.

The strong impression received from all the descriptions of Indian British entertainment in the pre-Victorian era is that it was redolent with extravagance and profligacy. Many correspondents attest to this, commenting that about four times as much food is placed on the tables as would happen in England: 'In short, a scandalous waste of provisions, or rather of our money.'[65,66] Another reality was that most food, and in particular meat, had to be over-ordered because of the risk that some would deteriorate in the climate, and that the large quantity of uneaten food after a formal dinner could only be thrown away. One might fondly imagine that the table servants and other staff would have benefitted from it but, as many were Hindu, they could not consider it at any price, except perhaps in the case of the outcast pariahs (dalits).[67] Some British in India were scandalised by such gross waste but, inevitably in that atmosphere of fatalistic short-termism, most just airily skirted the issue, and continued as before.

Chapter 7

Leisure, Pleasure and Endeavour

In the spare time available to a woman in India, which seems to have been rather less than most imagine, one of the most compelling desires was to get down to writing a letter home, or bringing one's journal up to date. Better still was the chance to savour a letter from a close friend, or from family. These could be few and far between, and delivery was especially subject to seasonal delays. During the European winter months the north-easterly monsoon prevailed in the Indian Ocean and prevented the arrival of ships from the Cape, therefore delaying the longed-for letters. This could last for a six-month stretch, and when added to the four months or so that it took a ship to sail from home, the delay in news from friends and family was extreme. In practice, ships often timed their long journey to coincide with the end of this monsoon so that the maximum delay would still only be six months, but this would have seemed long enough. It is little wonder that, with the passing weeks, mounting anxiety was felt as to what bad news might eventually arrive. Unexpected bereavement at home was inevitably the main worry.[1] As ships eventually came in, so letters would arrive in bundles. In 1802 Elizabeth Gwillim records the arrival of six letters from her sister Hetty in England, all of which had been written eight months before.[2] Sometimes these were a bit sketchy, perhaps dashed off out of duty, but anything that provided some connection with home and loved ones was a pleasure to receive: 'Of equal value with so much gold'.[3] Although she wrote, 'A Chit-chat letter, which seems to place us amongst you all, is what we most desire to receive'. Brief notes caused some indignation: 'A ridiculous little shabby note from James, for which he may expect a good trimming when I have more time to write. This letter to come 15,000 miles consists of six lines of business, and two more of apologies for not making it shorter!'[4]

Delays could be occasioned by numerous factors, such as war, disasters and weather, but the addition of these undoubtedly exacerbated the already existing feelings of isolation and homesickness, which were more or less universal among British women living in India at the time.

I wrote to you my dear Anne by the Auspicious, a ship that hath a fair name, and is bound from Calcutta to dear Liverpool. I have a letter half written to dear Phoebe, but I have little spirits to go on as it is so long since I have heard from you, your last letter was dated more than twelve months ago, since then how many things may have occurred. I cannot account by any means for this silence, but I suffer from it. Another ship has got to the Presidency, called the Cornwallis, but no letter for me. Ere long I must resign my journal since I cannot hope it will be interesting to hear from one so totally forgotten.[5]

Although there is some self-pity here, it arises from homesickness, a sentiment felt even by someone as privileged and cosseted as Emily Eden, surrounded in India by luxury, and much of her family. In referring to the six years she would spend there, she wrote home mourning the fact that she would miss the youthful years of the younger members of the family, and likewise her own youth would have gone before she returned home.[6] For the intelligent, acerbic lady that she was, this was an uncharacteristic slip into melancholia, but equally felt by so many of her peers. It is no surprise to learn therefore that, in 1837, Julia Maitland wrote at much the same time as Emily Eden, but at the other end of the country:

We have just received all your letters, which were more welcome than ever letters were before. In England, with your daily post, you little know the eagerness with which we poor Indians look out for our monthly despatch, nor the delight with which we receive it. For some days before the mail is expected all Madras is in a fever, speculating, calculating, hoping, almost praying, that it may arrive a few days, or even a few hours before the usual time; and when it is known to be 'in', the news travels like wildfire in all directions; peons are despatched from every compound to wait at the post office and bring the letters the instant they are given out, in order to gain an hour upon the general postmen; all other interests and occupations are forgotten.

In one letter from the beginning of her time in India, Elizabeth Gwillim has drawn a little sketch of herself seated at her writing desk, skirt billowing over the edge of a formal Georgian chair, bonnet on head, and surrounded by portraits of her family, all topped by a grand one of her mother. It is as if she is indicating the detachment she feels, with a need to project herself in her

156

mind back to familiar home territory, reaching out with the warmth and love she felt for all her relatives, but in particular her beloved mother.

There was, of course, no other means of communication. It was either word of mouth, or else thoughts and hopes committed to scarce and expensive paper with a quill pen, often by candlelight, and consigned to a ship in the packet, bound for home. The paper itself was often obtained from England, as the Indian version was of poorer quality, and often too absorbent for the ink at that time. The quills may also have been obtained from home, but cut, shaped and trimmed by the user with a sharp penknife. When a ship came in that was headed for Europe, a notice was posted, and orders distributed, to indicate that a packet had been opened for receipt of letters. This packet was a few miles away for many, such as in the Presidency fort, but any letters had to be collected there for onward carriage to the ship. Not surprisingly, a flurry of anxiety ensued and a dash to get letters written, or finished, before the packet was closed. Sometimes this was earlier than expected because the ship needed to sail prematurely. Although there was knowledge of planned sailing times and dates, there always remained a modicum of uncertainty. Elizabeth Gwillim described an occasion when a ship had lain at anchor for nine months off Madras when, quite suddenly, there was a mere twenty-four hours' notice of sailing. The attack of quill upon paper must have been audible all the way out to sea. The urgency could clearly be harassing and, at one time, Mary Symonds described having 'only half an hour allowed me to prepare and send this. The ship which carries it is an American, going to New York.' Elsewhere she said, 'I have three people standing by me and hurrying me to conclude.'[7] Unfinished letters were continued at leisure, completed when another ship was set to leave, and could stretch over a number of days. Mary's sister, Elizabeth, on one occasion completed a letter over five sittings which turned out to be almost 10,000 words; virtually a formal dissertation, and all scratched away with a feather.[8] Some individuals wrote prodigiously, given the awkwardness of the materials available. Sir Thomas Stamford Raffles is recorded by his uncle as writing 200 letters in one day with his own hand and, as if that wasn't prowess enough, he would additionally dictate at the same time to not one, but two, secretaries.[9]

We take it for granted these days, but the desire to communicate is intensely strong, and was perhaps even more so in the eighteenth and early nineteenth centuries, when England seemed as far away as the moon. Deep in the thoughts of the British in India lay the ever present concern that one might never see home, or family, again.

Apart from sending letters, there was the desire to send gifts or useful items to family or close friends. There are numerous references to this in the correspondence of the Symonds sisters. All sorts of items were despatched, but a regular favourite was lengths of material such as muslin and other cloth for making gowns. The sender would cut their extra material and off-cuts into pieces for several waistcoats, the final product being made up when they reached home. Kashmiri shawls with extraordinarily fine decorative needlework were often sent home along with these parcels of cloth, and were prized and valuable gifts for friends and family in England. Unset jewels such as amethysts and opals, along with mother of pearl snuffboxes and china thimbles are mentioned and, more prosaically, packages of seeds for planting, and even potted trees. The comment was sometimes attached that these would only be of use to the professional horticulturalist: 'For private gentlemen's gardeners would either give them away or never take pains to raise them.'[10] Exotic foodstuffs, such as fine porcelain jars of ginger from China, or preserved nutmegs were also sent, and all these items had to be carefully packaged for the long journey. Sometimes they were carried home by acquaintances and, not unexpectedly, there were instances of being let down by some such person, or items being lost along with the ship that carried them, or else damaged in transit. On eventual arrival in England the goods had to be collected from the East India house, although duty had to be paid first. Then, as now, this rankled:

> *If you get the brown beads from the India house without any trouble I wish you would show them to Mrs Toussaint and tell her that I think she could introduce them very prettily for Court... . I hope Lizzy and Mary will receive their two longtailed gowns safe. I stitched them up without cutting the muslin to cheat the Customs House officers.*[11]

Naturally enough there was a reciprocal flow of packaged goods from Britain to India. This was sometimes a result of anticipated need, but mainly a response to requests for items that needed replacement. The variety was wide, with a tendency towards apparel, such as 'elegant lace caps with yellow ribbons', or 'narrow satin ribbon, particularly white, for making shoe roses and such sort of ornaments.' Breathlessly unpacked also, were cloaks, dresses, petticoats, pairs of gloves, an eclectic range of millinery and even 'one pound of Windsor soap as it is very dear here'. A particular request was for 'pairs of dress, and undress, fine large black silk stockings', and '12 dozen pair of white silk stockings; very smart ones; as the open clocks stretch better and it is such a fatigue to drag on one's stockings in this country.' [The clocks were patterned inserts on the inner and outer surfaces near the ankle. They were decorative but, if of lace, and of an open-work pattern, they stretched more easily over the foot.] Fine leather goods, such as shoes and gloves, were much better obtained from home.

Please to let us have six pair each of coloured kid shoes, and some green Morocco for me; six pair for each of us of white kid gloves, and twelve pair each of the finest Limerick gloves of a light yellow in colour will be enough. Each glove must be put in a separate paper for in the ships the leather heats, and all our gloves were sticking together. We were obliged to tear them asunder.

The desire for goods from home was unquenchable, and various. A basket of writing paper, 'gilt and ribbed', Hamburgh Huccabic (Huckaback) linen for making towels, fire irons (surprisingly for India) and even 'some more of the Wedgewood breakfast cups, two dozen teacups and one dozen coffee cups, with saucers, and two teapots to match.' One could be forgiven for thinking that the regular flow of shipping backwards and forwards over many thousands of miles between Europe and India had little to do with trade, and the movement of personnel, but was more devoted to the maintenance of the British in India in a style which attempted to mirror their counterparts at home as closely as possible.

Fashion was a concern for Indian British women, just as it would have been if they lived in England. This was not necessarily because it was a preoccupation, but because they would have wished to look good if they were single, and had to find a partner or, if they were married, to retain a semblance of continuing attractiveness, not only to their husbands, but to themselves and the whole community of either sex. Two hundred years ago these were inevitable concerns for women, where life was so dependent on men but neither can the effect of peer pressure be overestimated – then as now. It was likely to have been a regular subject of conversation, just as it was a regular subject of discussion in letters home. On first arriving in India most women were enthralled by the variety and quality of fabrics to be found there, particularly the decorative embroidered work and similar such items. We have already met the very fine shawls from Kashmir, but the cotton and linen goods were just as exquisite, as Elizabeth Gwillim records in a letter home.[12]

Near here [Madras] *is full of manufactures of chintzes and counterpanes and palanpos, as they are called, with painted clothes for women of the richest patterns. I call them painted for so they literally are; one person draws all the outline, and others put in the colours sitting on the ground, and they will come to your house and paint you any pattern you like on a sheet, or what cloth you choose to give them. I need not tell you how permanent the colours are. They indeed get brighter the more they are washed, though they lay all clothes to dry here on the sand, which takes out all English colours.*

Although the earlier Indian British men often took on Indian dress, this was fairly uncommon among the women, especially after the turn of the century. Few would have had the courage to step out of line in this respect and risk the opprobrium of men, and society in general. The fabrics were another matter, the fine, lightweight and very cool (in the traditional sense) muslins of India lent themselves well to the high-waisted gowns with long, loose, flowing skirts universally seen on Jane Austen screen characters.

Because of the length of time it took to travel the vast distances involved before steamships or the overland route became more usual, the fashions worn in India were a good year behind those in London. The Indian British womenfolk were well aware of this, and were therefore ever on the lookout for up to date information. Local newspaper proprietors were therefore at pains to publish the latest London fashions, and these were given a regular column in the weekly gazettes of Madras, Bombay or Penang (Prince of Wales Island). Doubtless they were pored over, with sterling efforts made to update the wardrobe and impress other women. There follows an example of such a column from the *Prince of Wales Island Gazette* of April 1812, giving 'General Observations on the Dresses of Persons of Taste from La Belle Assemblée, London, of the present Month, July 1811' – a full nine months before publication. This was quite a long time in the fashion world of the late Georgian, and Regency, age.

OPERA DRESS

A blue satin robe, worn over a slip of white satin, let in at the bosom and sleeves, (which are short) with silver Moravian network. A tunic of Egyptian brown sarsnet or crepe, confined on the shoulders with diamond studs, and trimmed round the bottom with silver net, separated in small divisions, spangled by open work bells. A chaplet wreath green foil, placed twice round the hair, which is disposed in long irregular ringlets. Earrings of silver open work, studded with brilliants, resembling in form the bell of a child's coral. Shoes of brown satin, bound and sandalled with silver braiding. Long gloves of white kid.

WALKING DRESS
A round robe of white jaconet muslin, with a boddine of violet sarsnet,
trimmed with rich silk Brandenburgs of Austrian green, a half pelisse
of fine transparent muslin, with Bishops sleeves, fancifully tied with
green ribband and lace, ornamented with a green military plume; a
Chinese parasol, sarsnet, shot with green; gloves and shoes of York tan.

And another similar list in a different edition of the same gazette:

ANOTHER DRESS
A simple white muslin gown, made with a short train, and enriched
round the bottom with a superb border of ruby foil, made perfectly
plain, with a square back, and loose front, gathered into a band of
white satin; the shoulder straps are also of white satin, which continue
round the back. The sleeves are made short to cover only the top of
the shoulder, gathered into a band of white satin, with scarcely any
fullness, to correspond.

For the most part, this is a language all of its own, and near un-interpretable
to the modern mind, but it would have been very familiar to the women of
that era. An indication of what a woman actually possessed is given in the
inventories from existing will-books. These would have to have been
widows, and also women of substance, to have such an entry at all. If a
married woman died there was no will because her property had previously
all passed to her husband anyway. Eleanor Cope of Madras had a wardrobe
which contained a silk brocade gown and petticoat, a white satin sack half
trimmed with gold, a checked lute-string nightgown, a pink satin quilted
petticoat, four gowns of white morees, twenty coarse dimity (cotton woven
in stripes or squares) petticoats, fourteen ditto bedgowns, and twenty-four
shifts. Mrs Bromley, a lawyer's widow, had three muslin silver-flowered
dresses and numerous petticoats and shifts.[13] The will of the widow Elizabeth
Ure had, besides silks, gowns, caps, jewellery and silver in an inventory
extending to twenty-two pages, also fifteen pairs of silk shoes, fifteen pieces
of soap and, interestingly, four toothbrushes. (Inventory 9 August 1822)

Most households had a tailor, or *darzee*, who was invariably male,
regardless of whether he was working for mistress or master. He would have
been a Hindu of good caste, usually very capable indeed, and as comfortable
working with Western dress as oriental. The pressure on him to create new
out of old could be intense, and occasionally one reads of feminine outbursts

when the result was not exactly to taste, or not yet finished, and the garment being required that evening. The interest in new fashions extended beyond newspaper reports to an almost compulsive curiosity about what any newcomer to India was wearing, and these poor girls were regularly grilled by collections of ladies on the latest length of waist, or shape of sleeve or shoes.[14] Where possible, new dresses and other garments were sent for from home, although by the time they arrived they were almost certainly already out of date. This didn't stop a frisson of fascination among the European population when these items arrived, and dresses were often lent out so that a pattern could be taken from them; a practice still remembered by our parents and grandparents.[15] If the women felt uncertain about what was fashionable, the men were invariably hopelessly out of their depth, although still not above critical utterances aimed at their wives, or indeed any woman within range. In her journal, Elizabeth Fenton describes sitting next to a young army officer at a dinner in Chinsurah who described to her, in shocked tones, how he had 'observed a lady in conversation with some of the officers at the gate [of the parade ground] driving out in the same style of dress she would have worn at a ball, *her neck and arms quite uncovered*'. His reaction of prim condemnation gave way to one of agonised mortification when he realised that the lady he was referring to was none other than the one to whom he was speaking. Even when told that she was vastly more amused than piqued, he squirmed with embarrassment for the rest of the evening, probably to her silent satisfaction.[16] Those were not the days when one could readily laugh off a social gaffe but, then as now, it is a sensible axiom that men should never make any comment on a woman's appearance, unless it is favourable.

Soon after the advent of high-waisted, loose-skirted dresses, William Hickey recalls how in 1793 a Dutchman was taken aback by seeing a number of girls dressed in this fashion at a dance, and who expressed pity for the obvious embarrassment to their parents. When his neighbours could see no particular reason for this presumed discomfiture, he exclaimed to their great amusement, and his eventual blushes, 'Mein God, no reasonable cause of their uneasiness; is it not apparent that they are all with *child!*'[17] The style certainly concealed all sorts of variations in shape.

Women's clothes in India often became quite shabby it seems. One assumes that there were various reasons for this, not least that they weren't so easy to replace as they were at home. Sarah Robinson, the medical wife, wrote to her sister that she had worn the same formal dress for as long as six years. She was, in fact, so pleased with it: 'I find myself very fashionable'; that she disconcertingly threatened her sister with an identical one that she would make for her. Emma Roberts, that doyenne of Calcutta society in the early 1800s, happily commented on: 'The contrast between the splendid dresses of a London ballroom, fresh in their first gloss, with the tarnished, faded, lustreless habiliments exhibited in Calcutta.'[18] Elizabeth Grant, far away in Bombay, also found that dresses looked shabby more quickly in the Indian climate, and that she had to hope for new arrivals 'from my London dressmaker'.[19] Elsewhere she complained about the somewhat traditional, even fossilised, attitudes of men. She referred in particular to her husband who, as was often the case, was a good deal older than her and could not bear change, and 'Obliged me to appear very unlike the times, and look dowdy enough for many a year'.[20] One wonders whether the older husbands were tacitly fearful of their wives looking too attractive to other, younger, men.

Undoubtedly, one reason why clothes lasted so poorly, men's as well as women's, was the frequent need for washing owing to 'the process of perspiration', as Sarah Robinson delicately expressed it. In that hot climate, and with the completely unsuitable clothing of the time, most people must have been drenched. The women were somewhat better off with their light floating muslins, loose skirts, décolleté, and often bare arms. The men, on the other hand, must have suffered severely in their tail coats, waistcoats, shirts and breeches with stockings, even if everything was made of a light cotton material, but especially those burdened with a gown of office. Spare a thought for the judge, who would have been sitting with a host of others, packed like sardines in a steaming courtroom for a whole day at a time in full bottom wig and scarlet gown, under which were his usual clothes. An added factor was the vigorous approach to washing pursued by the average *dhobi wallah*; none of the gentle reciprocating sloshing-about in a stainless steel drum, but a violent and lengthy process of squeezing, slapping and slamming against hard stone steps, or rocks. The process hasn't changed for centuries but the results were, and still are, very fine, even if the life was beaten out of most garments. Elizabeth Gwillim wrote to her sister:

The borders of printed handkerchiefs disappear. Port wine goes clean out the first washing, and brown cotton stockings are no longer brown after one washing. I think you would envy me if you saw a washing of clothes come home. It looks all as if it was quite new, and the stockings are treated the same. I should buy them in any shop for real. They beat it on the pieces of rock, in the rivers where they wash, and the linens cut directly. As to hems, whether of calico or linen, about four or five washings beat them entirely out and they must be done again.[21]

Towels and waistcoats, among other things, soon developed frayed edges; no wonder the women's clothes looked a little shabby before their time.

The emerging change in personal attitude to the whereabouts of clothing manufacture is revealing. In 1827 Elizabeth Fenton wrote in her journal:

> It is, I must tell you, the extremity of bad taste to appear in anything of Indian manufacture – neither muslin, silk, flowers, or even ornaments, however beautiful. This at first amazed me; when I wanted to purchase one of those fine-wrought Dacca muslins I was assured I must not be seen in it as none but half-castes ever wore them.[22]

Until this time, Indian muslins were extremely popular in England, as they already were with the British in India. This was the age of muslin, and Jane Austen's correspondence and books make frequent mention of spotted, checked and cambric muslin. The best quality muslins came from India, especially Dacca in the north. The rate of manufacture, however, was much slower with the traditional Indian techniques than on the newly mechanised looms in England. Gradually, a burgeoning export trade from the Lancashire mills developed, giving rise to the bizarre paradox whereby cotton was imported to England, converted to a fabric, and then re-exported back to its origin – where such fabrics could not only be made anyway, but made very well indeed. An increasing desire to protect and encourage this new industry sprang up in the home country, leading to resistance against the importing of foreign-manufactured fabrics, such as from India, and a parallel resistance in that country to wearing the locally made ones. This all coincided with the expanding movement away from things Indian in other contexts.

Shoes were small, dainty and often made of satin. In the hot climate they grew tight over swelling feet, and it was fatal to remove them or one would be obliged to remain shoeless.[23] Because of their quality and inevitable scarcity, English shoes were precious; Indian copies were well made, but didn't last and would 'lose their shape directly'.[24] Fashion from the neck upwards was even more arcane. There were numerous cosmetics, but the requirement for a pale, porcelain complexion was achieved with a white lead-based cream, which had a number of toxic effects, including loss of eyebrows and a receding hairline. The pallid facial base could be garnished with a theatrical variety of potions: Rouge, Venus Bloom, and Mareshall Powder to name but a few.[25]

Until about 1800 however, the principal fad was for patches, which were peppered randomly about the face, or to cover some specific blemish. Some women became a bit carried away. On one occasion a woman had so extensively scattered these across her face, like a rash of mole hills, that an Indian prince whom she was visiting with her husband became rather exercised, and was moved to sympathise effusively, and to hope she would soon be 'rid of her boils'.[26] Hair and head were crowned with an array of caps, bonnets, and turbans, embellished with oddments. In the Symonds sisters' letters home there is reference to a bonnet with flowers, a cap with pink ribbon, a lace one with yellow ribbon, a blue bonnet and a sapphire-coloured velvet one, and also one made of white satin in which was planted 'a large creped white feather.' The permutations were extensive, and under all this there might be 'false foretops of hair', and an array of combs and pins. As so often before and since, the compulsion to conform created torment – but especially so in that climate. Elizabeth Fenton described in 1828 the anguish of a long hot dinner party and 'The inconvenience of my voluminous gauze dress, and the agony of my small satin shoes.' At last the time came when she could leave, and she described the bliss of stretching out in her palanquin where she: 'Pulled all my combs out, threw off my shoes, almost undressed myself, flung my pretty necklace and earrings on the mat, and shut my eyes until put down in my own verandah.' Fashion compliance can be torture.[27]

As any costume drama indicates, much time was taken up by needlework during the Georgian and Regency periods, some of which was complex and exquisite. As with music, it was a universal accomplishment. A few women made an industry of dressmaking in India. One such was Eliza Fay, who returned there after separation from her feckless barrister husband, and set up such a business. This succeeded for a while, but eventually failed, apparently from mismanagement; within a few years there were several such establishments in Calcutta, amounting to fourteen by 1840.[28,29]

When time allowed, after the convoluted organisation of a large household, another indoor interest was reading. Books were certainly available, or could be borrowed from friends. Those in existence depended wholly on what had come from England, and so there was a thriving exchange system. Copies were also printed in Calcutta, a blind eye being turned to any copyright issue. Walter Scott was extremely popular, and also Byron, whose thrilling romanticism was particularly popular with the women of the time. The Pickwick Papers had shot into literary prominence, and Emily Eden describes reading this with pleasure during her progress through Upper India with her brother. This was in 1837, only a year after its publication, and when Dickens was only 24.[30] That indefatigable diarist,

Fanny Parkes, describes the existence of a book society in Allahabad in 1832, although goes no further in discussing what actually happened in it. Nevertheless she was delighted with Allahabad which she describes as: 'One of the gayest and prettiest stations in India. We have dinner parties more than enough; balls occasionally; some five or six billiard-tables; a pack of dogs, some amongst them hounds, and (how could I have forgotten!) fourteen spinsters!'[31] Books didn't feature greatly in some people's lives, however, as Maria Sykes wrote from Bombay, when describing the arrival of young women in India aged no more than15:

> *When the intellect is sufficiently expanded to value improvement, but before time has been given for the acquisition of useful knowledge the adulation of men supersedes every desire for improvement. I one day asked one of these indolent beauties if she would like to read Waverley of Sir Walter Scott, which had just been lent to me. No, I thank you, she replied, I have no curiosity; I never read.*[32]

Newspapers were always popular, as a source of information about everyone and everything, but most especially about home. Bundles of year-old newspapers from England were consumed eagerly and, in dire circumstances, even those several years old.

Drawing and painting were accomplishments expected of any young woman in the Georgian, Regency and early Victorian eras. The temptation to depict India, and the life of its people in charcoal or watercolours was irresistible. Emily Eden frequently mentions places in her journal that she sketched or painted during her grand upper-India journey, and the results were eventually published on her return to England in 1844. A few years later Fanny Parkes also published, or made public, her illustrations of India in the hope of bringing knowledge of that country to a wider audience.[33]

There will have been so many such paintings lost or destroyed over the years, but some must still hang on a wall somewhere, isolated from their origin, and unrecognised. Some that have come to light since are of a very fine quality. Such are the extremely accurate and beautiful paintings of Indian birds by Elizabeth Gwillim, who died in 1807, before having the chance to return home. Her paintings are both life-sized, and taken from life, preceding Audubon by some twenty years. They are generally judged to be of high quality. Elizabeth was evidently a bird lover because a letter to her mother in 1803 contains several pages of detailed descriptions of the birds she had seen in southern India.[34] She was a prolific artist, and had to work fast – her living models could not be kept captive for long because they would not eat.[35] Elsewhere in her correspondence, she writes of her need for materials, always a problem for artists in India: 'Newman's cartridge paper and, above all, brushes; also Indigo, Umber and Vandyke Brown and Payne's grey, or Smith's grey;' elsewhere, 'Indigo, Prussian blue, Lake, Indian yellow.'[36] Such names are still familiar 200 years later; memories of an everyday childhood paint box. A collection of her fine paintings was found entirely by chance by a retired ophthalmologist (and avid collector) at a London dealer in the 1920s and is now in the possession of a Canadian University.

Much as with painting, most young ladies of that era were schooled in music. Keyboard, harp (and voice) were the main instruments, and these were all brought out from England, shipped in the cabins of their owners. Some would have been sold before the owner returned home, but the more precious items were shipped all the way home again. Mary, the wife of the Rev Charles Wimberley, was lent a Broadwood grand piano; something she certainly appreciated, and a rather uncommon and valuable acquisition in those earlier years of Broadwood's history, although one has to wonder how difficult it must have been to transport such an instrument many thousands of miles by sea.[37] Caring for a piano in the Indian climate was a problem. There are reports of pianos splitting in the heat, so the clearly musical Mary Wimberley would wrap hers in a blanket, and 'Put it by until the hot winds are over as already it is showing symptoms of having felt them.'[38,39] Despite this, four months later she opened it up, and wrote 'I fear that it is quite spoilt as scarcely any of the notes will sound.' If the piano survived unscathed, there was always the chance the sheet music wouldn't, being high on the bill of fare among the termite population. Inevitably, many stringed instruments, including the piano, went out of tune quickly and easily. Some households played them this way, possibly unaware of the discordance, but to the dismay of newcomers nevertheless.[40] Piano tuners were scarce, but many women quite happily tuned their own, and this tended to be the norm.[41] Just as there were military bands for regimental occasions and Governors' dinners, there were also groups of amateur musicians, or sometimes professional chamber orchestras. While today someone in their twenties or thirties might exercise their dexterity with computer games, or even home improvements, in the nineteenth century and earlier it was painting and music, and also needlework for the women. A high percentage of educated people could read music and play an instrument, if only to a modest standard. Musical soirées were common, and regularly referred to in women's writings:

Mrs Wiggins had a musical party. Miss Swinhoe sang, but not in such fine voice as last time. Mrs Littler played on the harp very well and very sweetly. A Mrs Abbott most disgustingly, as if bawling was melody. Lieutenant Andrews played the violin extremely well but his instrument rather squeaky.[42]

Singing was a common enjoyment. Many women would visit friends to practise duets with them, and after a dinner party an individual might be asked to perform, or groups might sing 'duettes or glees'; the men were quite as accomplished as the ladies.[43,44] It is unlikely such an invitation in modern times would be received with enthusiasm. While in Simla with her brother and his whole political and military entourage, Emily Eden describes visiting two acquaintances, a Mr and Mrs C, after dinner one evening:

I was to lie on the sofa and they were to sing, and so they did, beautifully, all sorts of things; she sings equally well in five languages, French, English, German, Italian, and Hindustani, and Mr C sings anything that is played to him without having any music.[45]

In the context of so many amateur musicians there was a need for tuition, just as much in India as in England, and accomplished players would offer their services to those lower down the ladder. There were also some rather more professional teachers, and one such was the enigmatic Miss Nina d'Aubigny von Englebrunner. She was especially interesting because she was German in an essentially British India, single and earning her own living. Nina was from an established old German and Huguenot family, and was something of a feminist intellectual. She was accomplished in four languages in addition to her own, and had an extensive musical education. She sang alto to a professional standard, and was highly skilled on the piano, harp and Italian guitar. She wrote several books about music, and taught all these instruments as well as singing in several countries, where she also performed professionally. Being unmarried, and her father being unable to support her any longer, she had to find employment, either that or a husband, but she obviously wasn't ready for that step. She and her sister Emilie travelled to England where there was a promise of better paid work, and there Nina found a job as a lady's companion, and thereafter as a partner in the ownership and running of a girls' boarding school. Meanwhile, sister Emilie sailed for Calcutta with her employer to continue her position as a companion there. Nina's school later failed, during her absence in Germany, as a consequence of her business partner's poor management, and so she too decided to make her way to India. There she joined Emilie and, after running her own finishing school for a while, and writing articles for German, French and British newspapers and periodicals, she took a job tutoring the youngest daughter of Sir William Burroughs. Burroughs was a not-entirely-loved judge at the Supreme Court in Calcutta. We have come across his older daughters elsewhere; the one scarified by William Hickey, and the other marrying Sir Thomas Strange, then Chief Justice in Madras. Nina got to know Sir William quite well, and he was keen to marry her, having recently been left by his wife. She was not the marrying kind, however, or certainly not to him. She later made a success of life by tutoring music, as well as performing, but she then fell ill and so, in 1816 and financially secure, she finally made the decision to leave India.

She had been in India for eight years, during which time she kept a diary in which she recorded her experiences. Having at first been favourably impressed by the education system in England, and its effect on British thinking and enterprise, she was less inspired by the British in India. She commented on the constant magpie chattering of the small talk, and the 'inclination of the English to do nothing'. Nevertheless this didn't inhibit her mischievously flirting with some of the young men. Her observations could be both wicked and witty. She commented about one young man, just arrived from England, that he was 'Full of life, poetry and youth; a pity that one of his dark eyes looks to the north during the time the other searches south, which may facilitate his talking sweetly to two belles at once.' The compelling thing about Nina von Engelbrunner is that she was dependent on no-one during her time in India, particularly not a man; didn't live for long with the only other family member, her sister, and made her own living throughout her time there. She did, of course, have a talent that was both respectable and marketable.[46, 47]

Other indoor pursuits enjoyed by women were cards, and collectibles. When they weren't playing music, singing, reading or writing, the card tables might be opened, especially after dinner. The journals of Eden and of West, and many other sources, refer to whist as probably the most popular game among the ladies. Others were piquet, vingt-et-un and loo. Many of the men gambled furiously, and not a few women as well, some of whom almost brought their husbands to their financial knees. In general, they were sociable games for a mixed four, and a good way to pass the evening after dinner and, as she often implied, a ploy in Lucretia West's case to avoid an obligation to play the piano, or sing, for the other guests. Collectibles, or the collection of curiosities, were a phenomenon of the time, right through into the Victorian period. They were especially popular with those women who had spent time abroad, in that their opportunity to collect something bizarre was obviously much greater than at home. They were the social equivalent of the botanical or zoological collections made by men who had taken on a role parallel to their day job, that is if they had one, and in the process became amateur scientists. The cabinet of curiosities was a talking point when receiving visitors, and afforded interest and pleasure to many women. It was no more than a hobby, that involved the collection of odd objects encountered during their lives in India, and which would eventually be taken home and proudly displayed to gratify the curiosity of visitors. Elizabeth Gwillim reports that Lady Clive was an enthusiastic collector.[48] Fanny Parkes certainly was. Contained in her cabinet of curiosities were 'skulls of alligators, crocodiles, hyenas and tigers, beautifully prepared,' a host of unspecified items and a scorpion that she had killed herself: 'a good fat old fellow'.[49] Julia Maitland in the *mofussil* north of Madras describes the finding of a cobra in her garden which she, or rather a servant, killed by dropping it into a bottle of neat spirits where it died from drowning, or even intoxication; quickly one hopes. The bottle was then sealed, and this 4ft monster was thus preserved as a curiosity on her desk, perpetually fixed in its death throe.[50]

Some women were astonishingly versatile and experimental in their leisure diversions and in the forefront, as one would expect, was the resolute Fanny Parkes. She could make articles from brass or silver, and was plainly skilful at turning wood. She could incise the wood to match a facial profile on a painting or drawing, and then cut the wood into a fine slice that could be mounted as a framed profile of the subject.[51]

A popular social diversion, in addition to dining and dancing, was amateur theatricals, and similar extravaganzas. These could be found in both small and larger settlements, and were as frequent as the energy and time that could be afforded by the chief participants – who were almost always men. It was not regarded as seemly for women to take to the stage in that era. Not unsurprisingly the standard was variable, but a good amount of labour went into the preparation. Fanny Parkes described going to the theatre in 1837 in Jelalabad, on the eve of one of her many journeys. The production was performed by privates in the Artillery, who built a theatre, decorated the scenery and formed the cast: 'The scenery is excellent, the house crowded; the men acted remarkably well; and the ladies, strapping artillery men, six feet high, were the cause of much laughter.'[52] One cannot but wonder if somewhere here was the beginning of the pantomime dame of today. Comedy and farce were the preferred format, but the classics were never far away. The women got in on the fun by performing in masquerades. These were not fancy dress balls, as one might suppose, but an opportunity to dress up and perform, which usually meant singing a few songs and adopting appropriate attitudes. Sophia Plowden, wife of a well-known Bengal civil servant, Richard Chicheley Plowden, later to become a director of the East India Company, clearly enjoyed making an impression in this way. In 1783 she wrote to her sister in England about fulfilling a long held ambition to act, with others, the part of a band of Kashmiri musicians. This she achieved, supported by a group of friends in Calcutta who were musically talented. One man 'was very musical and easily learnt to play the *sirindar*, or fiddle, of this country, and all my Persian and Hindustani songs.' Another played the sitar. Somehow it is hard to imagine a similar interest and capability in later Raj years. She went on to describe the essence of her performance in lengthy and indulgent detail. This was to beautify herself in Kashmiri fashion, including the wearing of 'long draws, or pyjamas, of dark green silk with gold small flowers fastened with a rose coloured string and gold tassels.' This was barely visible as she wore a petticoat over it, and over this a *shurta*, or muslin shift, and finally, a long sleeved dress decorated with silver gauze and rose-coloured satin. She also wore gold and silver slippers, and a 'turban of rose colour muslin with a silver tassel and a band of silver embroidery around it which fastened in front with a clasp of jewels composed of rubies, diamonds and emeralds.' Her hair was un-powdered and heavily plaited, and she wore swathes of jewellery garlanded about her chest, face, waist, arms and feet, with rings on her toes, and hennaed hands and nails. She was evidently quite pleased with the result – and with herself – remarking: 'The songs I sang were very pretty ones and the group were so admirably dressed that many people insisted on our being Hindustani. I received an infinite number of fine compliments on my appearance.' One must hope her audience were as generous with their sincerity as they were with their applause.[53] Thirty or forty years later, any such Indianization, particularly associated with the levity of a masquerade, would have been frowned upon by many. The rather starchy Lucretia West reported the contents of a sermon, preached by the chaplain in Bombay during her time there:

A thunderous sermon from Mr Davies; there was a play acted last week by amateurs which he of course condemns, & all parties. He certainly keeps my attention which neither of the others do; they are so prosy and sleepy. I am sure he does good. He must make [one]

*reflect a little & is I believe a very good well meaning man. We did
not go to the play; I do not fancy amusements or gaiety here.*[54]

Various other activities filled the remaining corners of their time. In her
journal, Emily Eden describes some of the jollities she and her brother got
up to in Simla in 1838. A particular feature of the time was the fancy fair.
The ladies of the place would manage stalls in a countryside marquee, which
on this occasion was in a rather fine valley near Simla called Annadale, now
a golf course and helipad. Each stall was labelled, such as The Bower of
Eden, or The Red Cow, holding odd items of clothing, jewellery and such
like, and all selling very fast to both Europeans and Indians alike. In addition
to this, there was a wheel of fortune and a lucky bag, both very popular. A
number of Emily Eden's drawings and paintings were auctioned, and later
there were sports events such as shying at a tin snuff box; the early nineteenth
century equivalent of a coconut shy perhaps. The European community
numbered just 150 people, but the whole event raised a record 3,400 Rupees,
equivalent to approximately £20,000 today – not bad for an afternoon's
equivalent to a church fete. The aim was entirely charitable, which would
have been both valuable to the community, and given some satisfaction to
Emily Eden, who raised a quarter of this from her artistic efforts alone.[55]

On another occasion, in the same valley, a small fête champêtre was
organised by six couples:

*They had bows and arrows, a swing, battledore and shuttlecock, and
a fiddle – the only fiddle in Simla; and they danced and eat all day,
and seemed to have liked it wonderfully throughout... . They give
another pic-nic next Thursday, and we are getting up some tableaux
and charades which are to be acted here* [the Governor's house]; *the
dining room to be turned into a theatre.*[56]

Outdoor leisure activities were relatively uncommon for women. While men
would ride or hunt vigorously, the modern concept of taking physical exercise
was not one that really existed for women. Although the word was used, it
meant little more than going out of doors. An evening stroll in one of the
coastal Presidency towns, along the esplanade, no more than a residential
seaside road, was a pleasure occasionally indulged in for an hour or so, but
not for the majority. As Lucretia West said in 1823: 'We are so unfashionable
we walk for an hour on the esplanade in a retired corner.'[57] Much commoner
was the evening or morning drive. The only exercise here would have been

getting in or out of a carriage. It was an event much enjoyed, and was inevitably an opportunity to see and be seen by those people out and about doing the same thing, as well as to enjoy 'the fresh air blowing on your neck and arms.'[58] Up and down a long road they would go, such as Mount Road in Madras, now Anna Salai, where the proud statue of Governor Sir Thomas Munro still stands. With a little imagination one can almost hear the sotto voce caustic wit sniped at other ladies' behaviour, or their attire, or else the murmur of envious chatter when faced by someone of particular standing or wealth. Not that this was inevitable. In 1809 Martha Sherwood wrote in Cawnpore:

> We generally went along the Sepoy Parade, where we met all the people of distinction in the place, and the varieties of equipages, costumes and living conveyances were really vastly amusing. There were officers in their plumed hats and gallant uniforms, riding for their very lives, with the syce [groom] panting by their sides, bearing in their hands the chowries [whisks] by which they defended the heads of their horses from the hosts of flies which always tormented them; elephants with their splendid howdahs; curricles and gigs, bullock-coaches laden with dames and babies; now and then a string of gawky camels; and, in great numbers, the open tonjon bearing the European lady in her elegant evening dress and lace cap, or veil, serving as a bonnet.[59]

Occasionally a pair of carriages would stop side by side, and the occupants would get out and walk and talk with their friends in the cool evening air.[60] Such a regular social event has now completely disappeared as a concept, and the modern networking equivalent is electronic, and detached.

The alternative to driving would be riding, which was for the most part an everyday event for men, but women were no strangers to it, especially if living in the *mofussil*. They didn't write much about it in their journals or letters, as the world of horses was such an everyday feature of their lives. However our ardent feminist Fanny Parkes obviously adored the freedom her horse gave her. It allowed her to demonstrate some of the activities and courage more commonly associated with men at that time. Flora Holman was similar; her reminiscences of her childhood in India in the 1840s were written down by her granddaughter many years later. She remembered relishing the opportunity for riding out every morning, and as a young girl galloping alone across the plains, despite the risks inherent in being right on the Afghan border in the North West territories.[61] Fanny had been given a beautiful Arab (horse) by her husband, which she cantered at six o'clock each morning on the race course in Calcutta or, in the evenings, on the drive in front of Government House. At the time she wrote down the interesting comment that:

> *So few of the gentry in England can afford to keep riding-horses for their wives and daughters that I was surprised, on my arrival in Calcutta, to see almost every lady on horseback; and that not on hired hacks, but on their own good steeds. My astonishment was great one morning on beholding a lady galloping away, on a fiery horse, only three weeks after her confinement. What nerves the woman must have had!*[62]

Much as for the manoeuvres carried out by the military, some women would get up at 3.30 to 4 o'clock in the morning to ride out in the cool darkness, before returning for another couple of hours sleep before breakfast.

For women, the universal style of riding was side-saddle, which accommodated their voluminous skirts, and any general notion of modesty. When Fanny Parkes visited the widow of the great Mahratta king, Scindia, in the camp to which she was exiled after his downfall, she also visited the zenana. Here, where no men were allowed, she demonstrated by request the manner of riding among European women. This caused great hilarity among the zenana women, who could not understand how this awkward style gave one any control of a horse. Their views seemed to be confirmed when they tried it out and all but fell off, clinging wildly to the saddle pommel, laughter evaporating. It was then Fanny's turn to change into Mahratta clothes, and sit astride a horse, something she would have found quite alien. In fact she relished the experience, expressing regret at the original development of the side saddle, and finding that riding 'en cavalier appeared so safe, as if I could have jumped over the moon.'[63] It is unclear whether she changed her style, but it seems doubtful that even Fanny Parkes would have confronted the established conventions of her times.

Many of her contemporaries were skilled horsewomen, as she was herself; but more so still were those who lived in the *mofussil* as the upcountry wives of soldiers or indigo planters, rather than the elegant and languid ladies of downtown Calcutta, Madras or Bombay. These women would be no strangers to trekking on horseback through rough country and, again, Fanny Parkes describes exploring the hill country above Mussoorie with a woman friend, roaming, camping and admiring the scenery. Many of the tracks were not only narrow, but also steep; snaking their way along the sides of precipitous gorges. They had already heard of two horses that had been killed in the company of a party of soldiers, slipping over the edge into a gorge. The two women were therefore wholly dependent on their agile, surefooted hill ponies, but one of these lost its footing, carrying Fanny's friend over the edge. By good fortune, it fell on its right side so that, being side-saddle, her leg wasn't crushed. Horse and rider slid down the sheer slope and 'but for a tree the lady and her steed would have been dashed to pieces.' She escaped unscathed, although very bruised – and probably also a bit damp having fallen into a mountain stream a while earlier. Although jaunts such as this would not have been familiar to every Georgian or Regency woman in India, they would have been on the spectrum of experience that needed to be tolerated if survival in that country was to be maintained.[64]

In the context of a near universal ability to handle a horse, it is no surprise that riding to hounds was quite common; then in Bihar as now with the Belvoir. In fact it was nowhere near so grand, and mostly pursued the humble jackal, an unloved and vicious creature. There are reports of packs of hounds in Madras in 1776, and jack-hunting was an excuse for a thoroughly good hack.[65] It was chiefly a male sport, but there is nothing to suggest that women did not occasionally enjoy the pursuit; and it is no surprise that our old friend Fanny would be out chasing jackals at times, although seemingly not with hounds. These were very expensive, and rather difficult to care for in that climate.[66] Women didn't get involved with hunting traditional game, but seemed to enjoy writing about it. The men were, of course, out shooting anything that moved – including, sometimes, each other.

The Indian countryside in those days was very different from now. There is barely a square metre today that is not cultivated; rice in the north, cotton in the south, wheat and vegetables almost everywhere. Two hundred years ago it was a very different matter. The landscape was significantly less populated, and there were vast tracts of wilderness or, as it was then called, jungle. Depending on the area of the country, there would have been acres of scrub with a dry, dusty undergrowth, and large areas of forest. This wasn't as dense as one sees in rainforest, but the variety and beauty of the trees was extraordinary, and still is in those increasingly scarce places that Indian wilderness still exists. The British would have seen several from the vast litany of tree names, so unfamiliar to the Westerner; the teak, with its plate-like leaves, wild mango, fig, the banyan, with its trailing aerial roots, the spindle-leaved neem, tulip tree, tamarind, with large pod-like bitter fruit, the sal, with its long straight trunk, quick-growing casuarinas, papayas and, if lucky, even the baobab, cashew or peepul. Beneath them could have been thorn bushes and, at the right time of year, flowering shrubs enough to excite the most dour of horticulturalists: jasmine, bougainvillea, and orchid among so many. Riding through this on horseback must have projected a feast of visual distraction, especially when the intention was to hunt the usual antelope, boar, and wild peacock, or other game birds. The cover afforded by this forest and brush-scape was perfect for that gilded emperor of the Indian outback: the tiger.

The tiger, of course, became the holy grail of the hunting Indian British. The women of earlier years had little to do with the activity, unlike their much later descendants, who occasionally joined in from the lofty protection of an elephant's howdah; but that didn't stop them writing about it in their correspondence, although not always favourably. There were numerous leopards in the jungle as well, and these still exist today, although in much smaller numbers, and only in the wilder areas, such as Chattisgarh. Remarkably, Eliza Draper in the 1770s made the statement in a letter to her cousin, 'Our field sports have something royal with em [sic] here – what think you of hunting the antelope with leopards? This I have frequently done – and a noble diversion it is.' Frustratingly, there the subject ends, and there are no details as to the practicalities. There is evidence, however, of the same technique being used today in Saudi Arabia. In India, regional Princes used cheetahs for the purpose until at least the 1930s.

Tigers were immensely common in India in earlier years. There are references to them throughout women's letters and journals, and not uncommonly they found themselves closer to these fine but alarming beasts than they would have preferred, especially if out in the countryside.[67,68] Hunting them had been the pursuit of Maharajahs and lesser royalty for centuries, glorified in innumerable miniature, and other, paintings. This continued among the princely class in the nineteenth and twentieth centuries but by then the British had acquired a taste for the sport, and tigers were shot in their thousands, and to the point of extinction. It is now rightly condemned and forbidden, although unfortunately poaching still continues. In the earlier Indian British years, hunting was encouraged, even requested, by native villagers and other country dwellers. This was because of the constant loss to their numbers from tigers looking for easy prey, or any prey at all, where competition for food was more intense, due to their then high numbers. Sarah Robinson refers to arriving at an evening halt on a long cross-country journey to learn that two men had just been killed at that spot.[69] Emily Eden heard of tigers regularly during her trek through upper India. On one occasion the men in her party were pursuing a man-eater who had taken seven or eight people from neighbouring villages.[70] Flora Holman, sometime in the 1840s, described her experience of travelling through open hilly country towards the northwest frontier, beset by tigers, wild elephants, leopards and black bears, and also 'black scorpions'. Fires were kept alight all night in the camp, to ward them off. One evening, they arrived at a village where there was much merriment, music and dancing, because a wedding was in full swing. At midnight however, 'Joy was turned to sadness, as the bride, aged ten, suited the taste of a tiger. He watched for her to be alone and, as she crossed from one tent to another, he took her.'[71] Inevitably there was no concept at that time of wildlife protection. If specific wild animals were causing a serious problem a solution was needed, and this meant hunting down the responsible culprit. This situation was a long stretch from hunting just for sport. Emily Eden wrote in her journal the following relevant passage:

W [her brother] *and Mr A have killed another dreadful tiger, or rather tigress, which they have hunted for and given up several times. She has carried off twenty-two men in six weeks, and while they were at the village, took away the brother of the chief man of the place; took him out of his little native carriage, leaving the bullocks untouched. They found her lair, and W. says they saw a leg and quantities of human hair and bones lying about it, and they saw her two cubs... . The next day she carried away a boy, and the villagers implored them to try again. They came to the remains of the boy, and at last found the tigress and brought her out by killing one of her cubs, and then shot her – but the horrid part of the story is that the screams of the boy who was carried off were heard for about an hour, and it is supposed she gave him to her cubs to play with. Such a terrible death! Altogether, W. and Mr A. have killed twenty six tigers – twenty large ones, and six cubs – which is a great blessing for the country they are in.[72]*

The line between hunting for necessity, and that for pleasure, was indeed a fine one; not a consideration that crossed the horizons of thinking at the time, and for many, hunting for fun was well on its way to becoming a firmly established sport. Sarah Robinson wrote in her journal from Secrole (Benares):

The General called yesterday morning; he was just returned from hunting tigers etc. He killed eleven tigers, nine bears, three wild buffaloes and lots of small game. Another hunting party had destroyed twenty-nine tigers, therefore I should hope that the whole breed will be extinct ere long.[73]

About the latter she was surely prescient, although with misplaced motives.

Travel to another part of India was relatively uncommon for any woman based in one of the Presidency towns. If it was necessary, the easiest way to reach another of these towns was to go by sea, a matter of two or three weeks sailing. Travelling across country was quite another matter. There were very few roads, and those that existed were mainly rough, unmade, and punishingly rugged. For a significant number of women it was necessary that they should make their way up country from Calcutta to the major towns further west, such as Patna, Benares (Varanasi), Allahabad and Lucknow, in order to accompany their military or planter husbands to the place where they lived, or were stationed.

Because of the non-existent roads, the first part of the journey was upstream along the Ganges river in large flat-bottomed boats, called *budgerows*, sailing, or being towed, as far as Allahabad if necessary, where the river Jumna joined it. After Calcutta, the flotilla of craft would glide past individual towns steeped in history even then; first Serampore, originally the site of the Danish East India Company, and later a missionary headquarters under the British, next Barrackpore, a British country residence catering for the Establishment of Calcutta, followed by Chandernagar, a French trading centre, shot into submission by Royal Navy ships just before the Battle of Plassey in 1757, and finally Chinsurah, which was originally a Dutch trading centre. All these have now merged into a widening oil slick of urbanisation. Quite a lot further up river there was the old capital of Bengal, Murshidebad, where the river was lined with stately palaces of mughal and later styles. Nearby was its more colonial annexe, Berhampore, with an altogether more administrative and cantonment flavour. The *budgerows* were themselves commodious boats on which there were cabins for sleeping, containing an adequate supply of furniture, and a saloon with a table large enough for eight, along with chairs, couches, writing desks and so forth. Venetian windows ran the length of these cabins, and the boat itself was equipped for sailing, but had about sixteen oars in case of necessity. Much of the time *budgerows* were travelling up river against the stream, and in that case they were often hauled along by ropes to the shore, pulled by the boatmen or *dandies*; an arduous business, especially where there was a headwind and a strong current. Hauling the boats against this, and around headlands, was often dangerous; banks undercut by the current sometimes came crashing down onto the *budgerows*, and several were sunk as a result.[74]

In addition to the accommodation boat, there was a cook boat, and one or more others containing luggage, furniture and the rest of the domestic paraphernalia, a sort of floating Pickford's. Travelling the 800 miles up to Benares was slow, but full of fascination for the voyagers, who admired the scenery and many ancient buildings, some ruined, whose nature seemed mysterious and not wholly understood. Nevertheless this was always a good opportunity to bring out the sketchpad and paint box. Things didn't always proceed smoothly. Mary Wimberley discovered that their baggage boat, a mile or so behind them, had sunk with the loss of books, clothes, personal possessions and much of their furniture, despite the boatmen diving and retrieving all they could.[75]

The Ganges was also full of sandbanks, and boats of every kind went aground on these, often driven onto them by the stream. The big heavy *budgerows* were hard to move, but by heaving on ropes, and driving off with poles, success was usual in the end. When Emily Eden was travelling into the northwest in 1837, the first part of the journey was again on the Ganges, except that in their case some of the *budgerows* were towed by a very early steamboat. This particular journey was done in style. The river section went as far as Benares (Varanasi), and then proceeded in a stately progress of 12,000 people, as well as camels, horses, elephants and mountains of baggage, all the way to Shimla. For more ordinary people, cross-country travel by boat was in no way as opulent as this extraordinary mission but, although arduous, was a diverting respite from the high temperature tedium of town life. The alternative means of travelling long distance was cross-country. The mode by which the majority of women travelled across the land depended on the terrain. If there was any form of track this could be by buggy (gig in England), which was a small carriage with two seats, two wheels and one horse or, at worst, by *hackery* (bullock cart). If there was no track, which was not uncommon, the women would travel by palanquin and the men would ride alongside on horseback. Sometimes travel would be to a neighbouring country town for a holiday, or at least a break from work and the big city. Lady Lucretia West recounts travelling from Bombay to a rented house in Poona for a short holiday with her husband, the judge Sir Edward West, the distance by road being about 90 miles today. There were five palanquins with eighty *hamauls*, or bearers, as well as five torchbearers because much of the travel was at night, during which the intention was that one should sleep in the palanquin. The journey took thirty-six hours, which included climbing the rugged Western Ghats; today it would take under three hours. A year or two later in 1828, Elizabeth Grant, the daughter of a judge who was a contemporary of Sir Edward West's, describes in her journal how the family went in a similar fashion into the hills, to a camp site in the Western Ghats. The retinue was large, with armed sepoys, bearers, servants, ayahs and so on. All of this was just for one family:

> *The luggage, tents, canteens, trunks, all on bullocks, peons and coolies running beside them to the number altogether of 50 or 60, with the beasts besides and our horses led. It was a long train winding round among the hills, always ascending and turning corners, and when night came on, and the torches were lighted and one was placed in about every fourth man's hand – the effect was wonderfully beautiful, the flames waving as the arms moved, leaves, branches, rocks, gleaming in turn among the dusky train that wound along up the steep pathway.*[76]

Daytime travel could be roasting, and was best avoided. Palanquins could heat up like saunas, and had to be cooled by having bowls of water thrown over them. Inmates would wear as little as possible, or as little as they dared.

Overland travel was far from being a stroll in the countryside. It was arduous, and difficulties were often encountered. The usual principle was to send a party ahead to the end of the stage for the day. This group would take with them a suitable amount of camping equipment (usually a large quantity), set it up, and start to prepare a meal ready for the travellers to arrive later in the day. The same thing would happen the following day, and so on in leapfrog fashion. There usually had to be two camp and cook teams, so that one of them could go on a day or two ahead, and give time for the first to pack up and, as like as not, travel through the night to get to the next stage ahead. They would take with them a change of *hamauls* (bearers) for the palanquins. The campsites were often extensive and comfortable, with furnished tents, adequate truckle beds, wall hangings and even carpets. Anyone who has done a tent safari in Africa will have some idea of the peace and beauty, as well as comfort, which can be achieved in an isolated spot that has been well chosen. Nearby water, a grove of trees and a distant undulating, beauteous landscape all add to the pleasure of arrival and relaxation. An alternative travel method would be in similar stages, but using the *Dak* bungalows of the very old Indian postal service, which by then the East India Company was subsuming into its own system. The bungalows were at stages on the main postal routes and were very basic, often empty, accommodation for postal employees, and any other travellers. In the earlier years many European women preferred to sleep in their palanquins, set down inside the *Dak* building safe from marauding animals, or predatory people. From the mid-nineteenth century the level of accommodation had improved, although it was still minimalist, and by then rudimentary catering was also on hand.

In 1815, Sarah, the somewhat reactionary and mildly overwrought wife of James Robinson, Assistant Surgeon, Bengal Army, travelled with her husband from Calcutta back to their home in Benares. They chose to go the 436 miles by road rather than river, because it was a shorter journey and they had been told it was excellent. They travelled in a buggy. In this they managed an average of 20 miles a day for about five days – little better than walking, but less effort. They then learnt that the young surgeon was badly needed on ahead at his base, so they decided to switch to the *dak* route, using just palanquins and bearers, and by this means they covered 350 miles in four-and-a-half days, or the astonishing feat of 75 miles a day on Indian feet alone – a feat indeed. There is no doubt that Sarah and James greatly admired and appreciated the efforts of the bearers, who also cooked their food. They appreciated rather less the behaviour of His Majesty's 24th Regiment, whom they met en route, and who had 'plundered the villages of all they could find, and the poor people fled as from a plague. The Kings Corps in this land are a degenerate breed; a set of lawless wretches who care for nobody.'[77] The Robinsons were, of course, attached to an Honourable Company regiment; so no prejudice there.

Sometimes travellers became lost, or other mishaps occurred on the road. This English family Robinson did not get stranded in a desert, but they did have some incidents which help us to understand the tribulations of overland travel at the time. Their route was deeply rutted, muddy and water-logged.

We found that in several places the road was destroyed and we had to get out while the syce [horseman] pulled the buggy through the places that seemed impassable from immense gaps, and water... . I every moment expected the springs would break and we should be left in the dirt. A fresh horse was put in; a little fiery Arab, but good natured and swift. He almost flew over the logs of mud and never minded our being nearly shaken into mummies... .We arrive suddenly at a massive gully, over which the buggy nearly plunges. Two syces prevented any disaster by quick action and led the horses through the gully and deep mud to the other side. A near disaster.

The buggy was clearly a compromise between comfort, speed and lightness, but not ideal for the conditions. The young couple were far from alone, however, being accompanied by a party reminiscent of a band of roving gypsies.

Our establishment was seven camels, one elephant (borrowed), three horses for the buggy, or rather four, though the fourth was very old, and James's saddle horse; one hackery, or cart, drawn by three bullocks, one palanquin in which my woman was conveyed, if I did not require it myself, a whole posse of armed servants, for they were very needful in a march over desert hills and plains uninhabited, and our own people, all old servants and eager to reach Benares; a few sheep and their shepherd, and my dear child's little dog, completed the party.[78]

Mary Doherty was a young army wife in Bangalore with two small boys, who was widowed in June 1820, her husband having been stationed there as Major of His Majesty's 13th Dragoons. Following his premature death she had no choice but to find the money to pay for accommodation on a ship back to England. First she had to return to Madras, which meant a journey of more than 200 miles overland in September of the same year, in the middle of the monsoon season. In the absence of any real roads this had to be by palanquin; she and one son in one, the other son and two nannies in another. The rain had been such that the water was rising fast, in and around any river, and departure had to be hurried. Early in the journey they arrived at a lake that had broken its banks and its containing wall, and the trail they needed to follow was found to go right through the middle of this. They crossed on a makeshift bamboo raft, which took an hour of precarious balancing, by which time it was dark, and they had no source of light. They also still had eight hours of travel before they would reach the *choultrey* (similar to a *dak* house, but not related to the postal system; an unmanned wayside inn of very basic type). Here they expected to find the next relay of bearers, only to discover that they had been purloined by someone else a few hours earlier:

Neither nanny nor myself could speak one word of the language and we were totally at the mercy of the palanquin boys who knew I had a

large sum of money in the palanquin with me. At last we reached it at
10 at night and found the choultrey occupied by a white soldier, more
than half tipsy, and his black wives and children all lying about the
floor asleep. In one corner our palanquins were placed.

Having found a nearby source of further bearers by the middle of the night,
the small party headed onwards through the rest of that night, and all the next
day. They crossed the Palar river 'which was so high as to oblige the
palanquin bearers to place the palanquins on their heads and they were often
carried off their feet by the current.' A little time later they ran out of food,
but eventually reached the top of the Eastern Ghats – at least 2,000ft up –
where they found that the next team of bearers had not turned up. In the
traditional manner of the British abroad, Mary pointed to her mouth to
indicate hunger, and clearly did a passable charade of a flapping hen, because
she was rewarded soon afterwards with a live cock, which was quickly
transformed into a very welcome curry. Only one of the two palanquins could
be got into the *choultrey*, and into this the children were placed. Mary and
the nannies slept on bedding on the floor, but their cook took a fancy to the
empty palanquin left outside, and settled down within it for the night. In the
middle of the night the indoor sleepers were woken by shrieks from the
unhappy cook who had become the object of intense interest to a tiger sniffing
and scratching around the palanquin. No doubt a cook smelt particularly
appetising, but the frustrated animal ran off amid the collective cacophony
from the whole household, who were only too aware that the *choultrey* had
no door, so that the tiger could have strolled in at any time.

The next day the small family party acquired some more bearers, who
carried them down the Ghat towards Madras. The way down was precipitous,
'But the poor bearers carried us safely down, though the poles of the
palanquins tore the flesh of their gallant shoulders.' Another change of
bearers, and again they were soon fording a river, with the water coming up
to the bearers' throats, and flowing through the palanquins. There were thirty
men to each one, sometimes having to swim, and although there was water
all around, the travellers by then had nothing that they dared drink.
Eventually, exhausted, dehydrated and hungry, they reached Madras, only
for Mary to have to negotiate a place on a ship home almost immediately, at
a price of £500 (an astonishing £20,000 today, at least) for a cabin measuring
10ft by 8ft for herself, her two children and their nanny. While such accounts
leave one impressed by the fortitude of female travellers in the pre-Victorian
years, one cannot help but be moved by at the tenacity, efficiency and loyalty

of the palanquin teams. There is little doubt that this was sincerely appreciated at the time, although it is evident that most of these men were more than glad of the employment. For many of them, any work, however hard, meant the difference between a contented family, or going hungry.

Women of that era were made of strong stuff. When Sir Stamford Raffles was in Sumatra in 1818 he made an excursion across country to make peace with a warring people who lived 50 miles within the interior, in a place that could only be reached through a dense and unexplored rainforest wilderness. The journey was arduous and dangerous, and involved the crossing of mountain passes whose whereabouts were unknown. The journey had to be done on foot, sometimes walking from before daylight until nine at night, and for up to thirty miles through wild country, as well as camping out in the open. To add to their enjoyment a torrential tropical downpour struck them from time to time. Apart from fifty coolies and six native officers, there were three British men and also Sophia, Raffles' wife, who came along of her own free will. She walked too, although was occasionally carried on a man's shoulders for half an hour. This journey would have been no mean accomplishment for a woman of her times, unused to walking much, and hardly dressed for the jungle. Nevertheless she accomplished it without incident, except that at one point she and one of the British men, an Edward Presgrave, found themselves separated from the main group and became completely lost in dense rainforest. Presgrave then fell into a pit from which he only extracted himself with the greatest difficulty. It was later entirely by chance that they once more came across the main party; otherwise it is more than likely they would be there still.

Two other areas of popular interest in which British women became involved in India were education and horticulture. Larger schools were run and supervised by men, especially those for boys. Many women, however, became involved in the organisation of schools for both girls and boys who were younger. There were plenty of poor within the British population in India, especially among the soldiers and their wives. Mortality in this group was high and consequently, there were many orphans. Where possible, these were congregated in orphanages, known as asylums, which were male or female, and often founded by a compassionate woman. One such was in Dinapore, created by Mary Sherwood, and there were a number of others, particularly in the Presidency towns. A good number of the children were of mixed race, and there were frequent instances of there being no funds to send them to England to be educated, which was the expectation of the children of better off families. Many were not even illegitimate, but faced a dire future without some support. Emily Eden wrote how shocked she was to learn of a palanquin containing three children, the oldest of whom was 9, being sent alone on a ten day journey to a school in Mussoorie; there being nowhere else for them to obtain any education and their parents being too short of funds to send them to England. They were completely unaccompanied, carried no papers or documents, and were just passed from one set of bearers to another across large stretches of country. After three days the bearers took it upon themselves to take the children to a European house, because they thought the children were tired. Here they were washed, dressed and fed, and later sent successfully on their way.

As the numbers of orphans, impoverished, or mixed race children increased, so the community responded hesitantly. By 1787 Lady Campbell, wife of the then Governor of Madras, had established a female asylum for mixed race children, under the control of twelve directresses.[79] The latter were found from the more established women of the Presidency, with the Governor's wife holding the most senior role, and the Chief Justice's wife, or the Commander in Chief's, being her deputy. Maria Callcott (formerly Graham) visited the Madras Asylum in August 1810 and commented:

It seems admirably conducted, and the girls neat, and very expert at all kinds of needlework. It is really gratifying to see so many poor creatures well brought up, and put in the way of gaining a livelihood. There is likewise a male orphan asylum, where the boys are brought up to different trades. If such establishments are wanted anywhere, it is in India, where the numbers of half-caste, and therefore half-parented children, exceed what one could imagine.[80]

The term half-parented is interesting. It either implies that the Indian parent is irrelevant, or that she has no idea who the father is. In the latter case it is unlikely that the child would even get as far as such a school, being regarded as wholly Indian. Even by 1810 a slight, almost instinctive, prejudice was beginning to creep in. Twenty-nine years later, when she revisited Madras, Julia Maitland commented that 'the poor female orphan asylum is as bad as ever.'[81] While some of the Madras women were involving themselves in its activities, a number of them would not cooperate by that time. There was now embarrassment and distaste among them, arising from the illegitimacy and mixed race provenance of the unfortunate inmates, as if somehow it was their fault, and which inclined many of these ladies to shun the institution altogether. This was 1839, by which time sanctimony and religious influence were beginning to prejudice the British against ordinary Indian people, their religions and their customs. The intolerance of Eurasian blood, with all it supposedly implied in the way of improper sexual practice, had by then grown to major proportions. It was also at this time that the influence of Bentinck and Macaulay was beginning to be felt, with their push towards educating the Indian people along British lines, and the adoption of English as the official language, rather than Persian or Sanskrit. As far as the children were concerned, these changes coincided with a growing interest in encouraging conversion to Christianity – many ladies longed to convert the 'heathens.' Julia Maitland opened a school in 1837 for native children in the up-country town of Rajamundhry, well north of Madras. The motives were elevated in principle, by teaching the children to read and write, but perhaps mildly subversive in practice in that they were taught English, in addition to Gentoo, but also some Christianity. She was, however, realistic enough to make the following comment, even if her aspirations remained fervent:

> *You must understand that we have no immediate hope of making Christians of these boys by our teaching, but we wish to do what we can for them, and I fully believe that, if schools were set up all over the country, it would go far towards shaking their Heathenism, by putting truth into their heads, at any rate, instead of falsehood.*[82]

In those intervening years, between their inception and the subsequent loss of interest, the orphan asylums provided a very worthwhile function. Who knows what would have happened to such children otherwise. The wife of the Chief Justice of Bombay, Lucretia West, in her journal between 1823 and 1825 described how she and other wives would visit the schools to hear the children read and spell, and also to supervise examinations and help with prize giving, notwithstanding her own personal timidity about being involved. She recorded:

> *This morning at 7 o'clock we went to lay the foundation stones of the two new central schools for the boys & the girls; Lady Chambers & myself for the girls & the Governor and the Archdeacon for the boys. We assembled I believe nearly all Bombay in tents; the children sang the morning hymn; we then laid the stones depositing an engraved brass plate & some coins and, with our silver trowels, I hope performed our work very elegantly.*[83]

It is hard to believe these efforts were not truly valued by the recipients, if only in retrospect. Some of these children would go on to work somewhere in the British community, but in future years, many of those of mixed-race would form the core of the impressive Anglo-Indian community that ran essential services, such as the railways, well into the twentieth century.

Horticulture and garden management was a preoccupation and joy for many women recently arrived in India, although some were inevitably keener than others. This was stimulated by the array of botanical wonderment present everywhere. Eliazabeth Gwillim in Madras busied herself planting seeds from England, which drew her a little closer to her much-missed family and her Britannic roots. She cultivated both flowers and vegetables, but struggled against the dry season, although she found that English vegetables grew well.[84] She happily produced turnips, carrots and French beans, and a host of others familiar to the English palate. She made a study of botany, having been given a large botanical library, and taken lessons from a Dr Shottler, who was a German missionary. Much of this related to her need to be able to name the plants and flowers that she painted, but she was obviously fascinated; a manifestation of her intelligent and enquiring mind, forever just a little frustrated at the inability to follow a more intellectual path.[85] Many other women must have felt the same, but it is equally likely many would have been happy to remain comfortably superficial.

She was a close companion of Dr James Anderson, an Edinburgh physician, who became the first president of the Madras Medical Board in 1786, and later became physician-general. Anderson was a passionate horticulturalist, besides his medical responsibilities, and planted a large stock of European mulberry trees as part of his scheme to establish a local silk industry. He imported apple trees, encouraged efforts to grow American cotton, and promoted sugar cane and coffee as profitable crops. He was locally much admired as a man of humanity who, in times of famine, supported starving peasants at his own expense. To this day there is a statue of him in St Georges Cathedral, Madras.[86] He had a large garden in which he carried out his horticultural experiments and which formed the basis of the original Madras botanical garden. He died in 1809 and sadly, when Maria Callcott (then Maria Graham) visited his garden only a year later she noted that it was 'now in a state of ruin'.[87] Elizabeth Gwillim spent a fair amount of time in Dr Anderson's garden, as well as her own, and they exchanged seeds, and cultivation experiences, although she would readily acknowledge that she received a net gain from his brain. In a letter home to a friend, shortly before her premature death, she wrote that:

His attention is wholly given to the fruit and forest trees of large growth. His great pride is having brought into this country the Bastard Cedar; it thrives here exceedingly; is found in every hedgerow and is certainly a great acquisition in a tropical climate. It is a native of Jamaica; its verdure is very fine and the foliage most profuse, even after the greatest drought the country can experience. Its leaves are food for the cattle when scarcely a blade of grass can be obtained.[88]

In a wholly different part of India, and from a rather different social sphere, the fragile and rather old-fashioned Sarah Robinson, doctor's wife, was equally enthralled by her small bungalow garden in Benares. She relished the arrival of the rains. 'I shall now be every day busy sowing flower seeds. The orange trumpet flower is now in full splendour, the Allemande is next in gaiety, and the superb Amaryllis; their season approaches.'[89] Such is her enthusiasm that she orders new plants from the Botanic Gardens in Calcutta, almost 500 miles away, among them being Taberia Montana Coronaria, Gardenia Florida, Lily Asphodel, Ixora Coccinea, Lantana Trifolia and a host of others. She was either addicted to long lists of Latin names, or very knowledgeable indeed – probably the latter. She acquired uncommon, or particularly beautiful, plants from other British people as well and was obviously proud of her garden: 'When those [plants] I expect from the Botanical Gardens arrive I shall be rich in floral wealth.' Not as rich as she thought: 'Half were missing, presumed stolen by the boat people to light their fires!' Nevertheless the *budgerows* from Calcutta still brought 108 large earthen pots containing Camellia Japonicas, Ficius Elasticus (rubber tree), mahogany trees, coffee plants, and multiple fruit trees. An additional problem in her garden, apart from drought and disease, was the locust-like predations of large flocks of birds on any fruit tree. This occurred despite a boy being hired to run about shouting and banging his stick all day. The birds even devoured the mangoes, despite each fruit being contained in a small wicker basket. Eventually she was sure she had found the answer, by arranging for a skilled Artillery marksman to arrive in the evenings, and 'Slaughter all before him'.[90]

Like many people living in the fairly rural *mofussil*, she and her husband kept animals as well; or rather they were kept for them by a gang of employees. A friend had given them six fine breeding sows, when he left the area, and these arrived by boat in Benares itself. As the Robinsons lived a few miles distant at Secrole, and the pigs were too fat to walk more than a few steps, they were individually transported in state to the house, each in his or her own carriage, or more precisely, ox cart. As one might expect, Fanny Parkes was also no slouch as a smallholder. Not only did she grow corn, trodden after harvest by her own oxen, but also cows, which were eventually destined for the table. Not content with these alone, she kept buffaloes and various types of goat. She was happily proud of her self-sufficiency. An interesting detail that she records in her journals is the manner in which grain was stored in rural India. Large pits were prepared in the ground, and the walls of these were dried and hardened by burning a fire within them for several days. Having been filled with grain, they were then covered over and carefully disguised to prevent them being found by any marauding army. The effectiveness of this concealment much depended on the ability of the *soonghee*, or smeller, in such an army to sniff out these secret underground granaries. Bizarre as it seems, these grain diviners must have been a real asset to a hungry army on the march, although they threatened devastation to the owners of the grain they came across.[91] For the ordinary people of India famine was never far away.

Chapter 8

Indian Impressions

The pre-Raj era of Indo-British relations was to a large extent one of social and cultural fusion. It was even political, in the sense that many of the disparate states and kingdoms that made up Hindustan, or the Indian nation, formed alliances with the British, more specifically the East India Company, and paid for military support against their predatory neighbours with land as well as cash. The fusion, and the interest, was mutual, unlike that of later years, especially the post-Mutiny Raj era, when the attitude was more one of fission, with an emphasis on social division and Victorian hegemony. In both eras a newcomer to the subcontinent was generally amazed and delighted with what he or she encountered, but in the fusion period this persisted, with a mutual fascination, respect and benefit that could last a lifetime. In the later fission years the initial interest became one of a more detached curiosity, ever aware of complete British domination and control.

Even now, if one visits India, one of the most delightful sights is the appearance of the people. Not so much the men, who today mostly wear a uniform of long trousers and a long-sleeved shirt, but the women, who continue to wear what they have always done, namely the sari, or the salwar kameez. Things would not have been very different 200 years ago, although then they would have perhaps carried more jewellery and hair adornments. The pioneer British visitor would have been just as startled and delighted, then as today, at the emergence of a woman from a tumbledown, knocked-together shack wearing a spotless sari of bright orange, yellow, green or scarlet as graceful and lissom as if she were a butterfly emerging from its chrysalis. As Julia Maitland noted in 1837:

> *In the midst of all this dirt and discomfort some little bit of tinsel would peep out at every opportunity: women covered with ornaments from head to foot, peeping out of the mud-hovels; men with superb Cashmere shawls looking quite beggarly from rags and dirt. This is Eastern splendour, a compound of mud and magnificence, filth and finery.* [1]

INDIAN IMPRESSIONS

It is no surprise that British men found the women attractive, but so too did many of the women, although often with some reservations because they were seen as competition. This brought out the odd caustic comment in which they were dismissed as dirty and disease-ridden, at least with respect to the lower castes but, as ever in commentary about that country, those observers with intelligence and interest were endlessly impressed by all they saw, and only rarely took defensive refuge in sarcastic repudiation. The latter was often for public consumption, whereas their letters and journals revealed their true impressions, especially about particular individuals.

> *I had heard of Mulka's beauty long ere I beheld her, and she was described to me as the loveliest creature in existence. Her eyes which are very long, large and dark, are remarkably fine and appeared still darker from being darkened on the edges of the eyelids with* soorma. *Her forehead is very fine; her nose delicate and remarkably beautiful – so finely chiselled, her mouth appeared less beautiful, the lips being rather thin. According to the custom of married women in the East her teeth were blackened, and the inside of her lips also, with antimony.... . Her figure is tall and commanding; her hair jet black, very long and straight; her hands and arms are lovely! Very lovely.* [2]

And from Elizabeth Fenton's journal: 'the soft, wavy folds of muslin which they roll round them in such a manner – it realizes the idea of the drapery on an antique statue; their free and untaught attitudes are so graceful, I am sure I never walked or rode out without again admiring them.'[3] Many such British women thus wrote admiringly of the beauty of Indian women, not without a tinge of envy sometimes; for a man to react likewise was met with icy disapproval. Some women, however, could not feel any admiration for the country and its people, and in 1837 Julia Maitland asked an acquaintance what she had seen of the country and the natives since she had been there. She received the response; 'Oh, nothing! Thank goodness, I know nothing at all about them, nor I don't wish to: really the less one sees and knows of them the better!' She elsewhere wrote how everyone in Madras tried to make it as English as they could, without much success but, in the process, did away with as much as possible that was interestingly Indian.[4] There were other extremes, such as the admirable Mrs A, wife of a comfortably off British landowner, who would regularly walk through a village giving comfort, and whatever else she could, to the poor and ill, dressing injuries and sores that would repel most people, and rescuing children from famine;

a sort of early British Mother Theresa, improbable though that seems for the early nineteenth century. Even then, many men and women would have avoided any such close contact.[5] One still sees this polarisation of attitude towards India today. Visitors to the country are either horrified by the clamour, crowds, squalor and poverty, or they are overwhelmed with fascination by the excitement, history, architecture and colour that is all around them. Even a Governor-General's sister, the imperious Emily Eden, wrote towards the end of the pre-Victorian era: 'in my life I never saw such a civil, submissive set of people... . They are civil creatures, and I am very fond of the natives.' A little patronising perhaps, but her impressions come across as genuine.[6]

In further pursuit of their fascination with the lives of Indian women, the more intrepid British women would seek a visit to a zenana, the home of the multiple wives and concubines of an Indian man of some wealth and importance. Such places were completely off limits to all men, other than very close relatives, and British women were therefore uniquely placed to study this culturally very different social institution, which was quite beyond the experience of any European, not that this inhibited the fantasising of the more fevered male. Although it is likely that several women from pre-Raj India would have visited a zenana, few wrote about it in their letters home, or in their journals. In 1804 Mary Symonds wrote to a friend in England, describing a visit to an unspecified such place, in which she observed that:

The ladies have a great many cushions and pillows to support their bodies and limbs, as they throw themselves about in various attitudes, forming beautiful groups. They wear a great quantity of thin drapery which does not conceal the person much...The house contains about three hundred women and children; one of which is her daughter, a widow of about six and twenty. She is tall and strong, beautifully proportioned, and I think if she had the European red and white complexion she would be the handsomest woman I ever saw...Fifteen or twenty of the other women are the Begum's [eldest and senior wife] son's wives; forty or fifty more are their concubines, and all the rest are slaves. A concubine amongst the mussulmans is not a contemptible person; though inferior to the wives, she has many rights and privileges in the house and is entitled to a part of the man's property when he dies. Every lady is attended by about eight women constantly. One holds her betel box, which is a little gold square casket; another prepares the betel leaves and presents them to her, a third holds a little gold vase, which is sometimes set with jewels, for their mouths are constantly filled with the red juice of the fresh betel, which they never swallow [i.e. a spittoon]. *Two more servants attend with fans to cool her, and keep off flies; a sixth holds her handkerchief; and the others give her water, which she is continually wanting to rinse her mouth from the betel, and which they keep in a silver or gold ewer, and present in a glass or gold cup.*[7]

If one thought that the wealthier British lived a lavish lifestyle, it was nothing compared to even the minor rajahs and princelings in the differing states of India.

Mary Symonds goes on to describe how crowded the apartments were, how there was a strong odour from the oils with which they anointed their hair and bodies, and how cruel they could be to their servants. She also wrote:

I think the worst of all is that the great, and apparently delicate, ladies themselves are in their hearts as ferocious as tigers, capable of shocking deliberate cruelty. They spend a great part of their time in quarrelling with each other, and a still greater part in idle childish sports in which the slaves and all join, sometimes dressing themselves with skins and running about on all fours like antelopes, tigers etc. At other times they dress the animals in their clothes.[8]

Evidently one woman had dressed her favourite cat with as many of the finest jewels as she could attach, only for it to slip over the zenana wall into the teeming life of the city outside. The cat was later returned, but had somehow mislaid the jewels.

The ever inquisitive and impetuous Fanny Parkes visited numerous zenanas, in Calcutta, Lucknow, Khasganj and Delhi. In particular she was intrigued in 1835 to meet Baiza Bai, widow of Maharaj Daulatrao Scindia, leader of the great Mahratta dynasty based in Gwalior. Following his death she ruled in her own right as Maharani until deposed by her adopted son and exiled to Fatehgar, in British territory near Cawnpore and Lucknow. Fanny seemed to hit it off with Baiza Bai, particularly as they had a mutual interest in, and knowledge of, horses and it is here that she learnt to ride astride in the Mahratta fashion. Her description of the zenana is a little more gracious than that resulting from Mary Symonds experience, the possible difference being that the latter was Muslim, whereas Baiza Bai was in Hindu purdah, which was somewhat less strict. Interestingly, during Fanny Parkes' conversations with her, they found mutual similarities between the privations of purdah and the zenana, and the considerable restrictions placed at that time on a married Englishwoman. In each case this was particularly so for a widow. Under Hindu law, widows had to give up all their jewellery and fine clothes, remain in constant mourning, and were denied food of any quality, and even a bed. Remarriage, however young, was completely forbidden. In response, Fanny described how an English widow was 'turned out of the family mansion on her husband's death, to make room for the heir, and pensioned off'. She spoke too 'of the severity of the laws of England with respect to married women, how completely *by law* they are the slaves of their husbands, and how little hope there is of redress.' When questioned, she added peevishly that it was 'men who made these laws'.[9]

In such discussions lay the germ of Fanny's burgeoning feminism which, to her mind, added a righteous justification to her already strong compulsion to travel far, and alone. One wonders how gratified she would have been if she had known of the practice of matrilineal succession in at least three Indian tribes, especially the Nair of Kerala, but also scattered through other parts of the world. By this means, the line of inheritance passes from a man, especially a ruler, to the offspring of his sister, and not his wife, thus preserving a linear succession strictly through the female side of the family. The men were therefore no more than an instrument of power, and a source of genetic material to leaven this feminine lineage. This would probably have appealed greatly to Fanny's feminist inclinations, although she might have been rather less impressed, even affronted, by the implied derogation of female behaviour in the alternative explanation, mentioned by Eliza Draper in a letter to her cousin:

> *Some very extraordinary customs prevail in this Malabar country, such as a King's sister's son succeeding to the throne in preference to his own children, and it arises from their indifferent opinion of their wives' chastity and then the dignity they say (poor souls) descends in a right line, for each monarch is certain whom is his sister, tho he cannot pretend to discern whether the Queen's progeny ought to style him father.*[10]

About five years later Emily Eden and her sister, also Fanny, found themselves with the whole British entourage in Gwalior, where her brother was due to meet the younger Scindia, the Mahratta leader. Here she too was invited to visit the zenana, where Scindia's child bride, the ranee, was

'Covered with gold tissue, and clanking with diamonds. Her feet and hands were covered with rings fastened with diamond chains to her wrists and ankles.'[11] The upshot of the meeting was that the Eden sisters were presented with large quantities of the 8-year-old ranee's jewels. 'I had a diamond necklace and a collar, some native pearl earrings that hung nearly down to the waist, and a beautiful pair of diamond bracelets, and the great article of all was an immense diamond tiara.' Previous experience had shown that rejection of such items, or an attempt to return them, was met with great offence. As it was against East India Company policy to keep any gifts they were initially accepted, but thereafter whole collections would pass into the hands of the Company, who obviously profited greatly, although many items were later used as presents to other Indian princes, at other official meetings.

In earlier years, mixing with Indians socially was much more part of life than in the later Victorian years. There seems to have been less class distinction: 'We talk a great deal to the servants, some of whom are very good and intelligent.'[12] Needless to say there was indifference among some, who were only interested in having life 'as like home as possible.' It was then not uncommon to entertain Indians of some standing in one's house. Mary Symonds wrote of a local Nawab being invited to breakfast with the Gwillim household. He duly turned up with sixty men in attendance, and was a 'very fat, tall young man; rather of a lively countenance; he talks a great deal and eats voraciously.' The next day he sent round nine elephants for their entertainment, 'all richly caparisoned, and their faces beautifully painted in scrolls winding in the course of the muscles.'[13] The Victorians lost so much interest from the absence of this sort of social intercourse, although they would never have recognised this at the time. In earlier years it was common to be invited to dinner, along with music and dance, or 'nautch', in the house, or palace, of a local rajah or prince, or even just a very wealthy man. The after-dinner entertainment of music and nautch dancing was really aimed at the men, particularly the nautch, and many a White Moghul had a posse of nautch girls to dance for him in the evenings. Women were often invited to these events in Indian households, but it is doubtful that they appreciated the dancing as much as their male counterparts. The intricacies of Indian classical dance are largely lost on Europeans today, although most appreciate its beauty of form, balance and elegance. Julia Maitland, commenting in 1837, wrote of how the girls were 'most graceful creatures, walking, or rather sailing about, like queens ... waving their hands, turning slowly round and round, and bending from side to side: there were neither steps nor figure as far as I could make out.' When it came to the music, her opinion was rather firmer:

Then they sang, bawling like bad street-singers – a most fearful noise, and no tune. Then we had a concert of orchestra music, with different-looking instruments, but in tone like every modification of bagpipes – every variety of drone and squeak: you can form no idea of such sounds under the name of music.[14]

When Emily Eden and her entourage were entertained in a Rajah's pleasure gardens, with fountains playing, and everything lit up for the occasion, her comment was ever pungent, but nevertheless perceptive: 'People may abuse nautching, but it always amuses me extremely. The girls hardly move about at all, but their dresses and attitudes are so graceful I like to see them. Their singing is dreadful and very noisy.'[15] It is all the more striking and impressive that Warren Hastings, a full fifty years earlier, was a patron of Indian music, employed his own musicians, and clearly had considerable admiration for it. Even today, there are many who would understand and support his taste, particularly with the music of sitar or santoor.

Appreciation of art and architecture was widespread. Many women wrote glowingly to their relatives at home about the wonders to be seen and studied. Maria Callcott (Graham) covered many pages with her descriptions of the cave temples and carvings of Elephanta Island, near Bombay and, a thousand miles away, on the other side of India, of the rock carvings and temples of Mahabalipuram, south of Madras. She describes the Hindu effigies of Vishnu, Shiva and Parvati and, like many before and after her, she sketched them in detail. Never to be outdone, Fanny Parkes travelled by *budgerow,* alone except for a bevy of boatmen, up the river Jumna from Allahabad to Agra in order to see the Taj Mahal, defying storms, torrential rain, constantly going aground and coping with alarming leaks, to achieve this end. She allocated a whole chapter of her journal to describing her objective, which she did with impressive accuracy and sensitivity. 'It is not its magnitude; but its elegance, its proportions, its exquisite workmanship, and the extreme delicacy of the whole, that render it the admiration of the world.'[16] There follows much detail, as one would expect, but it is hard to improve on this initial tight description. Many other women saw the Taj in those more distant years, but few wrote about it.

In more recent years, and especially throughout the Victorian period, there was increasing neglect of India's beautiful and ancient monuments, although still much general admiration. There was little significant damage done, apart from a brief episode of spiteful defacement after the Mutiny, but it was common for delicate inlay work and wall paintings to be covered with whitewash where British army officers had taken over such buildings to make a more comfortable mess space, and for some of the more precious inlaid stones to be gouged out. Stories that the British government was considering selling off the Taj Mahal's marble appear to have been apocryphal.[17] Even as early as 1835 Fanny Parkes recorded the playing of bands, and the dancing of quadrilles, on the marble terraces of the Taj Mahal, which she thought wholly lacking in good taste and disrespectful to this great mausoleum to a much loved queen. She even relates, one suspects with a modicum of relish, how one particular lady fell over the parapet of the terrace to the inlaid pavement 20ft below, perhaps a victim of the rather more than usually vigorous finale step of the quadrille.[18] India had to await the arrival of Lord Curzon in 1899, then newly appointed Viceroy, before a serious interest was shown in the enormous amount of exceptional architecture and art which was India's patrimony, and attempts were made to restore and preserve it for posterity. It is probably true to say that neither Victorian men nor women had reacted to India's art with effusive admiration until that time, but simply maintained a detached curiosity. The same is true of art in any situation, and in any epoch, but in the early years of India's colonisation, the writings of most educated men and women are overwhelmingly effervescent with fascination. It was in the central part of the Indian British epoch that interest seemed to lapse.

One of the greater interests among such women was reserved for the religious and social practices of the Indian people. This was, nevertheless, not without a frisson of indignation caused by their committed Christian sensibilities. This was parallel with official reaction, whereby the East India Company had encouraged tolerance of Indian religions in its early years but acceptance later giving way to Victorian prejudice, encouraged by men such as Macaulay. There can be little doubt that what most gripped these women was the extraordinary strangeness of Indian religious practice, with its attendant noise, colour and clamour, and the perplexingly strange rituals so completely different from what they were used to at home from an Anglican church choir, formal vestments, and priests intoning from an austere and lofty pulpit. No wonder some couldn't cope, and denounced all Indians as heathen. Many were enthralled, however, and wrote about it extensively in their letters home, having witnessed ceremonies, festivals and religious rites, and read as much as they could about Hinduism and Islam.

One such was our enquiring friend Elizabeth Gwillim, who wrote long descriptions amounting to hundreds of words with a passionate fascination; rather more so than her younger unmarried sister who was busy probing the

197

social whirl. As Elizabeth said in a letter home to her mother: 'I shall leave the White people to Polly and tell you a little about the Black people.'[19] And so she did – but at length, not just a little. One has the impression that such writing was generally reserved for friends and relatives at home. Anything for public consumption was described with more detachment and amused curiosity, as if one shouldn't be seen to show too much interest.

Early in her time in Madras, Elizabeth described Pongal to her mother in England, a four-day Tamil festival seen in southern India, particularly in the city where she lived, and which was centred on the rice harvest and feasting. The quality of the food that was prepared for it, over several preceding weeks, could provide a propitious sign as to the fortunes of the year ahead and, as with so many Hindu festivals, the whole event was aimed at appeasing the deities to ensure advantage for the future. For someone who was perennially homesick, she revelled in a sort of escapism in these events, and recorded them minutely in her letters. Fanny Parkes was just as observant and captivated, and just as loquacious. It is possibly no coincidence that both women, being childless, perhaps had more time and inclination to delve into the world around them. Elizabeth described in some detail the existence of the three deities; Brahma the creator, Vishnu the preserver, and Shiva the destroyer or avenger. She interestingly mentioned at the same time a prevailing European philosophy that Hinduism could therefore also contain the notion of a Trinity, indicating perhaps that such a concept was the inheritance of all mankind. One might, these days, be tempted to suggest that this was nineteenth century Christian conceit. In the same letter she described how Hindu worship is divided between these deities, but that temples only existed to Shiva and Vishnu. Individual allegiance to one or the other was determined by family tradition. Her descriptions go much further than this and are interestingly detailed, impressively accurate, and could be regarded as a testament to the quality of thinking of a woman of that time, denied the full education available to her sex. While recording these details she was also tackling the Hindu language, and the local Gentoo (Telugu). Would the same intelligent enquiry have been common in later Victorian years, one wonders?[20]

In the same letter from 1802 she described three consecutive nightly visits to a great festival celebrating the marriage of Shiva, and therefore presumably the Maha Shivarati.

The God is carried out each night in a different way: one night he rides on a bullock, and on each side of him one of his wives, also on a bullock. The next night they ride out on horseback; a third night on elephants; a fourth in European carriages, and so on. On the last night he is carried out without his wives as a Pandaram, or religious beggar.

Setting out at 10.30 in the evening, she and her companions travelled the 3 miles to witness these revelries, on roads that 'were crowded with men and women coming from all parts.... . They brought us sweets and fruit, garlands of flowers of a kind of white jasmine around our necks, and from a silver ewer sprinkled our handkerchiefs with rosewater, giving each of us a ball of the same flowers as the garland to hold in our hands.' If nothing else, this seems to indicate, among that company of women at least, a mutuality of appreciation; a warmth of shared respect. They were then invited to watch some of the better dancing girls, whom Elizabeth described in terms that define her admiration of their attractiveness. They too could understand only too well why young British men of that time were generally drawn to Indian women, even if they disapproved in principle.

They are very richly dressed, their hair is combed smooth, parted in front, and sweeping round the corners of the forehead with a fringe of fine work in gold and small jewels edging this sweep of the hair, and lying on the forehead. They wear a conspicuous piece of jewellery on the middle of the forehead, and various ornaments in the nature of clasps; one piece of gold like a small saucer finishes the back of the head and, between this and the front ornaments, wreaths of coloured natural flowers were twisted several times round. The back hair is plaited, and hangs down to a great length, mixed with gold and pearl tassels and flowers. Their ears are covered with ornaments; as many as possible hung in the ears, and others suspended from bands in the hair.... Their dancing is very little like ours; they never step [dance] upon the toes but keep the knees bent and tread on the outside of the feet. They dance for an hour within the space of a sheet of paper. The feet however all the while in constant motion. The action of the other part of the figure is extremely graceful. It is sometimes voluptuous, but never affected.

She continued to describe how vast numbers of people followed the processions of people and carriages, dancing all the way with undeniable grace and solemnity. Rather surprisingly, she then went on to say, 'one can

199

hardly be surprised that they are unwilling to give up these shows for a better religion, the fruits of which do not appear very good in the examples our people who come out here give them.' This was something of a backhander to the East India Company establishment and its employees. Clearly Lady Gwillim was not impressed by some of the behaviour and attitudes of her contemporaries.

Some twenty years later, during her own personal quest to discover India, Fanny Parkes wrote of her experience of observing the great mela, or Hindu festival, at Allahabad. This lies at the conjunction of the Ganges and Jumna rivers and has immense religious significance for Hindu people. To bathe in these waters is almost a passport to paradise. As Fanny says, 'the holy waters are convenient for washing away a man's sins, and as efficacious as a papal bull for this purpose.'[21] She was herself particularly struck by the ash-smeared religious mendicants, or sadhus; naked grey wraiths punctuated centrally by a rag. One of these was:

> *Remarkably picturesque, and attracted my attention. In stature he was short and dreadfully lean, almost a skeleton. His long black hair, matted with cow dung, was twisted like a turban round his head... . His left arm he had held erect so long that the skin and flesh had withered, and clung round the bones most frightfully; the nails of the hand, which had been kept immovably clenched, had pierced through the palm and grew out at the back of the hand like the long claws of a bird of prey. His horrible and skeleton-like arm was encircled by a twisted stick, the end of which was cut into the shape of a cobras head.*[22]

One has the feeling she would have added him to her cabinet of curiosities if she could. She also described how such men had the right to enter any house, even where a woman might be in purdah, or in the zenana, and so concealed from any other man except her husband, and that if a sadhu had left his slippers at the door, even the husband couldn't enter his own home. What might have occurred in those circumstances is implied by her next remark, that such men 'have the character of being great libertines.' The picture is reminiscent of the reported habit of Maltese catholic priests visiting a house, and leaving a warning umbrella for the husband at the door; no doubt manifesting his spirituality inside, but perhaps not his celibacy.

Apart from the generalities of religious practice, individual beliefs and customs often caused astonishment, such as the degree of reverence accorded to snakes, and especially the cobra. If the servants of a house were asked to kill a cobra that had intruded onto the premises, there would later be a nocturnal ceremony to the sound of drums, with wailing and weeping, and the washing in milk of the burnt bones of the snake in the hope that the perpetrators might exculpate themselves of any guilt associated with its death. By this means they hoped to avoid the wrath of the gods, especially Kali.[23] Fire was another venerated entity and if it spontaneously occurred in a residential area it was regarded as an act of God, over which man had no power. Elizabeth Gwillim reported instances where Indian people had made no effort to protect their belongings from the flames, or even themselves, on the principle that the event was preordained. Often no attempt was made to douse it, and individuals would willingly submit themselves to a death by fire in the belief that the Gods had willed it, and that they would reap rich rewards in heaven as a result.[24] This is not very detached in concept from the circumstances of widow burning, or sati, which so appalled the British that it was eventually banned under the governorship of William Bentinck in the 1830s, and not without some support from leading Indian citizens.

Another curious religious practice intertwined with Hindu social custom, noted by Elizabeth, was the complete lack of respect for the unmarried state, at least at that time. Much as women became socially inferior when widowed, and forbidden to remarry, even if widowed in childhood, so bachelors had little status either. If a man died before he was married, it was thought impossible he would achieve salvation, and so the usual funeral rites were not offered. Elizabeth described to her mother how a man condemned to death in Madras for murder was taken through the entire marriage ceremony on the night before his execution. 'He was dressed in flowers and perfumed like a bridegroom, and the family were up with him the whole night; his sword adorned as the bride. All this was done in order that the funeral ceremonies might be performed which are thought necessary to salvation. Upon enquiring, we found this was a common practice where a person is in imminent danger, which you must allow a man is who is going to be hanged.'[25]

Idiosyncrasies such as these, along with the whole panoply of Hindu religious practice, were obviously fascinating to some British women of the eighteenth and early nineteenth centuries, just as it was anathema to others, especially in later years. No doubt the men reacted similarly, the policy of the East India Company in the years before the 1820s being one of tolerance and understanding, aimed towards the maintenance of a stabilising social symbiosis between East and West. This was the era of orientalism. From the

1820s onwards, the reformist movements of evangelicalism and utilitarianism were creeping in, and Christian proselytisers in the shape of the missionary movement were becoming strongly motivated to convert Hindu and Muslim souls to Western religion, away from what they believed to be the ignorant superstition of their own beliefs. According to some contemporary historians, it is likely that the missionaries' collective activity was 'socially disruptive, forcing alien values and spiritual teaching on a resistant population and the sepoy army units.'[26,27] None of these reformist aims, which also included education, language and bureaucracy, were meant to be punitive. The political and religious leaders of the Victorian era truly believed that they had a sort of trusteeship of India, and that they were improving the wellbeing of a primitive society and perhaps, as a parallel goal, assuaging some of the guilt induced by the less pleasant events of British military expansion on that continent.[28] Just as the Victorians wanted India to be a Britain abroad, so they wanted the Indians to become more British within it.

Elizabeth Gwillim, while pursuing her anthropological leanings, was interested in the Indian caste system, in a vague comparison to the class system in England. Most women's knowledge of the Indian people was confined to those with whom they most frequently came into contact: their servants. In another long letter to her mother, she described the existence of the four castes, but in particular described the outcasts, or pariahs, now known as dalits. Defining these as people who had formerly dropped down from a higher caste, because of some offence to Hinduism, she described them with uncharacteristic censure as:

> *Dirty, lazy, saucy, vicious and extravagant for if they gain ever so much money they live in vileness till it is spent. They sometimes make a formal marriage but the bond is dissolved at the pleasure of either party. Chastity is a virtue they know nothing about. If they have any well-looking girls they dispose of them to European gentlemen, that is the mother does, for they are like the beggar children in London, all fatherless.*[28]

She indicated that these girls were often later discarded, but didn't draw the obvious conclusion, that the circumstance of both groups of desperate unfortunates was as much due to uncaring male behaviour as to underlying class.

Those Indians from a higher caste impressed many women, who pointed out from time to time that they deserved better respect than was sometimes offered by the British. As Julia Maitland wrote in 1838: 'A little politeness pleases them very much, and they have a right to it. The upper classes are exceedingly well bred, and many of them are the descendants of native princes, and ought not to be treated like dirt.'[29] Some of the senior servants regarded themselves as gentlemen, but they were by no means always treated as such. There is not much written evidence that women treated Indians badly, including their servants, but in their letters home they sometimes reported on how shocked they were by the pitiless attitude displayed by the occasional man. There may perhaps have been the odd woman who went this far as well, but there is nothing recorded. In her journal, Lucretia West wrote vividly of instances in Bombay that she knew of, particularly cases of flogging, which she likened to the horrific practices that occurred in the West Indies.[30]

Mentioning some horrible instances of a Mr Stewart sending all his hammauls to Mr Grays to be flogged because he could not make them understand his language, and of an Hon. Thos. Moore he was travelling with hitting a servant 20 times in the face and knocking him down because he had not provided milk, which he had no directions or business to get. Another, and worse, story of a Mr Horne at Surat knocking his servant down by blows in the face, then stamping upon him and kicking him in the face with his iron heels and, to conclude, taking off the stirrup and beating him in the face with the iron part, and Mr Moore the same day knocking down a guide with the brass butt end of his whip struck upon the face, because the man said he was out of breath and could run no further, and he left him bleeding in the road. Is it possible that these can be men, and English men, who behave in this brutal way?

In Emma Roberts' book about life in India, she commented that 'raw young men, and sometimes even those who have not the excuse of youth and inexperience, are but too apt to amuse themselves by playing tricks with, or beating their luckless bearers, who are not unfrequently [sic] treated like beasts of burthen.' She added, almost jubilantly, that the bearers sometimes got their own back on such a man by putting down his palanquin, running off into the forest, and leaving him stranded in the burning, waterless heat.[31]

Undoubtedly such individuals were in the minority, and there were also many men, and women, who supported the cause of the ill-treated native Indian. Indeed Lucretia West's own husband was one of those Crown-appointed judges whose remit it was to bring British justice to the Indian people, as well as to the local European population. Nevertheless, as Fanny Eden observed in 1837, at the dawn of the Victorian age:

Those people [Indians] *must have been so very magnificent in what they did before we Europeans came here with our bad money-making ways. We have made it impossible for them to do more, and have let all they accomplished go to ruin. All our excuse is, that we do not oppress the natives so much as they oppress each other – a fact about which I have my suspicions.*[32]

The Eden sisters were adept at rocking Society's boat. In Simla they held a dance for Sikh envoys, which the English ladies of the town were expected to attend. They also gave full support to amateur theatricals given by the mixed race Anglo-Indian community. Neither of these went down too well in the increasingly prejudiced British community, nor did the idea that the Indian community should also be allowed to contribute to a charitable craft sale. Emily Eden's caustic response to this bias was that the 'blackness' of Indian hands would not come off on their 'fancy-work'.[33]

The extent to which some women reacted to the horrific famines that were an intermittent feature of Indian life in circumstances of insufficient rain and subsequent crop failure, deserves mention. In 1837-38 there was a devastating famine in northern India, centred particularly on Agra, which killed more than three-quarters of a million people, and many more livestock. This coincided with Lord Auckland's mighty march through these territories on his way to do business with Ranjit Singh, leader of the Sikh nation. Many have questioned whether continuation of Auckland's grand tour was wise in the face of such death and destruction. His entourage numbered thousands and must have further denuded the environment of available food, although his sister, Emily, suggested that it was obtained outside the area, and that much of it was given away anyway. Clearly both Eden sisters, and their tenacious camp follower, Fanny Parkes, were hugely moved by the enormity and horror of this event.

Some hundreds came for food yesterday, a thousand were fed today, but many of them are still lying round the camp, children who have not many hours of life left in them – some of the grown-up people too are nothing but skin and bone, their faces like skulls... . Almost all our native servants have adopted either orphans or children they have bought for a rupee or two – they generally keep them for the rest of their lives.

204

With people trying to live off tree bark and roots, but dying in their tracks as they crawled on the ground, such sights must have been a Somalian experience for onlookers. Some women, for instance Emily Eden, even tried to rescue individual babies. It had all happened before, in 1770, and again as late as 1943. On such occasions, famine mortality seems to accelerate beyond any ability of governments to intercede. Those in power feel helpless; but inevitably, the accusation that more could have been done is left hanging in the air.

Chapter 9

Health and Death

An emotion that the women of the latter part of the eighteenth century, and first half of the nineteenth, shared with men was fear. They carried this with them most of the time, in the darker avenues of their thoughts; learnt from acquaintances in England, and nagging away at them through the long journey to the Indies. That fear was of death and disease, at that time so very prevalent in India and elsewhere in the Far East. One might ask why they went at all, if the spectre of early death weighed so heavily on their minds, until one remembers that the other driving force was greed. The combination of fear and greed has long been a motivational dilemma in the striving for betterment seen even now in stock markets the world over. Less bluntly, greed was really just an indicator of hope and aspiration for many, the reasons for which are self-evident. Even the greed was born of fear; fear that their lives would be poverty-stricken failures if they didn't make a go of it somehow. There was then no social safety net to catch those who fell off the ladder. Inevitably the compulsion to seek security, success, and even riches, outweighed the prospect of premature death, but each person was only too aware that a spectral figure with a scythe lurked in the shadows at every step of their Indian lives.

It is a sobering fact that, according to reliable sources (BACSA – British Association for Cemeteries in South Asia), there are very many hundreds of thousands of European graves in South Asia, mostly British. Although the actual number of graves is impossible to determine, as many as two million has been quoted, the great majority of which are on the Indian subcontinent. Many are in tumbledown, overgrown cemeteries, all but lost to the outsider, apart from a few dedicated visitors. Many graves were hastily prepared in remote wayside plots, and have completely disappeared, and some cemeteries have been destroyed and built over. Apart from those that have been lost, there are as many cemeteries, if not more, that have survived and are gradually being restored and protected. Most of these can be visited by travellers, and the experience of doing so is poignantly evocative; an emotive glimpse of British history buried in a distant land.

Although mortality in England was high at the time, it was nothing like as high as it was in India. In the very earliest colonial period the average age of death for Europeans abroad (excluding children) was under 30 for men and 25 for women, although obviously this age rose steadily over time.[1] At a later date, London insurance companies rated the chance of survival in India as poor, and 100 per cent worse than in England. Wilkinson quotes a statistic where, of thirty young officers arriving in Madras in 1775, only sixteen were alive five years later in 1780.[2] Likewise, but well into the 1830s and 40s, dragoon guards stationed in the United Kingdom had an average annual mortality of 14 per 1000, whereas British troops in the area of Bombay experienced a mortality of more than 47 per 1000, nearly four times higher and almost all from disease rather than combat.[3] Mortality was equally high among the civilians, and it was not uncommon for multiple family members to succumb to India's pestilences or, from time to time, for a whole family to be wiped out. As Lucretia West commented with some finality on the death of a certain Lady Franklin: 'What a sad annihilation of that family.'

James Forbes was a civilian who went out to India in 1765 with eighteen colleagues, all of whom died many years before he returned to England eighteen years later.[4] This was by no means a unique experience and more than one group of a dozen or so teenage Company writers travelled the huge distance only to be decimated by disease in that hostile environment, often leaving just the one survivor. One such loner was William Makepeace Thackeray, the grandfather of the author of *Vanity Fair*. The death rate among the European population was, at one time, quite probably close to parity with numbers arriving in the country.[5] Those at home in England seemed at first not to notice the high death rate in India, noticing more, indeed being envious of, the wealth that could be garnered there. Their envy was often misplaced, as the overall chance of financial success was considerably offset by the chance of dying. The saying in India at the time was 'two monsoons', being simply no more than the average life expectancy of a newcomer (a griffin).

It is not easy to gain any clear idea of the mortality of women or children, but it was undoubtedly terrifyingly high, particularly for the children. This was one of the main reasons why they were sent home from a young age, provided their parents could afford it. Interestingly, very young children may have survived better in India than in England because of a lower incidence of infantile respiratory problems such as croup or pneumonia related to measles or whooping cough.[6] This would have been a consequence of the warm, dry atmosphere, but after a year or two the mortality rocketed. 'The mortality among children, in this country, is quite appalling. Many parents have had ten or twelve, and lost them all in infancy.'[7] Some idea of the danger to women and their offspring comes from the BACSA register of the graves and standing tombs within the famous South Park Street Cemetery in Calcutta.[8] This contains 2,655 names, which cover the years between 1770 and 1890, the majority being from 1800 to 1850. The numbers interred after the 1850s are small, probably arising from the rather better medical care and public health in later years. Together, women and children under the age of 12 comprise almost exactly half the population in the cemetery (fifty-one per cent), and the number of women significantly exceeds the numbers of children, being almost a third of the total. This suggests a disproportionately high mortality for women during that specific period in India, when there were many fewer British women than men; a high percentage of the male population being unmarried soldiers, or young traders and merchants. Such observations are inevitably a little unscientific, and may be distorted by the possibility that many men died out of the cities in the course of their business, so skewing the mortality rate towards a higher value for women. Nevertheless, they serve to emphasise the risk to the lives of these women who, one should remember, were in India largely at the behest of men. They would have died of the same range of diseases but, whereas men might die in battle, large numbers of women died in childbirth.

That child mortality was high there is no doubt; the figures speak for themselves. There are over 500 children buried in South Park Street Cemetery, and this is just one of India's innumerable burying grounds for the British. In the school in which Lucretia West carried out some duties, as mentioned in her journal, nineteen children died during an outbreak of cholera.[9] Additionally, in the five and a half years she was in Bombay she records the death of thirty-two of her coterie of friends. The last of these was her husband, who died from a fever (probably malarial) at the age of 45. Only two weeks later she herself succumbed to the serious perils of childbirth, leaving one lone orphan daughter to find her way home to England. Lucretia West and her contemporaries lived with this possibility constantly; no wonder her journal is peppered with expressions of fear, such as:

We drove in the evening to Colabar & witnessed the funeral of 2 privates of the Queens Royals. The burying ground was a melancholy sight; 2 rows of new graves; I suppose about 50 since we last walked there. It made us reflect on the uncertainty of life, & particularly in this climate, where one ought to be prepared to leave this life whenever it may please the Almighty to take us, as often the warning is so short.[10]

Death was so much a feature of that epoch, that today it is often tempting to assume that people became immune to grief and that life was cheap. This is almost certainly a glib exaggeration, and was certainly so in the case of a child, or for that matter for the loss of a husband or wife. The ordinary soldier may have become hardened as a consequence of his lifestyle and poverty, but this reaction was rare among the mainstream Indian British, who felt as deeply about the loss of a loved one as we would today. Some women wrote about the loss of their children in their journals or letters, or even just of the dread that this might happen. Mary Wimberley lost a baby son in 1837, the second such loss. 'All through the night we watched this too dearly loved child, expecting to see him expire. His thirst was agonising. He kept gradually sinking, until evening when Death was in his lovely eyes and no hope of any relief in this world.' Both she and her husband were grief stricken; he was unable to officiate at an impending church service, and she wrote:

A melancholy day indeed. We endeavour to bow to God's will but it is a hard trial and deep wound, for our lost darling was not only our joy and delight but the light of the whole house.[11]

With death all around them, the only means by which people could make sense of the pain and loss was to take refuge in religion, and to somehow find an explanation and solace in the belief that this was all Divine will, part of some unfathomable and mysterious plan of the Almighty. Mary Sherwood also lost her first two children as infants. She was prostrated with grief by both events, but in some strange attempt at self-explanation, she believed that the illness of the second was not merely a Divine trial, but a rebuke and punishment for her excessive love of her daughter: 'My God was preparing me to give up this idol also.'[12] Mary was something of an evangelical Christian, which might offer some understanding of her reaction, which we would probably regard today as deluded spiritual self-chastisement. Nevertheless, established religion must have been a wellspring of comfort and comprehension to many. How else could one understand and explain the premature demise of so many innocents in a context that held them to be the creationist product of Godly beneficence; how contradictory and pointless this might have seemed on deeper reflection?

One of the most poignant examples of maternal grief was that of Sophia Raffles, wife of Sir Stamford Raffles. After his partial fall from grace, and the loss of his Lieutenant Governorship of Java at the time the island was handed back to the Dutch in 1816, he was transferred to the isolated and somewhat hostile enclave of Benkulen in western Sumatra. This was well known to be a white man's grave, brimming with fever, and a place poorly suited to a family. Sophia had five children, the three youngest being born in Benkulen. In July 1821, after two happy years there, the much-loved oldest son Leopold died quite suddenly in an epidemic of fever, leaving both parents bereft and wretched. Desperate to get the others to England, but unable to find a ship to take them, they watched two of the others, Stamford and then Charlotte, succumb to cholera six months later, and within two weeks of each other. This just left little Ella, whom they managed to get on a ship home two months after the second tragedy. Raffles and Sophia were both severely ill at the same time, this being compounded by the deepest of grief. In Sophia's case this grief led to her prostration in a darkened room for almost four months, unable or unwilling to eat, or to see anyone, and neglecting everything and everybody. In the end she was gently, but firmly, reproached by a lowly Indian serving woman who persuaded her to open a window, and rejoin the world of the living. She describes this in her memoirs with undoubted gratitude, and some humility.[13] As a final ironic twist, they had another daughter, Flora, about eighteen months later, the only child remaining to them in the East, but she too died within two months. As if all this wasn't pain enough, some years later Ella also died in England, aged 19, just before her wedding. The sole survivor was Sophia, who had gone through the agony of witnessing the death of all five of her children, and also her husband who died in England in 1826, from a cerebral arteriovenous malformation, which he had probably had for a number of years.

The death of a child was not the only source of grief. Women, or their husbands, also regularly fell by the wayside, prey to one of India's terrifying diseases. Of the women whom we have come across in the preceding chapters, scarcely one was not affected by bereavement, or by death itself. Lucretia West has already been mentioned as having lost her husband, Sir Edward West, from an acute but not particularly brief illness, only to be followed soon after by her own demise. Judges didn't survive too well in India, several dying in the early 1800s in Calcutta and Madras, as well as Bombay. They were very senior in the civil hierarchy, being only just below Governor in status, and several Governors also died from local illnesses: death was no respecter of rank. Lucretia West was inconsolable:

At 6 this morning the minute guns began to fire; each seemed a death blow to me, and at seven I went to church with my beloved Edward and saw him put into his grave. Good God, what a moment, one only longs to be there also.[14]

And:

I have endeavoured to write down the last dreadful week of my adored husband's life. There I must stop; the last week I have seemed so lost, and my nerves so shattered I have scarcely the power to do anything, and seem as if I must close my eyes to the future. I dare not look forward, only back to the last 6 blessed years of my life. Yesterday was the 6th anniversary of our wedding; I feel so alone, so deserted and quite tremble when I think I have no one to look up to, and to my God I now look for my only happiness and support, and pray that He will [be] a father to my poor fatherless child, or children, should God in his mercy grant that I survive my confinement.

He didn't. Two weeks later she and her new baby joined her husband. They are both buried in the Anglican church in Poona.

Elizabeth Gwillim died in 1807. No cause is known, and nothing appears in the letters home written by her and her sister. Some have conjectured that the stress of seeing her husband unreasonably criticised by his colleagues, and the Madras government, contributed to her final illness. This seems emotionally speculative, and it is much more likely that she fell victim to one of the several prevalent fatal illnesses. After all, people were dying all over the place, stressed or not. She is buried in St Mary's Church, Fort St George, Chennai (Madras) under a flagstone near the north door, carrying an inscription rather austerely engraved in Latin. She left no children, but a now valuable legacy in the shape of her fascinating letters, and some very fine watercolours of Indian birds.

Sarah Robinson, who wrote such long, and often unanswered, tracts to her sister in England, died in July 1818 aged 34. The final communication to her sister was written by a friend, and was a notification of her last illness and her death; her husband, 'stunned by this severe and sudden bereavement', was too overcome to take up his pen. Among other things he was no doubt anguishing over who was to give this shocking news to their young son Alexander, aged about 9 and alone in England. Less than a year later, Alexander was once more to hear the same grievous story, this time about his father, then aged 33. Both parents lie in the same tomb in South Park Street Cemetery.

Elizabeth Fenton, then Campbell, watched her young army officer husband die in just twenty-four hours. Expressions of grief cascade through the pages of her journal over the next six months, but by twelve months she was persuaded to marry her husband's best friend.

211

Mary Doherty was another army wife with two young children, who lost her husband in just five days, to an unknown illness. He was attended by three doctors on the last day, but died quickly despite the usual alchemy of bloodletting, leeches, blistering and mustard poultices. His wife was in a state of shock afterwards and then fainted, not surprisingly, when one of the doctors returned to open the body, and she was asked to leave the room. No abnormality was found, which would not be surprising to modern understanding. The biological events of so many acute infective illnesses are apparent only at microscopic level. Mary was, of course, devastated, and even her husband's friends sobbed with tears, although they sat up all night to talk to, and comfort, her. Later: 'I went to see my dear husband. He was laid in his coffin, such a beautiful smile on his countenance, I was sure his soul was in heaven. I kissed his cold lips and I covered him up and I never saw him more.' From her journal it is clear that her desolation was absolute. 'In about three weeks I was able to walk about the house... . No words of mine can describe the irreparable loss myself and babes had sustained. He was unequalled in every relation in life.'

If women were not dying themselves, or watching their children or husbands prematurely part with life, they were certainly ministering to friends and neighbours in the same situation, and sometimes writing about it in their journals. Such entries, or the letters written home to near relatives, were often graphic, and written with typical Regency prolixity and drama:

Death was now rapidly approaching: she [the dying friend] *held a hand of James* [Surgeon husband of the writer] *and one of mine, and when the shade of mortality had dimmed her eyes, she still felt my hand by my ring and, while her strength sufficed, put it perpetually to her cold lips, repeating prayers, thanks and blessings. Of her husband, heartbroken Capt. S., she took leave in a most affecting manner, and besought him to retire, as his audible distress overcame her fluttering spirits... . At her request I saw her laid in her coffin. I performed with my own hands the last duty and wrapped her in her burial garments. Serene was her fair face, and the traces of beauty remained there. I followed her to the grave and many tears I shed over it. She died at the age of 27.*[15]

Sometimes such detail could be disconcertingly explicit, especially to parents far away in Britain. The description of the last hours of Mrs Forbes Farquharson, who died of perhaps malignant malaria, or typhoid, is an example. She was pregnant at the time, which magnified the distress, but there are no holds barred in the description of events by her husband to her parents in distant Aberdeen. He made such bald pronouncements as 'Repeated doses of medicine had scarcely any effects in opening her bowels, so an additional dose was administered which operated copiously.' Elsewhere, 'An additional dose (of Calomel) was given which she threw up almost immediately. Vomiting much increased the bearing down pains.' And later, 'There came on the most alarming fever and frenzied delirium to such an extent that it required Dr McDonnell, myself, an [sic] European woman and two black girls to hold her to her bed. A blister was applied to the nape of the neck...' not a comfortable procedure. Can this have been reassuring to learn months later, and so far away? At least the writer goes on to say, 'I have been thus particular in mentioning to you everything which took place because I feel that, in your place, less would not be satisfactory.' It is hard to imagine any way in which it could actually have been satisfactory to learn such detail, added to hearing of the loss of a daughter and, bearing in mind she was pregnant, an infant grandchild as well.[16]

The cause of all diseases was effectively unknown at that time, and only the barest clue as to their supposed nature can be gained from the lay writings of the day, and not much more from the professional. The level of understanding and knowledge was primitive, extraordinarily so by modern standards. An understanding of the aetiology and pathogenesis of any disease was then based, not on evidence from scientific experiment and analysis, but on supposedly rational philosophical musings, tempered perhaps by some empirical observation of the beneficial effects, or otherwise, wrought by a surgical intervention, or by some concocted medicinal therapy. Fevers, fluxes (diarrhoea), headache and apoplexy, among others, were believed to originate from a disturbance in the four supposed humoral factors in the body; a theory which dates back 600 years BC to Hippocrates and was popularised during the Roman era by Galen. He emphasised the belief that blood was the constantly produced liquid of life, and that disease was due to a plethora, or putrefaction, of this blood and that improvement in health would only result from releasing a proportion of it. So arose the barbaric practice of blood-letting by all sorts of means, but especially by opening a vein with a lancet, or fleam. These theories endured century after century, well into the nineteenth, and long after luminaries such as the great John Hunter, father of modern surgery, and a strong believer in experimental observation, had pointed out the danger and inadequacies of releasing this important circulating body fluid.[17,18] Remarkably, they continued to be formally taught in the medical schools well into the 1850s, and long after Hunter's denouncements. They, or at least the therapeutic manoeuvres they gave rise to, continued until such time as evidence-based practice became more generally accepted in the mid-1800s, after Hunter had shown the way many years earlier. Parallel to the traditional thinking, but a later hypothesis, was the belief that disease was caused by external factors that caused this plethora or putrefaction. These factors were held to be mainly atmospheric or climatic and, in the context of cholera in India, could be heavy rain or a sudden fall in temperature, or in the case of malaria, the 'miasma' caused by 'poisonous emission and pestiferous exhalations' from overcrowding, poor hygiene and rotting waste.[19] All these peculiar considerations are especially remarkable when one considers that this was the tail end of the Age of Enlightenment, some time after pioneering studies in mathematics, optics, electricity, magnetism and other topics, by great thinkers such as Newton, Priestley, Davy and Faraday.

Cholera tended to be an epidemic illness and was little known about until a devastating epidemic in Bengal in 1817, which gradually spread throughout India, and even into the West. It caused something around fifteen million deaths overall between 1817 and 1865, and 8,500 British soldiers succumbed in India during the same period.[20] Even as late as 1868 medical authorities still held that the cause was climatic, especially from the effect of rain and humidity on the soil. Military opinion supported this, from its observations that moving troops away from an affected area resolved the situation, little realising that, by doing so, they were escaping not the hazardous climatic disturbance, but the infected water which had always been the source of the problem in the first place.[21] The truth was slow to permeate the medical world, especially in India, but John Snow had already convincingly proved in London by 1855 that cholera was a waterborne infection.

For the Indian British, and no less so the Indian peoples, the illness was devastating. Although caused by a simple bacterium, this organism produces a toxin so powerful that it completely reverses the function of the small intestine so that it no longer absorbs salt and water, as well as the usual nutrients, but causes the cells in the lining of the intestine to secrete this in vast amounts giving the sufferer the rice water diarrhoea and abdominal cramps so characteristic of the illness. This fluid loss causes a massive contraction in the volume of body fluids, and blood, leading to the grey, shrunken, hollow-eyed patient with inelastic skin and a collapsing blood pressure, so familiar to the doctors of those days. Death was frequently sudden and very shocking, victims often being young and hitherto perfectly fit. As Elizabeth Fenton wrote soon after the untimely death of her husband, 'Oh to be in one day taken from happiness to misery! To remember that he who saw the sunrise in health and hope was, before the next morning, to be numbered with the dead, cut off in all the energy of life and enjoyment!'[22] The suddenness was frightening, and one regularly reads reports of a friend being invited to lunch, only to be invited in turn to his funeral by supper.[23] One typical instance is quoted by Wilkinson where an army officer in Cawnpore was playing billiards at 10 am, was then seized with abdominal cramps and nausea at 11 am, had died by 1 pm and was on his way to the cemetery by 5 pm.[24] The conventional treatment of the time would have been bloodletting, either by lancet, or with leeches or scarification of the skin. All that this would have achieved would have been further shrinkage of blood volume, so worsening the circulatory collapse, and hastening the end. The tragic irony is that most of these patients could have been saved, not with the powerful tools of modern medicine, but definitely with powerful contemporary knowledge. A simple mixture, in the right proportions, of salt and sugar mixed with water and taken by mouth is enough to switch the errant microscopic pumps in the cells of the intestinal wall back to normal, so that fluid and electrolytes become absorbed and retained again, instead of being lost. Nevertheless, it is without doubt better to prevent an outbreak of the disease in the first place. This can be achieved by good sanitation alone.

If the flux didn't get you, then there was a high chance that the other great Indian scourge, fever would. The vast majority of the time this meant malaria, whose depredations laid waste many tens of thousands of Europeans. The simple word 'fever' appears on many a memorial or gravestone throughout India and the East. At that time, and for centuries beforehand, fever had been medically classified into remittent, intermittent and continual. Remittent, by definition, got better, which was comforting, whereas continual was reckoned to be putrid (or malignant), nervous, or inflammatory. The third, intermittent fever, was further subdivided into other categories, one of which was tertian, or a fever that peaked every third day. This was even then recognised as being the commonest type in hot climates, and could have been nothing more than one of the common forms of malaria, which follow exactly this pattern. This intermittency was familiar to the British of that era; 'the attacks of ague and fever returned [to me] at regular intervals'[25]

As for causation, it was well recognised that fevers were more prevalent at certain times of the year, particularly during and after the monsoon, when there was a good deal of free water lying about.[26] The geographical situation was understood to be important, as well, in that a relationship to marshland, uncleared jungle, stagnant water and moist grassland was recognised, as also was a connection to the development and spread of canal irrigation.[27] It was strongly supposed that all these circumstances produced a poisonous miasma, or noxious atmosphere which somehow caused the fever. The term malaria means bad air, from the Italian *mala aria*, and was a word well known in British India from the early days. For more than a century the medical profession, and its patients, suffered under this misapprehension, and all treatment and prevention was aimed at avoiding, or casting out, this pestilential miasma. Some understanding of the environmental factors that promoted the disease was at least of benefit by suggesting the wisdom of moving accommodation away from such sites. Emma Roberts wrote about Berhampore in 1835, 'Every breath of air which visits it comes over swamps and marshy lands; it abounds with ditches and stagnant pools, those fruitful sources of malaria, and its too redundant vegetation is rank and noisome.'[28] Flora Holman's recollections to her granddaughter of her life in Peshawar, sometime after 1840, were similar. 'In the days when troops were paraded in the morning, in a malarial white mist lying over the valley, the mortality among them was deplorable. Peshawar was little else but a large cemetery. Many of the bungalows were built on graveyards.'[29] The military was particularly badly affected, as implied by the writings of the army surgeon's wife, Sarah Robinson, in her journal of about 1815. This further indicated the generally perceived notion of the origin of malarial fever:

Many young officers have died, and are dying, of the dreadful fever. It is a melancholy thing that owing to the misconduct of the Generals these losses take place. Had they led their brave armies directly into Nepal, the campaign in all human probability would have been ended in triumph long ago, and these gallant young men's lives spared, or else lost on the field of battle, which would have been less grievous to their surviving friends than this kind of living death that many now groan under from bad air and water, and a soil steaming with bad vapours.[30]

Whether death was really preferable from cold steel than from disease is arguable. It is improbable that many young men would subscribe to such romantic notions today, although an individual friend may well have better tolerated the quick loss of a colleague in battle, than the slow loss from disease.

The mortality from malaria was grimly awful, and children were (and still are) particularly vulnerable. As late as 1889 Bengal's Sanitary Commissioner calculated that malaria was responsible for three-quarters of all mortality in the province (of all races), amounting to almost one million deaths a year.[31] The greatest killer was from the Falciparum variety of the disease which could cause brain inflammation (cerebral malaria) with fits and coma, but also red blood cell damage with anaemia and even kidney failure. In 1895 the remarkable Ronald Ross, with painstaking work, was the first to identify the malarial parasite within the mosquito, leading eventually to an understanding of how the disease was transmitted and therefore some hope for treatment and, better still, prevention. This work, along with similar studies, could only occur as a result of new developments in pathological research, especially more sophisticated microscopy. This would have been unimaginable fifty years earlier, not just for technical reasons, but also because medical practice still needed to mature towards an attitude of experimental evaluation rather than philosophical conjecture. As the world now knows, he identified the malarial parasite in the female anopheles mosquito, demonstrating that this was the vector for transmission from an infected host via saliva injected at the moment of biting its victim. Appropriately enough he was awarded the Nobel Prize. It is ironic to reflect that the most cherished time of the day in India, the evening, was also the most risky; this was the time when one could seek cool air driving out in a carriage, or enjoy a languid dinner on an open verandah. It was precisely this time of day that the voracious anopheles mosquito would venture out to exchange its infected saliva for a nutritious dose of human blood.

Treatment in the eighteenth century, and much of the nineteenth, followed the traditional pattern of extracting the supposed putridity in the blood by bloodletting in one of its forms. Even when the ancient theories as to causation were losing ground, these measures were still in constant use, the rationale for doing so being conveniently transferred to the newer concepts of cause. Purging was another popular means of ridding the patient of these putrid humours. None of these treatments would have been very pleasant but doubtless the reassuring murmur on the lips of every attending physician might have been the blithe comment that the worse the medicine, the greater the efficacy, particularly in those days. In India and other hot climates there developed a practice, led by naval physicians, of giving large doses of Peruvian bark, following purging and induced vomiting, which seemed to have positive results in cases of malarial fever. Exactly how successful is unclear, as observation and recording was limited, but the most interesting fact is that this bark came from the cinchona tree, originally from South

America, but later grown in India. Cinchona was nothing other than quinine, a name almost synonymous with malaria, very effective in its treatment and still sometimes used today. Its use did not, however, conform to Galen's humoral postulate and so remarkably, tragically even, it fell out of favour.

Based on no sound evidence, a belief gradually developed that fevers had their origin in putrid bile, and thus originated in the liver.[32] Consequently, and especially in India, a range of different medicinal therapies were introduced. The chief among them was the mercury compound calomel. The available correspondence indicates that almost every patient was given this medication to a greater or lesser degree, and often to an extent that was frankly toxic by any standards, but especially those of today, where all contact with mercury is inveighed against. So the unfortunate patient put his or her trust in the medical profession, as almost everyone has over the centuries, and thereafter suffered in resigned hopefulness the indignities of bleeding, cupping, and the plentiful application of leeches. This latter was usually at the site of the main symptoms, for example the abdomen or the right temple, in the mistaken belief it would there have more effect.[33] In addition they were scarified, blistered, smothered with mustard poultices and encouraged to swallow numerous dramatic and toxic substances. Many patients were destined to die anyway. Therefore most of this therapeutic armamentarium was just dramatic gesturing but, in truth, it was no more than futile optimism. The irony is that patients believed in it. They had to, or all hope was gone. In the modern era, when medicine has never been of better technical quality, recovery is an expected result; somehow public confidence in doctors has waned in the face of a diminution in despair.

By the mid-1800s the use of mercury in medicine was still in use, but lessening, but bloodletting again held sway. Fortunately, the use of cinchona bark underwent a resurgence, to the inevitable benefit of many individuals suffering from malarial fever, although medicine in general continued to remain in the dark ages until a proper scientific approach gradually emerged. Both Elizabeth Gwillim and Elizabeth Fenton, in 1804 and 1828 respectively, record being treated with cinchona bark for fever and ague – both with good effect.[34,35]

Cholera and malaria were the two major health problems in India, but there were many other diseases that lay in wait for the unfortunate visitor. A dysenteric illness, or severe gastroenteritis, was almost universal and not too uncommon even today. Occasionally they could prove fatal because of severe dehydration or electrolyte disturbance, much like cholera, but vastly less severe. Improved sanitation and safe water were the key; something which the British never really achieved in their jurisdiction, it being since suggested that there was an inclination to concentrate medical and sanitary expenditure on colonial enclaves only.[36] Because of the developing preoccupation of contemporary medicine with the liver as the source of ill health, it is no surprise that liver complaints were diagnosed constantly. One regularly comes across the diagnosis of an abscess on the liver, an almost impossible clinical diagnosis in the absence of scanning technology, and not necessarily easy even at post mortem, so it is hard to imagine what this might have been; perhaps a gallstone complication, or a hepatitis – or maybe it was just an imagined concept based on contemporary theory.[37,38] There is a record for one such unfortunate young soldier in the *Madras Gazette* that 'his death was caused by an abscess in the liver, for which he underwent a Medical operation and died soon after.' Enough to bring a worried frown to the brows of the doctors, and a smile to the lips of any nearby lawyer today, but not at that far distant time.[39] The 'medical operation' would have been nothing more than bloodletting or cupping.

Other causes of death and disease would have included typhoid, smallpox and suicide. Smallpox is one of the few examples of medical success in India and arose from the work of Edward Jenner who, in 1796, recognised that milkmaids who had contracted cowpox never seemed to catch smallpox. He inoculated volunteers with the fluid from cowpox blisters, and found they were protected from smallpox, a process that became known as vaccination, and which gradually spread world-wide, eventually eradicating the disease. Many in India submitted to this, and in her journal, Lucretia West records the urgent vaccination of her small daughter by a doctor friend, who had heard that there was a smallpox outbreak in the area.[40] Another entry on the other hand, describes how her household staff were dropping like dominoes with it, and Fanny Parkes recorded an outbreak in 1837 that was laying waste to some of the Indian British, but to far more of the Indian population.[41] This she attributed to the Governor General, William Bentinck's, decision to suspend the vaccination department as an economy.[42] His decision was based on the experience that Indian people were indifferent or hostile to the procedure. Nevertheless, vaccination was rolled out across the country, and throughout the villages in subsequent years. The proportion of the population submitting to the procedure gradually increased, leading to an eventual decline in mortality. Harrison comments that 'the reduction of mortality from smallpox was arguably the only significant contribution to mortality decline in India that can be attributed to colonial medical intervention.'[43]

Infant mortality was troublingly high. In the 1860s it was said to be fifteen per cent within the British population in India, and was undoubtedly even more in earlier years. This was more than twice as high as the rate in England at the same time, but about five per cent less than that in the Indian population, so far as can be determined. Infancy was just the beginning of the problem; many children also died in later years, sometimes by the nurseryful; a source of huge anxiety to overseas young mothers.[44] As alluded to elsewhere, mothers too were dying in childbirth, particularly of post-natal sepsis, but also of rampant eclampsia (toxaemia), haemorrhage of various sorts, obstructed labour, malpresentation and so on. Medicine at that time was blankly unaware of either the causes or means of prevention of virtually all of these conditions. This would account for the fact that, while maternal mortality in the UK today is about eight per 100,000, in 1850 it was around fifty-five per 1000, or an astonishing 700 times greater.[45] It must have been at least the same, or even more, in early British India.

Apart from the risk of potentially fatal illnesses there were many other ailments that afflicted the early settlers. Many of these were a product of misdirected personal habits, a prominent one of which was overindulgence in food and drink. Possibly because thinness was equated with poverty and ill health, it was quite common for people to eat themselves into a state of podgy corpulence. Even the women might refer to themselves as fat or stout, implying health and well-being, and this attitude of mind continued well into the Victorian era.[46,47] On the other hand, overindulgence in certain foods was thought to be dangerous. A much admired young woman, called Rose Aylmer, died suddenly in 1800 from a bowel complaint 'brought on entirely by indulging too much with that mischievous and dangerous fruit, the pineapple, against eating so much of which I had frequently cautioned her', according to William Hickey.[48] He goes on to say, in his typically trenchant manner, that one of her lovers 'shortly after her premature death sought comfort for himself in the arms of a vulgar, huge, coarse Irish slammerkin, Miss Prendergast, sister to my friend'; presumably not a friend for much longer. In typical Hickey fashion he has, in a few short sentences criticised the dead reputation of one woman, and castigated the living reputation of another. Apart from the dangers of pineapples, Wilkinson refers to the death of a General in 1812 from a supposed excess of radishes, and of a beautiful young woman in 1782 from drinking, rather rapidly, two large glasses of very cold water, mixed with milk.[49] These extraordinarily improbable dietary causes of death simply bear witness to the straw-clutching ignorance of medical opinion of the day.

Alcohol consumption was, as we know, high. Here the doctors got things wrong in reverse. Ill health was not blamed on an excess; in fact wine, especially claret, was regarded as medicinal. Many records exist of fever being treated in this way. Fanny Parkes refers to her husband being given the choice by his doctor between the lancet or a bottle of claret. He wisely chose the latter. During the last week of a three-week fever, a friend of Hickey's 'had poured down his throat from three to four bottles of that generous beverage [claret] every four-and-twenty hours, and with extraordinary effect.'[50] Quite what was extraordinary is unclear, but I think one would conclude nowadays that he recovered not because of his treatment, but in spite of it. Nevertheless, the risks of alcohol were not unknown, especially by women, who had seen too many young men fall by the wayside from chronic overindulgence. As Elizabeth Gwillim frostily remarked, 'inebriation is, in this climate, certain destruction.[51]

The hot weather in itself caused some suffering. Although heat exhaustion would undoubtedly have occurred, the totally inappropriate mode of dress for the climate would have been a major contributory factor. Too many layers of fabric closely applied to an overheated sweating skin, which may in turn be none too clean, caused blockage of the sweat glands. This led to a highly irritant red rash known as Prickly Heat – an understated term for an exasperatingly intrusive condition. 'We both had boils and terrible prickly heat which, to a person so irritable as Mr G, is a perfect misery.'[52] The same Mr G. (Sir Henry Gwillim) is recorded elsewhere as 'rolling on his own floor, roaring like a baited bull', for the same reason.[53] This unpleasant inconvenience could have been so easily avoided by good sense, and the adoption of an oriental mode of dress. For the majority, however, that was not the British way; so logic was defied, and discomfort prevailed.

What of the doctors who ministered to these suffering Indian British? Originally they were drawn from the ranks of the armed services, but in the mid-eighteenth century the East India Company employed its own medical staff to meet the needs of Company servants, especially those of its own army. This became the Indian Medical Service, which in 1785 consisted of a statutory 234 surgeons, but by 1824, after decades of war and expansionism, had risen to a total of 630.[54] A good fifty per cent of these were Scots from the excellent, but then less exclusive, medical schools such as Edinburgh and St Andrews. In general the social and professional standing of medical officers in India appears not to have been very high.[55] Before 1857 the European elite often looked down on them; 'to many of whom you would not, I think, like to trust your cat.'[56] Frequently, however, they also brought additional skills that were sometimes of value or interest to the community, such as an expertise in botany or zoology. Dr Anderson of Madras, who has been mentioned earlier as a physician and noted horticulturalist, was one such individual.

The income of an assistant surgeon was at subsistence level, but an improvement in his standard of living could be achieved by promotion, or by trade, speculation and even prize money. What is more, he could benefit greatly from private practice among the company's civilian population, and occasionally medical practitioners became very wealthy. It wasn't always straightforward, however. As Sarah Robinson wrote to her sister:

> *We have a very welcome letter from Government to James* [Surgeon husband] *in answer to a question whether he had got a right to claim fees from the families of gentlemen in the Service. Lord Moira assured him he had such a right and I hope people in future will be a little less troublesome and pay better, for frequently he has been harassed and seized early in the day by fancied ailments, and in return was treated with vile ingratitude.[57]*

But elsewhere one can read a different viewpoint on Oriental British medical practice:

> *Many of your friends dying about you and nobody caring a curse for you when you are ill or well, besides the extravagance of doctors, and the enormous price of physic should you be unwell, more especially to a man who grouches almost every farthing he parts with! No physician visits under a gold mohur or 16 rupees, equal to two guineas. This you will think high, no doubt, but they deserve it in this country.[58]*

In both instances one can't resist the impression that attitudes haven't changed over the centuries.

Before the latter part of the nineteenth century, the responsibility of the Indian Medical Service was almost entirely to the British population, and not much personal care was given to the Indian people. Apart from anything else the numbers were unreachably large, and there was grave suspicion of Western medicine among the Indian population. Some public health measures, such as smallpox vaccination, were extended throughout the general population nevertheless. In the earlier years there was a distinctly Orientalist attitude within the profession, holding the view that there were aspects of Indian medicine from which the West could learn. Both the doctors, and even the company's Court of Directors, particularly recognised what might be learnt from the rich *materia medica* (range of medicinal therapy) of indigenous medicine.[59] However, after the reformist initiatives of

222

Bentinck towards the end of the 1830s, and later Macaulay, an Anglicist attitude prevailed whereby, after 1835, Western medicine was promoted as the hallmark of a superior civilisation, and Indian physicians were denounced for their 'shameless impostures'.[60] This all coincided with the parallel changes in education and language mentioned earlier. Nevertheless, at the same time, the new Medical College in Calcutta was formed as a shining initiative to train Indian medical staff to assist with the care of the army, but also to practice medicine among their own population. Before one warms to this apparent altruism, it should be noted that the aim was just as much to promulgate the superiority of European medical knowledge as it was to advance the medical care of the Indian people.

So often, the end point of medical care among the British in early India was not cure, but inevitable decline. If a patient recovered from an acute illness, it was likely to be the natural course of that infection or illness, and the medical ministrations were an uncomfortable, often unnecessary, adjunct. A patient would, nevertheless, expect some intervention, even if suspected by his physician to be hopeless. In such a manner the mythology of a valued medical practice perpetuates itself in the minds of the suffering public. When patients died anyway, which was so often the case, burial was swift because, in the absence of refrigeration and with temperatures up to 40° C, the dead loved-one rapidly became an unlovely embarrassment. Death was such a frequent occurrence that the ensuing burial was a well-oiled procedure. Burials were often at night – perhaps the torchlight procession added to the gravitas. Mournful funeral music, such as the *Dead March* from Handel's *Saul*, was often avoided because its constant occurrence was deeply depressing for anyone within earshot who happened to be ill, and probably not much less so for the healthy.

Mourning was quite limited, apart from within the immediate family because, again, it would have been an almost constant state; the machinery of death was always running. As Lucretia West wrote, with depressed resignation, in her journal, 'here people die one day, are buried the next, their furniture sold the third and forgotten the fourth', and elsewhere: 'one, to me, of the most horrible things in this country, that you are put in the earth almost before you are cold and are soon forgotten.'[61,62] Women did not usually attend a funeral, except in the case of their own husband, which even then was not inevitable, as it was believed necessary to protect their sensibilities. Husbands' sensibilities were not a consideration, and some of them occasionally prolonged the agony of bereavement and, by doing so, demonstrated their fervent regard for their deceased wives. One inconsolable man, so distressed by the loss of his wife at sea, resolved to preserve her corpse in spirits, in a barrel. Unfortunately the sailors got to it unseen and drank its contents. As a result several died from the toxic effects of this noxious embalming fluid – doubtless felt to be a fitting penalty at the time.[63] A certain Colonel Dyce was 'so inconsolable after the death of his wife that he kept the [her] poor body … always by him in a leaden coffin'.[64] In circumstances where attendance at a funeral was not possible, but one's presence was expected, it was usual to send one's empty carriage to follow the hearse. The owner would have been recognisable to all, if only from his insignia, but the sight of such a ghost carriage seems a peculiarly macabre thought today.

In the journal of her time in India, Maria Callcott wrote about passing the English burying ground in 1810, when returning from an evening drive in Calcutta.[65]

> *There are many acres covered so thick with columns, urns and obelisks, that there scarcely seems to be room for another; it is like a city of the dead; it extends on both sides of the road, and you see nothing beyond it; and the greater number of those buried here are under five-and-twenty years of age! It is a painful reflection, yet one that forces itself upon the mind, to consider the number of young men cut off in the first two or three years residence in this climate. How many, accustomed in every trifling illness to the tender solicitude of parents, of brothers, and of sisters, have died here alone, and been mourned by strangers! I do not know why, but it seems more sad to die in a foreign land than at home.*

Just how many women died while in India during those pre-raj years is unknown. Somehow, it is almost worse to have made that long journey to such a distant land to accompany a husband, father or brother, or perhaps in search of a hopeful alliance, only to find oneself alone again, a sad remnant of one of India's dreaded diseases. As Lucretia West poignantly noted on 9 April 1826, after so many of her friends in Bombay had lost their husbands: 'the ship, the *Lady East*, sailed away at half past two o'clock for dear England, holding a mournful cargo of widows.'[66] For too many of those British women in India, the sweetness of exploring a new country, with all its richness, beauty and wonderment, was soured by the harshness of destiny. How many young women, one wonders, went to India buoyant with hope and exhilaration, only to return bereft and dejected as widows? How many never returned at all?

Notes

Chapter One – The Voyage
1. Parkinson, C. N. p.125
2. Doherty, M. APAC MSS Eur C537
3. Parkinson, C.N. p.207
4. Roberts, E. p.263
5. Hickey, W. Vol. ᴵV p.358
6. Parkinson, C. N. p.267
7. Sherwood, M. p.228
8. Parkinson, C. N. p.274
9. The East India Register and Directory for 1821
10. Grant, E. p.215
11. Doherty, M. APAC MSS Eur C537
12. Wurtzburg, C. E. p.424
13. Parkinson, C. N. p.286
14. Doherty, M. APAC MSS Eur C537
15. Sherwood, M. p.232
16. West, L. APAC MSS Eur D888
17. Sherwood, M. p.233
18. Parkinson, C. N. p.288
19. Hickey, W. Vol IV p.373
20. Sherwood, M. p.233
21. Thomas Twining, quoted in Parkinson, C.N. p.290
22. Wurtzburg, C. p.22
23. West, L. APAC MSS Eur D888 1 December 1822
24. Sherwood, M. p.236
25. Parkes, F. p.4
26. West, L. APAC MSS Eur D888 1 December 1822
27. Grant, E. p.217
28. West, L. APAC MSS Eur D888 16 November 1822
29. Ibid. 7 January 1823
30. Ibid. 10 November 1822
31. Ibid. 1 December 1822
32. Stanford, J. p.32
33. Maitland, J. P.8,9
34. Barlow papers APAC MSS Eur F167
35. Wimberley diary APAC MSS Eur Photo Eur 072
36. Parkinson, C. N. p.248
37. West, L. APAC MSS Eur D888 12 October 1822
38. Wimberley diary APAC MSS Eur Photo Eur 072
39. Parkes, F. p.3

40. Grant, E. p.219
41. Parkinson, C. N. p.80
42. Wurtzburg, C. p.680-3
43. Sherwood, M. p.238
44. Maitland, J. p.27
45. West, L. APAC MSS Eur D888 January 1823

Chapter Two – Arrival and Establishment
1. West, L. APAC MSS Eur D888 8 March 1827
2. Sherwood, M. p.245
3. Doherty, M. APAC MSS Eur C537
4. Maitland, J. p.28
5. Callcott, M. p.85
6. Kincaid, D. p.42
7. Roberts, E. p.53
8. Gwillim, E. APAC MSS Eur C240 7 February 1803
9. Hickey, W. Vol. III p.214
10. Gwillim, E. APAC MSS Eur C240 5 February 1802
11. Hickey, W. Vol. III p.357
12. Gwillim, E.APAC MSS Eur C240 14 October 1801
13. Parkes, F. p.14
14. Ibid. p.19
15. Roberts, E. p.7
16. Eden, F. p.43
17. Gwillim, E. APAC MSS Eur C240 14 October 1801
18. Ibid. 14 October 1801
19. Parkes, F. p.112
20. Fenton, E. pp.13,71,212
21. Parkes, F. p.32
22. Gwillim, E. APAC MSS Eur C240 March–July 1802
23. Ibid. 3 August 1802
24. Ibid. 7 March 1804
25. Parkes, F. p.274
26. Eden, E. p.157
27. Gwillim, E. APAC MSS Eur C24012 August 1804
28. Robinson, S. APAC MSS Eur F492 1814
29. Callcott, M. p.19
30. Roberts, E. p.7
31. Raza, R. p.19
32. Parkes, F. p.14
33. Raza, R. p.91
34. Roberts, E. p.8
35. Fenton, E. p.15
36. Roberts, E. p.8
37. Gwillim, E. APAC MSS Eur C240 5 February 1802

38. Maitland, J. p.142
39. Parkes, F. p.38

Chapter Three – The Pioneer Women
1. Dalrymple, W. *The Last Mughal*
2. Hibbert, C. *The Great Mutiny*
3. De Courcy, A. *The Fishing Fleet*
4. Dalrymple, W. *White Mughals*
5. Keay, J. *The Honourable Company* p.234
6. Wurtzburg, C. Chap. 1
7. Wilkinson, T. p.99
8. Minto, *Life and Letters of Sir Gilbert, 1st Earl of Minto*
9. Keay, J. *The Honourable Company* p.135
10. Wilkinson, T. p.107
11. Hyam, R. p.116
12. Butler, Iris, quoted in *White Mughals*. Dalrymple, W. p.323
13. Dalrymple, W. *White Mughals*
14. Parkes, F. p.242
15. Heber, R. pp.362, 392
16. Hickey, W. Vol. IV p.141
17. Wilkinson, T. p.118
18. Dalrymple, W. *White Mughals* p.372
19. Wilkinson, T. p.46
20. Shustari, S. quoted in Dalrymple, *White Mughals* p.411
21. Robinson, S. APAC MSS Eur F492 1814
22. Raza, R. p.56
23. Draper, Eliza in Wright, A. *Sterne's Eliza* p.71
24. Grant, E. p.267
25. Hyam, R. p.60
26. Gwillim, E. APAC MSS Eur C240 15 October 1804
27. Ibid. November 1806
28. Ibid. 16 October 1804
29. Ibid. 4 March 1805
30. Ibid. 14 October 1804
31. Ibid. 11 February 1802
32. Nugent, M. Vol. II pp.55, 140, 147
33. Fenton, E. p.38
34. Dalrymple, W. *White Mughals* p.50
35. Palmer, W., from the Anderson Papers, quoted in Dalrymple, W. *White Mughals* p.52
36. Hyam, R. p.116
37. Orwell, G. *Burmese Days*
38. Hyam, R. p.119
39. Ibid. p.116
40. Eden, E. p.4
41. Wilkinson, T. p.120

42. Eden, E. p.91
43. West, L. APAC MSS Eur D888 12 March 1827
44. Roberts, E. *Scenes of Hindustan* p.43
45. Wilkinson, T. p.101
46. Eden, E. p.344
47. Roberts, E. p.40
48. Ibid. p.41
49. Sykes, M. APAC MSS Eur C799 1818
50. Ibid. 1810
51. Roberts, E. p.36
52. Raza, R. p.42
53. Hickey, W. Vol. IV p.114
54. Eden, E. p.293
55. Roberts, E. p.33
56. Ibid. p.38
57. *The Morning Chronicle*, London. 7 June 1815
58. Hyam, R. p.65
59. Roberts, E. p.19
60. Draper, Eliza in Wright, A. *Sterne's Eliza* p.9
61. Gwillim, E. APAC MSS Eur C240 7 May 1803
62. Ibid. 14 October 1804
63. Ibid. 7 February 1803
64. Ibid. 13 October 1802
65. Ibid. 28 January 1806
66. Smith, G. p.21
67. Postans, M. Quoted in Raza, R. p.166

Chapter Four – Housewife and Household
1. Vickery, A. *Behind Closed Doors: At Home in Georgian England.* 2009 p.193
2. Dodwell, H. p.201
3. Doherty, M. APAC MSS Eur C537 1820
4. Gwillim, E. APAC MSS Eur C240 3 September 1803
5. Draper, Eliza in Wright, A. *Sterne's Eliza* p.35 November 1767
6. Gwillim, E. APAC MSS Eur C240 March–July 1802
7. Parkes, F. p.116
8. Grant, E. p.230
9. Roberts, E. p.85
10. Maitland, J. p.78
11. Fenton, E. pp. 15,20
12. Gwillim, E. APAC MSS Eur C240 14 October 1801
13. Maitland, J. p.79
14. Gwillim, E. APAC MSS Eur C240 March–July 1802
15. Ibid. 12 February 1802
16. Ibid. 11 February 1802
17. Grant, E. p.270

NOTES

18. Fenton, E. p,213
19. Roberts, E. p.83
20. Ibid. p.88
21. Gwillim, E. APAC MSS Eur C240 3 August 1802
22. Ibid. 12 October 1804
23. Raza, R. p.80
24. Eden, F. p.13
25. Sherwood, M. Chaps 14, 15
26. Maitland, J. p.79, 86
27. Lawrence, H. quoted in Raza, R. p.54
28. Wimberley diary APAC MSS Eur Photo Eur 072 18 March 1834
29. Callcott, M. p.56 16 February 1810
30. Robinson, S. APAC MSS Eur F492/1 1814
31. MacPherson Papers. Centre of South Asian Studies, Cambridge
32. Wimberley diary APAC MSS Eur Photo Eur 072 14 July 1841
33. Gwillim, E. APAC MSS Eur C240 12 February 1806
34. Hickey, W. Vol III p. 272
35. Draper, Eliza in Wright, A. *Sterne's Eliza* p.35 November 1767
36. Lawrence, H. quoted in Raza, R. p.72
37. Waterfield, R APAC Photo MSS Eur 097
38. Wimberley diary APAC MSS Eur Photo Eur 072 30 July 1835
39. Dodwell, H. p.230
40. Heathcote, quoted in Holmes, R. *Sahib* p.476
41. Barlow Papers APAC MSS Eur F176
42. *Prince of Wales Island Gazette* 27 March 1813
43. Gwillim, E. APAC MSS Eur C240 *c.* September 1805
44. Doherty, M. APAC MSS Eur C537 1820
45. Holmes, R. p.486
46. Ibid. p.486
47. *Pearman's Memoirs*, quoted in Holmes, R. p.491
48. Lyttleton, N. p.79
49. Wilkinson, T. p.114
50. Fenton, E. pp.139, 155, 158
51. Stanford, J. K. p.71

Chapter Five – Society and Propriety
1. Vickery, A. *The Gentleman's Daughter: Women's Lives in Georgian England* 2003
2. Vickery, A. *Behind Closed Doors: At Home In Georgian England* 2009
3. Martin, J. *Wives and Daughters* 2004
4. Kincaid, D. *British Social Life in India* 1938
5. Dodwell, H. *The Nabobs of Madras* 1926
6. Raza, R. *In Their Own Words* 2006
7. Dodds, C. *A Manual of Dignities, Privilege and Precedence*
8. Low, (ed.) *Fifty Years with John Company* p.155
9. Fane, I. ed. Pemble, J. *Miss Fane in India* p.235

10. Doherty, M. APAC MSS Eur C537 1820
11. Fane, I. ed. Pemble, J. *Miss Fane in India* p.60
12. West, L. APAC MSS Eur D888 6 April 1824
13. Ibid. 1 Jan 1826
14. Roberts, E. p.36
15. Grant, E. p.268
16. West, L. APAC MSS Eur D888 28 April and 16 May 1825
17. Parkes, F. p.43
18. Roberts, E. p.110
19. Fenton, E. p.63
20. Grant, E. p.227
21. West, L. APAC MSS Eur D888 16 June 1826; 13 February and 13 March 1827
22. Ibid. 20 February 1823
23. Ibid. 5 February 1824
24. Robinson, S. APAC MSS Eur F492/1 1814
25. Wimberley diary APAC MSS Eur Photo Eur 072 4 May 1835
26. West, L. APAC MSS Eur D888 15 August 1828
27. Grant, E. p.226
28. Gwillim, E. APAC MSS Eur C240 18 October 1802
29. Ibid. 7 February 1803
30. Ibid. 2 October 1802
31. ODNB. Bentinck, William
32. Cocks, R. *The Journal of Legal History* 2002: 23. p.87
33. ODNB. Strange, Thomas.
34. Gwillim, E. APAC MSS Eur C240 2 February 1805 and 6 March 1805
35. Hickey, W. Vol IV p.343
36. Cocks, R. *The Journal of Legal History* 2002: 23 p.82
37. Gwillim, E. APAC MSS Eur C240 7 February 1803
38. Ibid. 11 February 1802
39. Ibid. 14 October 1804
40. Factory Records, Straits Settlements APAC IOR G/34/197,8
41. Cocks, R. *The Journal of Legal History* 2002: 23 pp.77-101
42. West, L. APAC MSS Eur D888 6 April 1823
43. Ibid. 4 February 1823; 7 March 1823; 12 August 1823
44. ODNB. West, Edward
45. West, L. APAC MSS Eur D888 27 August 1828
46. Callcott, M. p.18
47. Sykes, M. APAC MSS Eur C799 June 1810
48. Ibid. September 1812
49. Ibid. 1799-1812
50. Robinson, S. APAC MSS Eur F492/1 1814
51. Ibid. 1814
52. Draper, Eliza in Wright, A. *Sternes Eliza* p.63
53. Devine, T. p.251
54. Ibid. p.251 et seq

55. Gwillim, E. APAC MSS Eur C240 25 August 1805
56. Ibid. 15 October 1804
57. Robinson, S. APAC MSS Eur F492/1 1814
58. West, L. APAC MSS Eur D888 8 May 1824
59. Roberts, E. p.13
60. Robinson, S. APAC MSS Eur F492/1 1814
61. Gwillim, E. APAC MSS Eur C240 24 August 1805
62. Minto, G. *Life and Letters of Sir Gilbert, 1st Earl of Minto*
63. Wurtzburg, C. p.413
64. Ibid. pp.689– 694
65. Gwillim, E. APAC MSS Eur C240 10 September 1803
66. Ibid. 28 February 1804
67. Ibid.
68. West, L. APAC MSS Eur D888 24 April 1824
69. Gwillim, E. APAC MSS Eur C240 18 March 1802
70. Ibid. 14 October 1804 24 August 1805
71. Ibid. 6 March 1805
72. Robinson, S. APAC MSS Eur F492/1 1814
73. Sykes, M. APAC MSS Eur C799 1817
74. Wimberley diary APAC MSS Eur Photo Eur 072 22 July 1835

Chapter Six – Dine and Wine

1. Roberts, E. pp.65, 66
2. Fenton, E. pp.72,73
3. Yule, H. *Hobson-Jobson*.
4. Jameson Papers. Centre of South Asian Studies, Cambridge
5. Robinson, S. APAC MSS Eur F492/1 1814
6. Ibid. F492/2 1814
7. Madras Gazette, quoted in Wurtzburg p.355
8. Gwillim, E. APAC MSS Eur C240 29 January 1802
9. Roberts, E p.91
10. Gwillim, E. APAC MSS Eur C240 16 July 1802
11. Roberts, E. p.97
12. Gwillim, E. APAC MSS Eur C240 29 January 1802
13. Fenton, E. p.26
14. Gwillim, E. APAC MSS Eur C240 April 1803
15. Fenton, E. p.18
16. West, L. APAC MSS Eur D888 29 September 1826
17. Gwillim, E. APAC MSS Eur C240 28 January 1806
18. Gwillim, E. APAC MSS Eur C240 18 October 1802
19. Ibid. 7 May 1803; 29 January 1802
20. Ibid. 7 Feb 1802
21. Ibid.
22. Wimberley diary APAC MSS Eur Photo Eur 072 17 July 1827
23. Parkes, F p.132

24. Ibid. p.126
25. Eden, E. pp. 34, 38
26. Ibid. 30 November 1837
27. Madras Gazette. February 1817
28. Robinson, S. APAC MSS Eur F492/1 1814
29. Madras Gazette. January/February 1817
30. Gwillim, E. APAC MSS Eur C240 14 October 1801; 10 October 1804
31. Ibid. 3 September 1803
32. Wimberley diary APAC MSS Eur Photo Eur 072 7 September 1827
33. Grant, E. p.234
34. Parkes, F. p.79
35. Burton, D. p.205
36. Hickey, W. Vol III p.29
37. Wimberley diary APAC MSS Eur Photo Eur 072 9 April 1827
38. Parkinson, C. N. p.74
39. Malcolm, J Chap 30
40. Ibid.
41. Fenton, E. p.51
42. Robinson, S. APAC MSS Eur F492/2 1814
43. Dodwell, H. p.220
44. Hickey, W. Vol. IV p.191
45. Doherty, M. APAC MSS Eur C537 1820
46. Callcott, M. p.18
47. Maitland, J. p.37
48. Gwillim, E. APAC MSS Eur C240 7 February 1803
49. Roberts, E. p.97
50. Burton, p.214
51. Parkes, F. p.49
52. Fenton, E. p.250
53. Hickey, W. Vol III p.283
54. Parkes, F. p.149
55. Mutiah, S. p.172
56. Roberts, E. p.59
57. Sykes, M. APAC MSS Eur C799 August 1809
58. Gwillim, E. APAC MSS Eur C240 14 October 1801
59. *Prince of Wales Island Gazette.* 29 February 1812
60. Gwillim, E. APAC MSS Eur C240 10 September 1803
61. Eden, E. p.286
62. West, L. APAC MSS Eur D888 29 January 1824
63. Eden, E. p.272
64. Raza, R. p.114
65. Minto, *Life and Letters of Sir Gilbert, 1st Earl of Minto*
66. Maitland, J. p.37
67. Gwillim, E. APAC MSS Eur C240 12 February 1802
68. Roberts, E. p.99

NOTES

Chapter Seven – Leisure, Pleasure and Endeavour
1. Gwillim, E. APAC MSS Eur C240 2 October 1802
2. Ibid. 29 January 1802
3. Ibid. 3 October 1802
4. Ibid. 21 July 1804
5. Robinson, S. APAC MSS Eur F492/2 July 1814
6. Eden, E. p.181
7. Gwillim, E. APAC MSS Eur C240 28 July 1806 and 30 September 1806
8. Ibid. 24 August 1805
9. Boulger, D. C. p.131,105
10. Gwillim, E. APAC MSS Eur C240 November 1806
11. Ibid. 18 March 1802
12. Ibid. 7 February 1802
13. Dodwell, H. p.200
14. Fenton, E. p.17
15. Gwillim, E. APAC MSS Eur C240 August 1803
16. Fenton, E. p.214
17. Hickey, W. Vol. IV p.115
18. Roberts, E. p.26
19. Grant, E. p.264
20. Ibid. p.271
21. Gwillim, E. APAC MSS Eur C240 7 February 1802
22. Fenton, E. p.82
23. Ibid. p.251
24. Gwillim, E. APAC MSS Eur C240 7 February 1803
25. Dodwell, H. p.200
26. Draper, Eliza in Wright, A. *Sterne's Eliza* p.17
27. Fenton, E. p.251
28. Fay, E. *Original Letters*. And see Raza, R p.108
29. Raza, R. p.109
30. Eden, E. p.6
31. Parkes, F. p.130
32. Sykes, M. APAC MSS Eur C799 1812
33. Raza, R. p.182
34. Gwillim, E. APAC MSS Eur C240 1804
35. Ibid. 2February 1805
36. Ibid. 6 March 1805
37. Wimberley diary APAC MSS Eur Photo Eur 072 2 October 1835
38. Roberts, E. p.35
39. Wimberley diary APAC MSS Eur Photo Eur 072 8 April 1827
40. Doherty, M. APAC MSS Eur C537 1820
41. Wimberley diary APAC MSS Eur Photo Eur 072 13 July 1826
42. Ibid. 19 May 1837
43. Ibid. 2 August 1826
44. West, L. APAC MSS Eur D888 20 March 1824

45. Eden, E. p.303
46. Von Englebrunner, Nina. APAC Eur Photo Eur 323
47. Elsberger, M. *Nina dAubigny von Engelbrunner*
48. Gwillim, E. APAC MSS Eur C240 2 October 1802
49. Parkes, F. pp.36, 76
50. Maitland, J. P.74
51. Parkes, F. p.43
52. Ibid. p.302
53. Plowden, S. APAC MSS Eur B187 4 April 1783
54. West, L. APAC MSS Eur D888 14 September 1823
55. Eden, E. p.168
56. Ibid. p.287
57. West, L. APAC MSS Eur D888 September. 1823
58. Fenton, E. p.200
59. Sherwood, M. p.232
60. Grant, E. p.233
61. Holman, Flora. Centre of South Asian Studies, Cambridge
62. Parkes, F. p.17
63. Ibid. p.246
64. Ibid. p.326
65. Dodwell, H. p.224
66. Parkes, F. p.126
67. West, L. APAC MSS Eur D888 November 1825
68. Grant, E. p.277
69. Robinson, S. APAC MSS Eur F492/3 1815
70. Eden, E. p.281
71. Holman, Flora. Centre of South Asian Studies, Cambridge
72. Eden, E. p.282
73. Robinson, S. APAC MSS Eur F492/2 1814
74. Fenton, E. p.30; 55
75. Wimberley diary APAC MSS Eur Photo Eur 072 31 January 1826
76. Grant, E. p.253
77. Robinson, S. APAC MSS Eur F492/3 1815
78. Ibid.
79. Raza, R. p.129
80. Callcott, M. p.93 10 August 1810
81. Maitland. J. p.182
82. Ibid. p.89
83. West, L. APAC MSS Eur D888 5 May 1825
84. Gwillim, E. APAC MSS Eur C240 42, 43
85. Ibid. 3 October 1802; 7 May 1803; 16 October 1804
86. ODNB. Anderson, James
87. Callcott, M. p.89
88. Gwillim, E. APAC MSS Eur C240 1807
89. Robinson, S. APAC MSS Eur F492/2 1814

90. Ibid. F492/3 1815; F492/4 1815
91. Parkes, F. p.133

Chapter Eight – Indian Impressions
1. Maitland, J. p.95
2. Parkes, F. p.194
3. Fenton, E. p.117
4. Maitland, J. pp.41, 80
5. Callcott, M. p.78
6. Eden, E. p.18
7. Gwillim, E. APAC MSS Eur C240 14 October 1804
8. Ibid.
9. Parkes, F. p.248
10. Draper, Eliza in Wright, A. *Sterne's Eliza* p.51
11. Eden, E. p.374
12. Gwillim, E. APAC MSS Eur C240 7 February 1802
13. Ibid. 11 February 1802
14. Maitland, J. p.43
15. Eden, E. p.124
16. Parkes, F. p.179
17. Keay, J. *India Discovered* p.131
18. Parkes, F. p.184
19. Gwillim, E. APAC MSS Eur C240 16 July 1802
20. Ibid.
21. Parkes, F. p.136
22. Ibid. p.137
23. Gwillim, E. APAC MSS Eur C240 10 October 1804
24. Ibid.
25. Ibid. 12 October 1804
26. Bayly, C. *Imperial Meridian* pp.146-147
27. Lawson, P. p.151
28. Gwillim, E. APAC MSS Eur C240 12 October 1804
29. Maitland, J. p.113
30. West, L. APAC MSS Eur D888 15 March 1826
31. Roberts, E. p.210
32. Eden, F. 23 March 1837
33. Ibid. November 1838

Chapter Nine – Health and Death
1. Wilkinson, T. p.6
2. Ibid.
3. Harrison, Mark. *Public Health and Medicine in British India*
4. Parkinson, C. N. p.72
5. Ibid. p.73
6. Raza, R. p.49

7. Wilson, J. *A Memoir of Mrs Wilson*. Quoted in Raza, R. p.49
8. South Park Street Cemetery, Calcutta. BACSA
9. West, L. APAC MSS Eur D888 21 July 1826
10. Ibid. 21 October 1825
11. Wimberley diary APAC MSS Eur Photo Eur 072 23 July 1837
12. Sherwood, M. p.325
13. Raffles, Sophia, quoted in Wurtzburg, C. p.598
14. West, L. APAC MSS Eur D888 19 August 1828
15. Robinson, S. APAC MSS Eur F492/1 1814
16. Farquharson, Forbes. APAC MSS Eur D615. Letter from Bombay 16 August 1823
17. Arnold, D. p.76
18. Porter, R. *Blood & Gut.* p.59
19. Arnold, D. p.81
20. Ibid. p.84
21. Holmes, R. p.471
22. Fenton, E. p.90
23. Wilkinson, T. p.9
24. Ibid. p.13
25. Fenton, E. p.192
26. Harrison, M. *Disease and Medicine in the Armies of British India 1750-1830* p.92
27. Arnold, D. p.78
28. Roberts, E. p.106
29. Holman, Flora. Centre of South Asian Studies, Cambridge.
30. Robinson, S. APAC MSS Eur F492/4 1815 Arnold, D. p.84
31. Arnold, D. p.84
32. Harrison, Mark. *Public Health and Medicine in British India*
33. West, L. APAC MSS Eur D888 12 August 1828
34. Gwillim, E. APAC MSS Eur C240 15 October 1804
35. Fenton, E. p.192
36. Harrison, Mark. *Public Health and Medicine in British India* p.8
37. West, L. APAC MSS Eur D888 25 January 1826
38. Robinson, S. APAC MSS Eur F492/1 1814
39. Madras Government Gazette 9 December 1819
40. West, L. APAC MSS Eur D888 22 August 1826
41. Ibid. 30 March 1825
42. Parkes, F. p.290
43. Harrison, Mark. *Public Health and Medicine in British India* p.8
44. Chaudhuri, N. *Victorian Studies* 1988 31, no. 4: 517-535.
45. Chamberlain, G. J R Soc Med. 2006; 99: 559–563
46. West, L. APAC MSS Eur D888 28 February 1828
47. Gwillim, E. APAC MSS Eur C240 7 March 1804
48. Hickey, W. Vol. IV p.230
49. Wilkinson, T. p.180
50. Hickey, W. Vol IV p.267
51. Gwillim, E. APAC MSSEur C240 July 1805

NOTES

52. Ibid. 3 August 1802
53. Lord Minto, quoted in Wilkinson, T. p.180
54. Arnold, D. p.58
55. Ibid. p.61
56. Gwillim, E. APAC MSS Eur C240 24 August 1805
57. Robinson, S. APAC MSS Eur F492/1 1814
58. Kay, R. August 1819
59. Arnold, D. p.66
60. Ibid. p.69
61. West, L. APAC MSS Eur D888 3 Aug 1823
62. Ibid. 18 March 1824
63. Grant, E. p.237
64. Maitland, J. p.124
65. Callcott, M. 1 November 1810
66. West, L. APAC MSS Eur D888 9 April. 1826

Bibliography

Manuscript Sources
*Asia, Pacific and Africa Collection (APAC), British Library, London
   (formerly Oriental and India Office Collection, OIOC)*
Anderson Papers. BL Add MSS 45,427
Barlow papers MSS Eur F176
Factory Records, Straits Settlements. IOR G/34/197,8
Edward West Papers, including the diary of his wife Lucretia West.1822-28
   MSS Eur D888
Elizabeth Gwillim Letters, and those of Mary Symonds her sister. 1801-08
   MSS Eur C240
Farquharson, Forbes. MSS Eur D615. Letter from Bombay 16 Aug 1823
Maria Sykes – Commonplace Book. 1809-18 MSS Eur C799
Mary Doherty Journal 1818-21 MSS Eur C537
Mary Wimberley Diaries 1825-41 MSS Eur Photo Eur 072
Richard Kay Diary   1819 MSS Eur F349
Sarah Robinson Diary 1814-18 MSS Eur F492/1-4
Sophia Plowden Letters. 1783 MSS Eur B187
Von Englebrunner, Nina dAubigny. 1807-16 Eur Photo Eur 323
Waterfield, Robert. *A Grenadiers Diary* Photo MSS Eur 097

Centre of South Asian Studies, University of Cambridge
MacPherson Papers   1787 – 1820 Section T. Microfilm 9
Jameson Papers   1819 – 1820 Microfilm Box 5 No. 24
Holman Papers   1840   Small collections box 14

Original Papers
Cocks, Raymond. *Social Roles and Legal Rights: Three Women in Early
   Nineteenth-Century India.* The Journal of Legal History. 2002 Vol.23,
   No.2. pp.77–106
Harrison, Mark. *Public Health and Medicine in British India: An
   Assessment of the British Contribution.* Liverpool Medical History
   Society. 5 March 1998
Chaudhuri, Nupur. *Memsahib and Motherhood in Nineteenth-Century
   India. Victorian Studies* 1988 31, no. 4: 517-535.
Chamberlain, G, J R Soc Med. 2006 November; 99(11): 559–563

BIBLIOGRAPHY

Newspapers, Asia Pacific and Africa Collection, British Library, London
Prince of Wales Island Gazette
Madras Government Gazette
The Morning Chronicle, London

British Association for Cemeteries in South Asia (BACSA)
Chowkidar Biannual Journal
South Park Street Cemetery, Calcutta: Register of Graves and Standing
  Tombs: from 1767. Pub. British Association for Cemeteries in South
  Asia (London 1992)

Published Sources

Arnold, David. *Science Technology and Medicine in Colonial India. The
  New Cambridge History of India. Vol. III* (Cambridge 2000)
Bayly, Christopher. *Imperial Meridian. The British Empire and the World
  1780-1830* (London 1989)
Boulger, Demetrius Charles. *Life of Sir Stamford Raffles* (London 1973)
Burton, David. *The Raj at Table* (London 1993)
Butler, Iris. *The Eldest Brother: The Marquess Wellesley 1760-1842*
  (London 1973)
Callcott, Maria. *Journal of a Residence in India* (London 1813;
  Cambridge 2012)
Dalrymple, William. *The Last Mughal. The Fall of a Dynasty, Delhi, 1857*
  (London 2006)
Dalrymple, William. *White Mughals. Love & Betrayal in Eighteenth
  Century India* (London 2002)
De Courcy, Anne. *The Fishing Fleet. Husband Hunting in the Raj*
  (London 2012)
Devine, Tom. *Scotland's Empire. The Origins of the Global Diaspora*
  (London 2012)
Dodds, Charles. *A Manual of Dignities, Privilege and Precedence,
  Including Lists of the Great Public Functionaries from the Revolution to
  the Present Time* (London 1842)
Dodwell, Henry. *The Nabobs of Madras* (London 1926, New Delhi 1986)
East India Register and Directory for 1821
Eden, Emily. *Up the Country* (London 1866; 1930)
Eden, Fanny. *Tigers, Durbars and Kings. Fanny Edens Indian Journals
  1837-1838* (London 1988)
Elsberger, Manfred. *Nina dAubigny von Engelbrunner. Eine adelige
  Musikpädagogin am Übergang vom 18. zum 19. Jahrhundert.*

Untersuchungen zu ihrem Hauptwerk Briefe an Natalie zu ihrem Gesang (München 2000)

Fane, Isabella. [Ed. John Pemble] *Miss Fane in India* (London 1985)

Fay, Eliza. *Original Letters from India 1779-1815* (London 1925)

Fenton, Elizabeth. *The Journal of Mrs Fenton 1826-1830* (London 1901)

Grant, Elizabeth. *Memoirs of a Highland Lady* (Edinburgh 1898; 1988)

Harrison, Mark. *Disease and Medicine in the Armies of British India 1750-1830: The Treatment of Fevers and the Emergence of Tropical Therapeutics.* In: *British Naval and Military Medicine 1600-1830* Clio Medica 81: The Wellcome Series in the History of Medicine. Ed. Geoffrey L. Hudson

Heber, Reginald. *A Narrative of a Journey Through the Upper Provinces of India from Calcutta to Bombay 1824-1825* (London 1827)

Hibbert, Christopher. *The Great Mutiny: India 1857* (London 1978)

Hickey, William. *The Memoirs of William Hickey* (London 1919)

Holmes, Richard. *Sahib. The British Soldier in India 1750-1914* (London 2006)

Hyam, Ronald. *Empire and Sexuality: The British Experience* (Manchester 1990)

Keay, John. *India Discovered: The Recovery of a Lost Civilisation* (London 2001)

Keay, John. *The Honourable Company: A History of the English East India Company* (London 1993)

Kincaid, Dennis. *British Social Life in India, 1608-1937* (London 1938)

Lawrence, John and Woodiwiss, Audrey (eds) *The Journals of Honoria Lawrence: India Observed 1837 – 1854* (London 1980)

Lawson, Philip. *The East India Company, A History* (London 1993)

Low, Ursula. (ed.) *Fifty Years with John Company* (London 1936)

Lyttleton, General Sir Neville. *Eighty Years Soldiering, Politics, Games* (London 1927)

Malcolm, John. *Malcolm. Soldier, Diplomat, Ideologue of British India. The Life of Sir John Malcolm (1769-1833)* (Edinburgh 2014)

Maitland, Julia. *Letters from Madras during the Years 1836-1839* (London 1843; 2003)

Martin, Joanna. *Wives and Daughter. Women and Children in the Georgian Country House* (London 2004)

Minto, Countess of. *Life and Letters of Sir Gilbert, First Earl of Minto* (London 1874)

Muthiah, S. *Madras Rediscovered* (Chennai 1999; 2004; 2008)

BIBLIOGRAPHY

Nugent, Lady Maria. *A Journal from the Year 1811 till the Year 1815, Including a Voyage to and Residence in India, with a Tour to the North-Western Parts of the British possessions in that Country, under the Bengal Governement* (London 1839)

Orwell, George. *Burmese Days* (London 1935)

Oxford Dictionary of National Biography (ODNB)

Parkes, Fanny. *Wanderings of a Pilgrim in Search of the Picturesque* (London 1850)

Parkinson, C. Northcote, *Trade in the Eastern Seas, 1793-1813* (Cambridge, 1837)

Porter, Roy. *Blood & Guts. A Short History of Medicine* (London 2002)

Postans, Marianne. *Travels, Tales and Encounters in Sindh and Balochistan 1840–1843* ed. Raza, R (Karachi 2003)

Raza, Rosemary. *In their Own Words. British Women Writers and India 1740–1857* (Oxford 2006)

Roberts, Emma. *The East India Voyager, or the Outward Bound* (London, 1845)

Roberts, Emma. *Scenes and Characteristics of Hindostan with Sketches of Anglo-Indian Society. Volume 1* (London 1835; 2005)

Sherwood, M. *The Life and Times of Mrs Sherwood* 1775-1851 (London 1910)

Shustari, Sayyid Abd al-Latif. *Kitab Tuhfat al-Alam* (Hydrabad 1802; Bombay 1847)

Smith, George Loy. *A Victorian RSM* (London 1987)

Stanford, J. K. *Ladies in the Sun* (London 1962)

The East India Register and Directory for 1821

Vickery, Amanda. *Behind Closed Doors: At Home in Georgian England* (London 2009)

Vickery, Amanda. *The Gentleman's Daughter: Women's Lives in Georgian England* (London 2003)

Wilkinson, Theon. *Two Monsoons. The Life and Death of Europeans in India* (London 1976)

Wright, Arnold. *Sterne's Eliza; Some Account of her Life in India: with her Letters Written between 1757 and 1774* (London 1922)

Wurtzburg, C. E. *Raffles of the Eastern Isle* (London 1954)

Yule, Henry. *Hobson-Jobson: A Glossary of Colloquial Anglo-Indian Words and Phrases, Etymological, Historical, Geographical and Discursive* (London 1903; Oxford 2013)

241

Index

A

Age of marriage in early British India, 73, 74
Alcoholic beverages, 144-6
Anglo-Indian (Eurasian) women, prejudice against, 65
Attack at sea, passengers' experience, 35

B

Ball, The, 151
Barlow, Lady Elizabeth, 24
  Sir George and Lady Elizabeth, 98
  Sir George, Acting Governor-General, 24
Barry, Charlotte, 33
  Barry, Charlotte and William Hickey, 68
Bathing, 30
Bentinck, William, Governor of Madras 1803-1807, 111-2
Books, 165-6
Breakfast, 133-4
British women marrying Indian men, 78
British women, shortage of, 57-8
British-Dutch relations, 35-6
Burke, Edmund, 9
Burroughs, Sir William, Calcutta judge, 114

C

Callcott, Lady Maria,
  Arrival at Madras, 40
  Mothers, and children sailing home, 92
  Life in Bombay, 119
Cacutta, 38
Cape Dutch women, 61
Cape of Good Hope, 36
Cards, 169
Caste, 202
Children, 90-1
Cholera, 214-5
Christian influence, 202
Christmas, 138
Clive, Edward, Governor of Madras 1798-1803, 111
Cohabitation, British men and Indian women, 58, 60-1, 77
Collection of curiosities, 169-70
Cooling of houses and occupants, 47-8
Cornwallis, Lord, and legislation against Anglo-Indians, 65
Cotton trade, 10
Court of Directors, East India Company, 10
Crown-appointed judiciary in India, prejudice against, 114-117
Cruelty to servants, 203

D

Death, widespread prevalence, 209-13
Dinner, 135
Disease, main causes of, 213-4
  Other causes of, 218-21
Divorce, 97-8

INDEX

Doherty, Mary, voyage to India, 19,
    20, 23-7
    Arrival at Madras, 39
    Coping with bereavement, 99,
        212
    Cross-country travel, 182-4
    Daily routine, 105, 147
    Domestic bliss, 81
Dundas, Henry, Lord Melville,
    President of the Board of Trade
    for India, 113
Dutch in the East Indies, views of
    the British, 125-7

E
East India Company, 8-10
    Attitude to Crown-appointed
        judges, 117-8
    Attitudes to its writers, 56-8
    Early tolerance of Indian
        religions, 201-2
    Policy respecting women, 67
    Shipboard representatives, 23
East Indiamen, losses, 30
    Cost of passage to India, 14
    Life aboard, 14-9, 23-5, 27-9
    Passengers, 24
    Ships, 12-3
    Structure, 13
Eden, Emily, hill station life, 50
    Comment on young age of girls,
        73
    Observations on single women in
        India, 68-9, 71
    Painting, 166, 172
    Tiger hunting, 176-7
    Witnessing famine, 204-5
    Zenana experience, 92-3
Education, 92-3

Elpinstone, Mountstuart, 105-8, 117
Extravagance, 154

F
Fane, Isabella, 77
Fashion, 159
Fay, Eliza, 76
Fenton, Elisabeth, cold bathing, 49
    Bereavement and remarriage,
        101, 211, 215
    Changing attitudes to Indian
        fabrics, 164
    Domestic life, 81, 134
    Furnishings, Spartan, 52
    Prejudice against mixed-race, 65
Fire at sea, 34
Foodstuffs, 139-41
French social relations, 128
Funerals, 51-2
Fusion and fission between Britain
    and India, 9-10, 190

G
Garden Houses, 44
Gardner, William, 59
Government House, Calcutta, 43
Grant, Elizabeth, 109
Gwillim, Elizabeth and her sister,
    May Symonds
    Christmas, 138
    Comments on local dignitaries,
        111-3
    Comments on society, 148
    Comments on the Dutch, 125
    Correspondence, 154, 157-9
    Daytime routine, 81-2
    Death, 211
    Foodstuffs, 143-4
    Horticulture, 187

Houses, 43
Indian festivals, religions, customs and castes, 197-9, 201
Language learning, 85
Paintings, 166-7
Preferment in employment, 115-6
Servants and staff, 88-90
Visiting, 108
Young age of marriage of girls, 74-5
Young men and native women, 62-4, 129
Zenanas, 192-3
Gwillim, Sir Henry, 43
Judicial controversies, 112, 114, 117
Overwork, 95

H
Hastings, Warren, 9, 24, 59, 124, 196
Heber, Reginald, 59, 107
Hickey, William,
Berths aboard ship, 15
Charlotte Barry, 30, 59, 68
Comments on various women, 95, 101, 114, 162, 169, 220
Drinking, 146, 150
Extravagance of houses and furniture, 44-5, 52
Hurricane at sea, 30-3
Wine and water supply aboard ship, 21, 29
Hill stations, 50, 97
Hooghly River, 38
Horse riding, 173-5
Horticulture, 187-8
Household servants, 82-9
Hunting, 175-7

I
Ice-making, 149-50
India Bill, 1784, 10, 85, 103, 123
Indian architecture, 196-7
Indian religion, 197-201
Insects and pests, 52-3

J
Java, invasion of, 126
Jones, Sir William, 9

K
Kirkpatrick, James, 60

L
Language learning, 85-6
Leaving England by sea, 20
Letter writing, 155-8
Luggage necessary for a woman going to India, 17

M
Madeira wine, 35, 144-6
Madras, 36
Maitland, Julia, 52
Communication with Indians, 85, 203
Correspondence, 156
Indian dance, 195
Schools, and orphans, 185-6
Malaria, 215-7
Malcolm, Sir John, 120
Malicious gossip, 121-2
Marital fidelity, 95-6
Marriage market, 70
Masulah boats, 39
Medical profession, 221-3
Medical treatment, 217-8

Memsahibs and their influence on fraternisation, 66
Minto, Lord, 57-8, 126, 153
Missionaries, 67, 202
Monsoons, 36
Mortality rates among the British, 206-7
Music, 167-9

N
Nabobs and social climbing, 115
Nautch dancing, 195
Nugent, Lady Maria, 59

O
Ochterlony, David, 59
Opium, 10
Orphans, 69

P
Packages, sending to and from England, 158-9
Painting, 166-7
Palmer, William, 59
Parkes, Fanny, 47
    Domestic difficulties, 53
    Household staff, 82-4
    Ice-making, 149-50
    Interests, 166-170
    Riding, 173-4
    Travel through India, 196-7, 200
    Water, 144
    Zenanas, 193
Penang, 38, 146
Plassey, Battle of, 10
Point de Galle, 36
Postans, Marianne, 77
Privacy, lack of, 47

Promiscuity of young men, protection against, 62
Prostitution, 62

R
Raffles, Sir Thomas Stamford, 10, 34, 126-7, 157
Raffles, Sophia, 34
    Lost in rainforest, 184
    Maternal grief, 209-10
Ranjit Singh, 50
Roberts, Emma, 75
    Aspects of behaviour, 106, 203
    Malarial swamps, 216
    Marriage market, 70-2
    Meals, 133, 135
    Servants, 87
Robinson, Sarah, 51
    Clothing, 162-3
    Death, 211
    Dining formalities, 104
    Entertaining young officers, 131
    Fever, 216
    Gardens, 188
    Returning children to England, 93
    Roast porcupine, 142

S
Schools, 185-6
Sclater, Eliza, 61, 73, 92, 96
Scots in India, 123-4
Social precedence, 103
Sterne, Lawrence, 96
Storm at sea, 30-3
Strange, Sir Thomas, Chief Justice, Madras, 112-4
Stuart, Charles 'Hindoo', 58
Sykes, Maria, 70, 120-1

T
Theatricals and masquerades, 170-1
Tiffin, 81, 131
Toasts, 146-7
Travel, cross-country, 180-2
  River, 178-9
Trincomalee, 34

W
Wellesley, Richard, 9, 43, 58, 66-7
West, Lady Lucretia,
  British abuse of servants, 203
  Cross-country travel, 179
  Intentional breach of social
    protocol, 106-7
  Judicial controversies, 117-8
  Mortality in India, 207-8, 210,
    223
  Schools, 119-20, 124, 128, 138,
    153, 169
  Visiting, 107-9
  Voyage to India, 22, 30, 93, 132
West, Sir Edward, 30, 106-7, 117

Widowhood, 99
Wimberley, Mary, 29-30, 93, 132
  Bottling Madeira, 145
  Children, 93-4
  Death of infant, 209
  Domestic matters, 29-30
  Music, 167
  Social impropriety in a single
    woman, 132
  Voyaging up the Ganges, 179
Women's concerns for young men
  living alone, 129, 31
Women's social history,
  introduction, 10-11

Y
Young bachelors, 56
Young women, arrival in India, 61-
  2

Z
Zenanas, 192-3